"As Germany's news magazine treated its readers to a unique fusion of rigorous reporting and vivid storytelling. Now its reporters have deployed those talents to extraordinary effect in a gripping account of the cataclysm of September 11th. Along the way American readers will profit from *Spiegel*'s ironic hometown advantage: the magazine's editorial offices are located in Hamburg, the city where September 11th ringleader Mohammed Atta and many of the other leading hijackers apparently plotted the attack. As a result, *Spiegel* journalists have managed to draw a dense and compelling collective portrait of a handful of inconspicuous students who would ultimately become the world's most notorious terrorists."

—Christian Caryl,
Moscow Bureau Chief *Newsweek* Magazine

"Easily the most comprehensive reconstruction of the events of 9-11. It takes advantage of unparalleled access to police documents and reporting on three continents to paint a compelling portrait of the tragedy."

—Ian Johnson,
Berlin Bureau Chief, *The Wall Street Journal*

"I read every word of the daily newspaper coverage in the days and weeks after the attacks. Not only does *Inside 9-11* distill the events of that astonishing day into a highly compelling and coherent story, but it's full of intriguing details I haven't encountered anywhere else. This is a first-rate piece of work."

—Kurt Andersen,
author of *Turn of the Century*

INSIDE
9-11

What Really Happened

By the Reporters, Writers, and Editors of

Der Spiegel Magazine

Stefan Aust   **Cordt Schnibben**

Klaus Brinkbäumer   Ansbert Kneip
Uwe Buse   Dirk Kurbjuweit
Dominik Cziesche   Georg Mascolo
Fiona Ehlers   Cordula Meyer
Ullrich Fichtner   Alexander Osang
Hauke Goos   Alexander Smoltczyk
Lothar Gorris   Barbara Supp
Ralf Hoppe   Andreas Ulrich

Thomas Hüetlin

TRANSLATED FROM THE GERMAN BY
Paul De Angelis and Elisabeth Kaestner,

WITH CONTRIBUTIONS FROM
Margot Dembo and Christopher Sultan

St. Martin's Paperbacks

First published in Germany in *Der Speigel* magazine and in book form under the title *11. September Gesschichte eines Terrorangriffs* by Deutsche Verlags-Anstalt

INSIDE 9-11

ISBN: 0-312-98748-X

Printed in the United States of America

St. Martin's hardcover edition published 2001
St. Martin's Paperbacks edition / September 2002

St. Martin's Paperbacks are published by St. Martin's Press, 175 Fifth Avenue, New York, NY 10010.

10 9 8 7 6 5 4 3

To the victims, heroes, and survivors of September 11.
The world will not forget.

CONTENTS

Foreword   ix

PART I: A CHRONOLOGY   1

    Attack from the North   3

    Attack from the South   63

    Search and Rescue   112

PART II: IN THE "HOUSE OF FOLLOWERS"   155

PART III: AFTERMATH   203

Appendix

    The Hijackers and Their Helpers in Germany   253

    Chronology of the Attacks   255

    Timetables of the Hijacked Flights   261

    Excerpts from the Terrorists' Manual   262

    Atta's Last Will   305

    Primer for Terrorists on Suicide Missions   308

    The Bin Laden Videotape   314

FOREWORD

Significant days in world history are like turning points of fate; people remember them for years and even decades later, telling each other over and over again where they were, and what they were doing and thinking at a specific moment in time. Those who turned on their television on the morning of September 11 around 9 A.M. Eastern time and saw United Flight 175 crash into the South Tower of the World Trade Center—the North Tower of which was already burning from the explosion caused by American Airlines Flight 11—and who later saw both towers collapse will never forget those images. People will still be talking about September 11 at this century's end.

What they will say will of course be determined by what happens in the intervening years. It may be that September 11, 2001, will be seen as no more significant than the night of April 15, 1912, when the *Titanic* sank. How good that would be. It may be that September 11 will enter history as the day mankind first began to learn how the nations of the world could eliminate the sources of terror. That would be even better. It may be that September 11 will be seen as the beginning of a long and increasingly violent battle between irreconcilable forces. That would be history's most terrible judgment.

Nothing will ever be the same—these words were repeated everywhere after September 11, so widely that they lost meaning. In fact much is the same as it was before the attack on the World Trade Center and the Pentagon. Yet a great deal of what we knew or assumed before the attack is no longer of much use. And those unaware of what they don't know are useful tools to terrorists.

Terrorists want to spread fear through violence, and thus to force us to think about things we haven't thought about. In this, the September 11 hijackers have succeeded: we now think about Islam and about terror. We understand that Muslims living in Arab countries may view globalization as Americanization, may feel debased by arrogance, marginalized by prevailing economic trends, and isolated from the world. We understand that Islam is a religion that has appealed to the world's dispossessed, and that Muslim extremists have learned how to channel frustration into rage and rage into action.

When the Islamicist movement first gained power in Iran in 1979, some of us thought it of no great concern because we understood nothing about religion. When terrorists tried to topple the World Trade Center in 1993—failing because they misunderstood how the buildings were constructed—we might have dismissed it as an act of insanity. Seven times (that we know of) over the succeeding years, Muslim extremists have tried to blow up airplanes, tunnels, or ships, in an effort to kill as many people as possible. They have succeeded three times. In the other four the attacks were discovered in time.

By 1996 Osama bin Laden stopped concealing the true targets of his attacks: America and its allies, soldiers, and citizens. The goal was first to clear Saudi Arabia and its oil fields of American military personnel, then to take over Pakistan and its atomic arsenal, and finally to make the world tremble in fear and terror until the Islamicist agenda dominated public life in many nations.

The attack was an attack on our way of thinking. New questions emerged from the ruins in New York and Washington. We now know that a troop of unobtrusive yet fanatically committed Islamic terrorists roams the world, willing to sacrifice their lives for what they believe. The questions are, How can we stop them from growing in number and from viewing us as their enemy? What has gone so badly wrong with life in their native lands? Is it a matter of too much globalization, or too little? How quickly will we understand that no two Muslim countries are alike? Did the attack create an opportunity for globalization? Or will it turn the United States into the world's policeman?

The questions seem endless. But a tragedy of the dimensions of September demands new answers. Such terror is very different from the social revolutionary terrorism of the twentieth century. Acts of religious terror are not done for the sake of farmers, workers, students, or oppressed and hopeless peoples; they are done in the name of God. But God will not reply to them, *This is not what I had in mind.* Allah does not make demands, and so terrorists who kill in His name need not negotiate with any earthly power. Their goal is to eliminate the unfaithful, not to convert them. But is that the extent of what the hijackers wanted? Did they, could they, think about the consequences of their deed?

By looking at the hijackers' stories, and listening to what people have to say about them, this book seeks some answers. The terrorists were not raving lunatics, or starving, or desperate. They did not emerge from caves. They were, as we all are, children of globalization. They spoke several languages and they knew something of the world.

They differed in the degree of intensity of their religious beliefs but were united in their world view. That view was that the West had been corrupted by greed, sin, and selfishness. And that the Islamic world was an oasis of faith and culture—but an oasis threatened and humiliated by the West, and by the United States in particular. They misunderstood the West as they misunderstood Islam; in one they saw only destruction, in the other only decline.

xi

They took themselves for the servants of God. As His earthly deputy, Osama bin Laden was the perfect agent to enthrall them: educated, rich, worldly, charismatic, fanatic—not someone who had to fight; someone who *chose* to fight. You could find his likeness among some of the nineteen hijackers, holy warriors for whom jihad was something like what doing drugs, or body piercing is to Western youth.

Who among the hijackers was merely following orders? Who formulated the plan to commit mass murder? Where did the money for the nearly two years of preparation came from? All this remains unclear. Even the videotape of bin Laden found in Jalalabad, Afghanistan, raises more questions than it answers. The tape has the feel of a staged performance, as if in this conversation with his dinner guest, the Saudi Arabian comrade-in-arms Ali Saeed al-Ghamdi, bin Laden is trying to show that all along he had been the one pulling the strings of the September 11 attack. Yet he seems to know less about the operation than those who did it. For example, he says he had already learned on September 6 that the planes were going to hit the World Trade Center on September 11. However, the hijackers began buying their tickets for these flights as early as August 26.

The theater of destruction offered to the world on September 11 was larger than structural engineer bin Laden could ever have dreamed. Shock is of course one goal of terrorism; the greater the number of people in shock, the better. That is why the attacks of September 11 are to date the most perfect act of terror in history. First you attract the media to a place like the World Trade Center with the crash of the first plane, then you deliver unforgettable images of terror twenty minutes later with a second plane. It was an idea that almost could have been thought up by the Hollywood screenwriters from whom the Bush Administration sought advice about potential terrorist scenarios after September 11.

Describing in detail the preparation and execution of an act of such cold-blooded calculation may help us understand exactly what sort of enemy threatens us.

Giving the stories of those who survived it consoles us. They show how the will to live and pure chance can foil the most successful terrorist plot. The stories of the emergency personnel—the firemen, policemen, security officers, emergency medical workers—offer us hope. They show how duty and courage can redeem a day that seemed to so many as the beginning of the end.

The lives of thousands of people—secretaries, stewardesses, window washers, stockbrokers, chefs, bond traders, janitors, carpenters, and computer technicians—from over sixty-two countries intersected on September 11. Three thousand died, but more than three times that number survived.

The task of disentangling the threads of fate of so many people has been both tense and arduous. Interviews with the families and friends of the perpetrators, with survivors from the World Trade Center, New York City firefighters, airport security personnel, and with police investigators in several countries were just as important as the evaluation of thousands of documents: tapes of the radio messages between the cockpits of hijacked planes and air traffic controllers, tapes of cell-phone conversations carried on from within the planes, of emergency calls to the police and fire departments, including those made from within the World Trade Center. The background of the Al Qaeda network was illuminated by new evidence from investigative and intelligence agencies around the world.

The reconstruction of the events of September 11 has been a collaborative effort, involving reporters, editorial staff, researchers, fact checkers, and production editors. The authors would like to thank Udo Ludwig, Erik Schelzig, Holger Stark, Georg Bönisch, Erich Follath, Heike Kalb, Bettina Stiekel, and our colleagues in New York, Sabine Schenk, Kerstin Linke-Muller, and Angelika Wrubel, for their research and contributions. Without the work of fact checkers Klaus Falkenberg, André Geicke, Stephanie Hoffmann, Angela Köllisch, Wilhelm Tappe, Peter Wahle, and production editors Lutz Diedrichs-Schneider, Hermann

Harms, Anke Jensen, and Manfred Petersen, this book would be full of mistakes. Our gratitude extends as well to Claudia Jeczawitz, Christiane Gehner, Matthias Krug, Michael Rabanus, Martin Brinker, Michael Walter, Ludger Bollen, Cornelia Pfauter, Jens Kuppi, and Claudia Conrad, and to Helma Dabla and Runhild Höfeler.

This book would not have happened without the support of the editors-in-chief of *Der Spiegel*—Stefan Aust, Martin Doerry, and Joachim Preuss. And without the still youthful vision of the founder and original publisher, Rudolf Augstein, who brought to the editorial floor diverse talents in investigation, analysis, and storytelling, our efforts would have been scattered rather than unified.

We're also pleased to thank everyone at St. Martin's Press who, with the help of an excellent translation by Paul De Angelis and Elisabeth Kaestner, made this American edition a reality: our publisher, Sally Richardson, our editor, Tim Bent, and Julia Pastore, Amelie Littell, James Sinclair, Steve Snider, Karen Gillis, and Susan Joseph.

The dedication contains our final and most important expression of recognition and gratitude.

—CORDT SCHNIBBEN

PART I

A Chronology

ATTACK FROM THE NORTH

New Jersey, September 11, 4:40 A.M.

Jan Demczur did not need an alarm clock. He had a schedule, a plan. The day, the month, the year—his life—were divided into panes of glass. For the last ten years Demczur had been working his way through the World Trade Center as a window washer. He cleaned nonstop, over and over again from the beginning, even weekends. All part of his plan. Demczur had come a long way but hadn't yet reached his goal. Some day he wanted to be a real American. That was why he had to get going so early.

Jan Demczur was forty-eight years old. He had a Polish accent, a Polish face, and an American house, only half of which belonged to him. He had two daughters and a wife, still sleeping. It was Tuesday and he would start on the 48th floor, like every Tuesday. He had plans for the month, for the week, and for the day. All worked out by himself. *They* provided the panes of glass; *he* worked out the plan. He'd been working this job for ten years; he didn't need to waste time.

Demczur went into the bathroom and shaved. Then he got dressed. Outside, Interstate 78 was already humming, but now, just before 5 A.M., you still noticed the breaks between cars headed for or emerging from the Holland Tunnel. Another twenty minutes and the breaks of silence would

3

give way to a constant, noisy din. Demczur's small house was only a few blocks from the highway. It was noisy here, but a tree grew right outside the window.

At 5:20 Demczur pulled the front door shut behind him. No one heard. Everyone was asleep.

Portland, Maine, About 5:00 A.M.

Mohamed Atta woke up for the last time to the sound of small aircraft in a motel 105 miles northeast of Boston and 280 miles northeast of New York City. Cessnas and Pipers had been buzzing around the two runways of the nearby Portland airport since 5 A.M.

Atta's (no-smoking) room in the Comfort Inn was furnished with fake Andalusian furniture, dark dressers, elaborate bedside tables, carved bedposts, easy chairs, and blankets in bright summery colors.

To the right of the door were the toilet and tub, to the left a small wash alcove set into the wall, a poisonous neon light flickering above it.

Do not leave your house unless you are washed and clean, for the angels will forgive you if you are clean. That was what it said in the terrorist "primer" later found in Atta's suitcase.

If Atta followed the primer's commandments, he shaved that morning, threw water over his face, washed up for the last time. Did he undo the waxed wrapping and use the one-ounce wafers of motel soap, one for the face, the other labeled "deodorant"? Did he smell of fruity Comfort Inn Botanical Shampoo on September 11?

At 5:33 A.M. he handed in his pale blue key card at the reception desk. At his side was his night's roommate, Abdulaziz Alomari. They didn't have breakfast, but hurriedly left the motel. Waiting outside was a blue Nissan Altima from Alamo Rental Cars in Boston, with Massachusetts plates, number 3335VI.

4

Minutes later, the four-door Nissan pulled into the Portland airport's parking garage.

At 5:43 A.M. Atta and Alomari were in the lower level of the elongated steel-and-glass building, checking in for US Airways Flight 5930 to Boston, a flight operated by Colgan Air.

At 5:45 they passed through security one flight up: an X-ray image of their bags unsettled no one.

New Jersey, 5:30 A.M.

For Jan Demczur, it was a ten-minute walk through his neighborhood to the PATH train that would take him from New Jersey to New York. The driveway in front of his garage was still glistening and wet. That would be forgotten in the course of the day. The forecast was for good weather. Demczur breathed in the morning air. For a few years the weather hadn't mattered so much because now he worked exclusively inside. It was his reward for seniority; he had worked for American Building Maintenance longer than any of the other fifteen window cleaners at the World Trade Center.

Turnover at work was high. Most of the window cleaners had arrived only recently in America. There were Yugoslavs, Albanians, Turks, and the Irish, but only one Pole. Two of them worked the window washing machines located on the towers. Years ago Demczur had had that job too. You got a good view up there, but otherwise it was boring. Only the two top stories and the nine lowest had to be done by hand, since the machines didn't reach there. But Demczur didn't have to get out there anymore. For the last three years he had worked only inside the North Tower—he had specialized.

At this hour of the day the PATH train to New York was nearly empty. At 5:50 Demczur got off at the World Trade Center, five stories below ground level. He took the escalator up. He was almost alone. The stores in the underground shopping passage were still closed. At 5:54 he swiped his card in the time clock on Lower Level One, North Tower. He took the elevator to the 3rd floor where, like the other window cleaners, he had a locker that held his work things and his tools—pail, rags, detergent, and squeegee. A few of his coworkers were there, though not all. They started work at different times, and often one would oversleep. Demczur ran into Rako Cami, an Albanian who worked the machine on the roof of the South Tower, and Fabian Zoto, who cleaned the windows on the observation deck every morning before the first visitors arrived. The regular operator of the machine on the North Tower was on vacation and his substitute seemed to have overslept again.

It wasn't easy finding reliable workers. They talked for only a minute; it was still early. Demczur combed his hair again, to the side, the way he'd parted it since he was a boy.

Portland, Maine, 6:00 A.M.

After a fourteen-minute wait at Gate 11, Mohamed Atta and Abdulaziz Alomari boarded the nineteen-seat propeller-driven Beech 1900, destination Boston.

The plane took off at 6:04, only slightly late, and headed out into the half light over Casco Bay. Atta and Alomari sat next to each other, surrounded by unsuspecting commuters. At 6:17 the beaches began to glitter. It would be a clear day—cloudless, warm, windless.

The sky smiles, my young son, it was written in the "primer." *Open your heart, welcome death in the name of God.*

It was only late afternoon of the day before that they had driven from Boston to Maine. At Logan Airport they had climbed into their rental car, taken Route 1A from the big airport traffic circle, leaving behind them the car showrooms, furniture stores, Laundromats, Dunkin' Donuts, Wendy's, and myriad convenience stores—America zipping past like one great supermarket.

The trip through Massachusetts and New Hampshire into

southern Maine takes an hour and a half on the six to eight lanes of I-95. Their Nissan merged into the quiet stream of traffic. Driving along unhurriedly, they crossed Piscataqua Bridge, located about halfway between Boston and Portland, and reached South Portland shortly after five. Atta and Alomari registered at the Comfort Inn, 90 Maine Mall Road, at 5:43 P.M. Because they were leaving again very early the next day, they paid the $149 for the room in advance. Their last evening began.

They spent it like people who have a long life ahead of them and lots of time to kill. They drove their car along highways flanked by bluish, shimmering supermarkets, hamburger drive-ins, and car dealerships. Sometime between 8 and 9 they were spotted at a Pizza Hut on the Maine Mall Road. Their last meal.

At 8:31 P.M. the surveillance camera inside the Fast Green ATM in the parking lot at Uno's Chicago Bar & Grill caught pictures of them: In the foreground Alomari can be seen making faces, feigning an expression of helplessness, then laughing broadly as if enjoying himself.

Atta stood behind him, a short man with a flat face who in the video always seems bored, gray, and washed-out. Both were filmed through a strip of mirror above the ATM panel. They look like two buddies getting money on a Saturday night for a bout of drinking—average types, regular guys, maybe at worst small-time crooks.

Atta made his last purchase between 9:22 and 9:39 P.M. at the Wal-Mart on Payne Road in Scarborough, south of Portland. Video cameras show him going in and out through the store's glass doors. He was wearing a black-and-white polo shirt, and when he left he was carrying a plastic bag.

No other security camera took their picture that night, no eyewitness reported seeing them. At some point they returned to the Comfort Inn. At 10:23 a waning moon rose in a clear, starry night.

The evening before you perform your deed: Shave all excess hair from your body, perfume your body. Recite the verses about forgiveness. Remember that this night you must

7

listen and obey because you will confront a grave situation. Get up during the night and pray for victory; then God will make everything easy and protect you.

It took fifty minutes for the prop plane to reach Boston. The flight was smooth; there were breakfast rolls encased in plastic, coffee, soda. Atta and Alomari might have been tourists, sales reps, sports officials. Their covers worked. For years they had used the disguise of assimilated, secular Muslims. Atta was wearing a bright blue short-sleeved shirt; Alomari's shirt was beige. Both carried medium-sized shoulder bags; their hair was cut short, no beards, no jewelry.

As soon as you board the airplane and have taken your seat, remember that which you were told earlier. God says that when you are surrounded by several nonbelievers, you must sit quietly and remember that God will make victory possible for you in the end.

For years already Atta and Alomari had had an appointment with God. Their education had been difficult and challenging. Now the time had come. There was no turning back.

How did the attackers live for so long undiscovered in the hated country of the godless? How did they get in and get out, and where did they stay? Who trained them as pilots? What were they looking for in the decrepit motels at the end of the Las Vegas strips? Why did they pick fights over bills of less than $50 in greasy bars just before the Big Day? What would have become of the attackers without the document forger of Falls Church, Virginia? Could Josh Strambaugh, Deputy Sheriff of Broward County, Florida, have averted the whole nightmare way back on April 26, 2001, when he pulled over Atta in a red Pontiac, by arresting him for driving without a license?

Newark, New Jersey, June 3, 2000

Fifteen months before Mohamed Atta slammed that jet into the North Tower of the World Trade Center, he stepped onto

American soil for the first time at Newark Airport; it was a warm, sunny Saturday. Atta, thirty-three, was Egyptian, son of a Cairo lawyer who had raised him to hate Jews. The FBI assumes that Atta spent several days in Prague before his departure. It is thought that while there he met with an Iraqi agent.

Marwan al-Shehhi, presumed pilot of the plane that crashed into the South Tower, entered America on May 29, 2000, aboard a Sabena Airlines flight from the United Arab Emirates via Belgium. Like Atta, he landed at Newark. And, like Atta, he was in possession of an HM1 student visa that permitted him to attend a flying school. Al-Shehhi, twenty-three, was born in the United Arab Emirates, the son of an Islamic preacher. He arrived in Germany as an eighteen-year-old on a military scholarship, studied German at the Goethe Institute in Bonn, visited a schoolmate, and later moved to Hamburg.

Ziad Jarrah, the presumed pilot of the plane that would crash in Pennsylvania, arrived in Atlanta, Georgia, on June 27. Jarrah was twenty-seven, Lebanese, from a respectable background: a popular guy who liked to drink and study hard.

Jarrah also held a student visa, and the people who met him during the coming year found that he bounced through life, like someone from whom a burden had been lifted, like someone who no longer needed to ask deep questions about the meaning of life.

The three men knew one another from Hamburg, where they had learned German and studied city planning, electronic engineering, and airplane construction. There they had become fanatic Muslims. There their plans had crystallized—plans to take part in something the likes of which the world had never seen before.

When your work is done and everything has gone well, everyone will take each other's hands and say that this was a deed done in the name of God.

Before they entered the United States, all three reported to German authorities that their passports were missing. Any suspicious stopovers in "rogue states" were thus expunged from their passports and personal profiles—a good idea, since the three had not come to seek their slice of the American dream.

Shortly after arriving, they got in touch with Hani Hanjour, the presumed pilot of the plane that would crash into the Pentagon. The thirty-two-year-old Hanjour was from Saudi Arabia and had first come to the States nearly ten years before.

Fifteen months before the attack, the most important members of the four terror teams, the four pilot ringleaders, were all in the United States. Atta, Jarrah, and al-Shehhi remained on the East Coast, in Miami. Hanjour spent most of the coming year out west, in California and Arizona. Their assignment for the next few months: learn how to fly a plane.

Venice, Florida, August to December 2000

Mohamed Atta and Marwan al-Shehhi parked their car on the grass of Huffmann Aviation. Straight ahead lay the flat, one-story building. In the middle was the reception desk, to the left the offices of the flight instructors, to the right a narrow hallway leading to the Cockpit Café, which always smelled of coffee and hamburgers. Through windows of the Cockpit visitors could watch student pilots taking off and landing. Nobody was surprised that two men with Arabic names were registering for flying lessons. That's not unusual here.

The flight training needed before you can apply for a commercial pilot's license costs about $9,000. It takes four months and assures a lot of foreign students a good job back home. By the time they pass the exam, student pilots have spent somewhere around 250 hours at the control stick of an airplane and are entitled to fly an Airbus or a Boeing. Rudi Dekker, flight instructor and owner of Huffmann Aviation, is proud of the fact that pilots from around the world are trained in the United States.

Atta and al-Shehhi began their training on a Cessna 152, a single-engine propeller-driven plane that is common to flight schools. The Cessna 152 is a good-natured plane; it forgives most student errors and one would have to be pretty inept to get into serious trouble.

Atta learned. He learned how to turn on the main switch, activate the starter, speed up, and pull the stick back after 250 yards and take off. He learned how to turn left, bank right, how to descend and how to land again. He struggled through the maze of symbols on flight maps and charts, learned the correct way for a pilot to talk with air-traffic controllers—how to report in and sign off—how to interpret a weather report, and he did it all without making a fool of himself.

In the course of his training Atta moved up from the Cessna 152 to a Piper Warrior and finally to a two-engine plane. Like the rest of the flight trainees, Atta read three thick books on flight theory.

Rudi Dekker didn't particularly like Atta. He often walked moodily among the airplanes, making it clear to everybody that he wasn't there to make friends. After a while his sullen face got on Dekker's nerves. He took Atta aside and advised him to change his attitude.

In October Atta and al-Shehhi switched for three weeks to Jones Aviation Flying Service in Sarasota. Once again Atta came across as unpleasant and aloof. Flight instructor Tom Hammersley says, "Atta always knew better." The terrorists went back to Huffmann. There, Anna Greaven found reasons not to like Atta either. She was also a student and often flew with him. Most of the time she felt like waving her hand in front of his face to pull him out of the frightening rigidity that gripped him while flying. He reminded her of a robot. Al-Shehhi seemed the exact opposite. Greaven compares al-Shehhi to a clumsy bear, always laughing, following Atta around like a bodyguard.

At the start of their training Atta and al-Shehhi lived with a couple named Voss. The Vosses' house is on the outskirts of the city, and it's obvious from just looking at it that the only thing Charles and Drucilla—Dru for short—want in life is peace.

In front of their house—a collection of thin-walled rectangles covered by a flat roof—stands a snow-white plaster fountain. Cherubs dance at the foot of it. Charles and Dru Voss are proud of their fountain. At night floodlights illuminate it. Snow-white pebbles cover the ground behind the fountain and around the house like a line of defense. More white plaster statues guard the front door. They, too, are illuminated.

Atta and al-Shehhi lived in a long rectangular wing connected to the rest of the house by a narrow passageway. One of their windows looked out onto the fountain and its cherubs. They stayed there only briefly. Charles Voss became upset about a flooded bathroom; also, his tenants walked through the house with dripping wet hair. After a week he asked them to look for a room elsewhere. Four months after they started flight training, Mohamed Atta and Marwan al-Shehhi received their pilot licenses.

Meanwhile, in Venice, Ziad Jarrah had learned to fly. He started his training at the Florida Flight Training Center, a flying school as small and unassuming as Rudi Dekker's. He too learned to fly in a Cessna 152.

Arne Kruithof, the owner of Florida Flight Training, liked Jarrah. Kruithof says he would have had no hesitation about flying with Jarrah. He was always on time, usually in a good mood. He was helpful to others when they had problems, and when they were depressed he would cheer them up.

His fellow students took pictures of him: Jarrah laughing, Jarrah solving a tricky navigation problem, Jarrah partying and infecting everyone else with his bonhomie. In one group photo he stands at dead center, like a man around whom everything else revolves. Evenings the students and flight instructors often sat together in the 44th Squadron, a bar right next door.

Kruithof believes it's important that pilots feel comfortable around other people. After all, they have to spend an enormous amount of time crammed with them in the tight quarters of a cockpit. To his students he holds forth on the importance of teamwork, the pilot as role model, the need for self-discipline, and why beer cans lying around a student pilot's room is not acceptable.

Hanging on the wall behind the worn brown sofa in the lounge is a fax sent to Kruithof by a European airline. It's only one page long but asks a lot of questions: Is the applicant dependable? Can he work as part of a team? Can he take criticism? Can he get things done? What are his weaknesses?

Kruithof receives such inquiries regularly. He is not only a flight instructor; he also provides evaluations and recommendations when his students apply to an airline for a job in the cockpit. Kruithof quickly reached his assessment of Ziad Jarrah: "the perfect candidate."

Jarrah's mission in America, like that of the other conspirators, was a difficult one. He had to be prepared to live for more than a year in the land of the enemy. He had to be ready to obey his enemy and cheerfully accept instruction in all the skills he and his fellow assassins needed to accomplish their mission. He had to get to know his enemy, to party with him, laugh with him—and at the end of it all still be able to kill him.

Jarrah, too, passed his flight test without difficulty.

Scottsdale, Arizona, August to December 2000

Hani Hanjour, the presumed pilot of the plane that smashed into the Pentagon, had problems learning how to fly.

Hanjour lived in Scottsdale, Arizona, while in flight training at CRM Airline Training Center. The school has an excellent reputation.

Hanjour had every kind of problem—with takeoffs, landings, midair turns. He was nervous and distracted, couldn't concentrate. After three months of intensive instruction he still didn't have the private pilot's license that trainees normally obtain after four to six weeks. Finally, with a great deal of luck and many flying hours behind him, Hanjour managed to pass the commercial pilot examination.

A delicate-boned Saudi with the eyes of a puppy and a sparse mustache, Hanjour first came to the United States on October 3, 1991. He went to Arizona, where he finished a language program. He returned to Saudi Arabia at the beginning of 1992, only to come back to the United States in 1996—this time for good. At first he lived with the Khalils, an Arab-American family in Hollywood, Florida. The Khalils knew little about their houseguest and suspected nothing about his motives for coming to America. Adnan Khalil teaches English at the local college; his wife, Susan, is a friendly middle-class housewife who at the time was taking care of their three-year-old son, Adam.

Susan Khalil, then forty-five years old, helped the helpless Hanjour fill out applications for various flight schools. He hardly spoke a word of English and was constantly blushing beet-red. Adnan, affable and cheerful, cooked opulent Arabian-style meals for Hanjour and encouraged his houseguest to watch television to improve his English. But it didn't help. It seemed to Susan as though Hanjour were withdrawing into his shell. America intimidated him. His helplessness was most evident when he was with women.

It was easier for him to relate to little Adam. For hours he romped and played with the boy, teaching him Arabic words and letting him ride on his back. As often as he could he went to the Dar Ulum Mosque, located in a converted supermarket, a gray, unattractive building at 7050 Pines Boulevard. Susan Khalil, a practicing Protestant, was amazed at her houseguest's inflexible piety. She told her husband, "That poor boy must have a serious problem. I wonder what it could be."

A week after Atta and al-Shehhi received their pilot's licenses, they rented six hours on a Boeing 727 simulator at SimCenter, Inc., in Opa-Locka, north of Miami. Mostly they practiced making midair turns, showing no interest whatsoever in takeoffs and landings. Considering the 250 flight hours they had to their credit, they had become adequate pilots. This was the last time, according to all available evidence, that Atta and al-Shehhi sat in a Boeing simulator.

Nine months before the attack, the pilots seemed to have overcome their biggest challenge: how to fly a plane. To stay in training they would repeatedly rent planes—in Florida, Georgia, and Maryland.

Now began the next phase of the undertaking: preparation for the hijacking and remaining inconspicuous while waiting for the fateful day.

Arrangements for financing the attack were in place. According to the FBI and CIA, the approximately half a million dollars for the operation would come via messengers and wire transfers—mostly from the United Arab Emirates, but also from other countries, such as Bahrain. It arrived in many small installments so as not to arouse suspicion. On July 4, 2000, for example, just under $10,000 was deposited in account number 573000 259 772 that Atta and al-Shehhi had opened at the SunTrust Bank in Florida. The money came from someone named Isam Mansur in the United Arab Emirates. On August 30, there was another deposit of $19,985. This time the money came from "Mr. Ali." On September 18, $69,985 was deposited, this time from "Hani." Altogether the money in the account amounted to just under $110,000.

Hamza Alghamdi, one of the terrorists on board the plane that flew into the South Tower, opened an account in Hollywood, Florida, into which a hitherto unknown accomplice deposited money using traveler's checks purchased in Bahrain—sometimes $3,000, sometimes as little as $1,000. And, through an account at HSBC Bank in the Emirates that belonged to pilot al-Shehhi, some $100,000 was deposited between July and November of 1999, almost all by wire transfer.

Small amounts. Different accounts. Different points of origin. No regular pattern. Perfect.

To take care of daily concerns, the leaders counted on their "logistics men," as the FBI called them after the fact—men who took care of lodging, clothing, food: Khalid al-Mihdhar and Nawaf Alhamzi. The two were supposed to become pilots as well but didn't have the right stuff.

Al-Mihdhar, a short, wiry, and agile man, probably came from Yemen. Alhamzi, powerfully built, was from Saudi Arabia. Alhamzi's father, Mohammed Salim al-Hamzi, owned a supermarket in Mecca and was prosperous enough to be able to offer his son a trouble-free future.

Both men had been in the United States since January 15, 2000. Before that they were in Kuala Lumpur, the capital of Malaysia, where they met with intermediaries of Osama bin Laden.

The group in Kuala Lumpur was suspected of having organized the suicide bombing attack on the United States destroyer *Cole*. A videotape of their meeting in Kuala Lumpur had been recorded by the Malaysian secret service and in a roundabout way eventually landed in the hands of the CIA; it led to al-Mihdhar and Alhamzi's being put on the United States Immigration Department's "watch list." But this was done much too late—not until August 21—twenty months after al-Mihdhar and Alhamzi were already in the United States and only twenty-one days before September 11.

San Diego, December 2000

The two logistics men lived in San Diego, California, in the tastefully modest Parkwood Apartments, 26401 Mount Ada

Road. Alhamzi's telephone number is still listed in the San Diego telephone book: (858) 279-5929. The Parkwood Apartments are close to the bustling commercial strip of San Diego, and al-Mihdhar's apartment is located on the ground floor—just as the Al Qaeda handbook prescribes.

This 180-page-long terrorist manual written in the name of Allah makes everything clear from its first page: *Islamic governments have never and will never be established through peaceful solutions and cooperative councils. They are established as they always have been by pen and gun, by word and bullet, by tongue and teeth.*

Lesson 4 in the handbook gives a detailed twenty-two-point explanation of a proper terrorist apartment. It must not be near a police station or other government office. Curious neighbors must not be able to see inside. It must have locks that can be changed. And above all, it has to be on the ground floor to allow escape in case of a surprise raid. Terrorists in training are also urged to conduct business during normal working hours so as not to arouse the suspicion of neighbors.

In this, al-Mihdhar and Alhamzi would not be altogether successful.

First they aroused suspicion at Sorbi's Flying School because they were so adamant about learning to fly but did not show the slightest knack for it. They offered flight instructor Richard Garza additional money to train them to fly jets. Garza refused and became suspicious, but he didn't report them to either the CIA or FBI.

In the meantime a few of their neighbors at Parkwood Apartments were starting to wonder about the two men's behavior. There was no way to conceal the fact that even after months of living there al-Mihdhar and Alhamzi still had no furniture, instead sleeping on mattresses on the floor. Yet they were seen constantly walking about with briefcases, cell phones glued to their ears. Sometimes a limousine would come pick them up. But before anyone could call the police, al-Mihdhar and Alhamzi moved out.

The fact that, contrary to Al Qaeda terrorist instructions,

they then sought lodging in an Islamic neighborhood may indicate that either they were increasingly nervous or felt pressed for time.

After the training of the four suicide pilots was successfully completed, it was up to al-Mihdhar and Alhamzi to prepare for the arrival of the other terrorists. The FBI divides them into three groups: "pilots"—Atta, al-Shehhi, Hanjour, and Jarrah; "logistics men," like al-Mihdhar and Alhamzi; and finally the "strongmen"—men without special talents other than being capable of killing as many of the crew or passengers as necessary or inciting fear as necessary to keep everyone else on board in check.

Did these men need to know all the details of the suicidal plan? It is doubtful. In the view of their leaders it was probably safer and more practical to let the killers on board think this was simply a "normal" hijacking. The fewer who knew, the lower the risk that one or the other of the "strongmen" might have a slip of the tongue or lose his nerve at the thought of impending death.

Dubai, United Arab Emirates, March 2001

It is not yet known who signed up the twelve men, whether the purpose of Atta and al-Shehhi's twelve trips (to, among other places, Madrid, Prague, and Amsterdam) was personally to recruit strong, battle-tested men, or if they were supplied through agents of Al Qaeda. One thing is certain: that the "strongmen" entered the United States between March and June 2001, in small groups, from Dubai.

The killers included Salim Alhamzi from Mecca, Saudi Arabia, probably a brother of logistics man Nawaf Alhamzi. He and Hanjour and the logistics men al-Mihdhar, Majed Moqed, and Nawaf Alhamzi would be on the plane that smashed into the Pentagon. Moqed was the son of a Bedouin tribal prince from near Riyadh and attended law school at King Saud University.

The other arrivals were: Ahmed Alghamdi from Baljurshi

in the Saudi province of Baha, who called his family for the last time a few months before September 11 and asked them forgive him his sins and to pray for him; and another Saudi, Mohald Alshehri, who attended the Islamic University in Abha for one semester and then moved to Riyadh, eventually disappearing into Chechnya. These two arrived on May 28 in Miami on a flight from Dubai via London. Hamza Alghamdi, also from Baljurshi, arrived on May 2 via London and Washington, D.C.

Along with the Saudi Fayez Ahmed these three strongmen would crash into the South Tower of the World Trade Center under their leader and pilot al-Shehhi.

On board American Airlines Flight 11, which Atta would fly into the North Tower, were Satam al-Süqami from the United Arab Emirates; the brothers Waleed and Wail Alshehri—the older one a physics teacher; the younger a student with psychological problems. The Alshehris were two of eleven sons of a successful businessman from the city of Khamis Mushait. In addition there was Abdulaziz Alomari, also from Saudi Arabia. He was the last to arrive in the United States, probably under an assumed name and using a stolen passport.

The plane that would take off forty minutes late and later crash in Shanksville, Pennsylvania, had only three strongmen on board. While Ziad Jarrah took over the cockpit, these three men would fight a life-or-death battle with the passengers: Saeed Alghamdi, who arrived in Orlando, Florida, on June 27 from the Emirates; Ahmed al-Haznawi; and Ahmed Alnami. We have a little more information about Alnami, who was twenty-three, than we do about the others. He made a pilgrimage to Mecca in August 2000 and then disappeared. His father and mother have little to say about their son—except that he turned into a religious fanatic two and a half years before, becoming an imam, a prayer leader at the mosque in Asir, which is a high honor for someone so young.

Fifteen of the nineteen terrorists were from Saudi Arabia;

most were the sons of well-to-do families, sons of super-market owners and tribal princes.

They came from the kingdom that houses and protects the holy places of Islam and is at the same time a filling station for the Western economy. A fifth of America's oil imports come from Saudi Arabia. As the leader of the OPEC cartel, the Saudi government also ensures stable oil prices.

No wonder that the ruling Saud clan has business links that reach into the highest political ranks in the United States. At the same time, Saudi Arabia has invested billions of dollars into Islamic wars of liberation the world over. A rift cuts through the country, even through individual families. Most of the fathers and mothers of the conspirators had no notion what their sons were up to.

Nowhere else could Arab terrorists obtain entry visas to the United States with such ease. Michael Springmann, former head of the American consulate in Jiddah, said, "My job was supplying visas to terrorists." During his time at the consulate the terrorists involved were those whom the CIA and Osama bin Laden recruited together, first for training in the United States, then to go into action in Afghanistan against the Soviets. The terrorists saw it as only right and just to twist such a grand old tradition to their own purposes.

Florida, Spring and Summer 2001

Managing the logistics for nineteen men who don't look like average Americans, who don't all behave like Americans—and yet who aren't supposed to be conspicuous—is no simple matter. They need places to sleep and to eat breakfast; they need clean socks, driver's licenses, medicine for diarrhea; and they have to pray five times a day. They must not drive through red lights, come down with appendicitis, or get into fights.

The four leaders, with help from their logistics men, developed a highly obfuscating choreography of changing apartments with a single goal: invisibility.

Evidently they had learned from al-Mihdhar and Alhamzi's mistakes in San Diego, when suspicious neighbors started asking questions. The terrorists rented many small apartments and motel and hotel rooms—preferably on the cheaper side, like the Bimini in Hollywood, Florida. Mostly they paid in advance—$650, for example, for a tiny attic apartment in a dingy house at 1818 Jackson Street in Hollywood, Florida, that Atta rented from May to June. This was the kind of place meant for immigrants, late-blooming hippies, and students who can't afford anything better.

Otherwise they moved into apartments in gated communities like Hamlet Country Club in Delray Beach, north of Miami, where al-Shehhi found a home for two months at 401 Greenswald Lane. The rent was $6,000. Here you could live in both comfort and privacy.

In this way the terrorists scattered across the densely populated eastern coast of Florida between Miami and Daytona Beach, where every other place name ends in "beach," where there are enough flight schools and sunlight to stay in shape. Besides, hordes of young tourists vacation here; a few young Arabs in khakis and polo shirts didn't attract attention. Only in their motel rooms would they wear the traditional Arab *thaub*, the yellowish tan knee-length smock. Besides, there was a whole host of fitness clubs to choose from, where the attackers could bodybuild or, like Jarrah, do martial arts.

Coral Springs, April to June 2001

Tara Gardens Condominium, at 10001 West Atlantic Boulevard, served as the terrorists' headquarters from May to July. The white two-story building has thirty-eight apartments, surrounded by fan palms.

Atta and al-Shehhi rented Apartment 122 for $840 per month. They spent most of their time crouched in front of the computer, sometimes using flight simulators. These programs were favorites of "God's Warriors"; in Kabul, Osama bin Laden's fighters used to while away the time with them. Among the wreckage found in the Al Qaeda bunker after the capture of the Afghani capital in November was the user's guide for Microsoft's Flight Simulator 98.

The laundry room of the Coral Springs apartment complex provides extensive facilities for the tenants. Here one could often find al-Shehhi; apparently he did the laundry for the whole team. Sometimes neighbors wondered how two men could use that many shirts and pants. None of the men was ever seen at the swimming pool, which is surrounded by a six-foot wall; Atta, however, was often seen standing in the parking lot, smoking one Marlboro Light after another. Clean-shaven and well-dressed—pants creased, button-down collars—he could have been a young, serious engineer or teacher; perhaps a little too grim, but unremarkable.

The hijackers erected an effective deterrent against the curiosity and affability of the Americans. When neighbors attempted to engage pilot al-Shehhi in a little small talk, he responded bluntly, rudely. Atta, too, ostentatiously lowered his gaze as soon as a resident crossed his path and seemed about to greet him. Even among themselves the men never exchanged a word outside their apartment.

In the spring of 2001 the prospects looked promising: Atta and al-Shehhi had organized their team brilliantly. Sometimes they were here, sometimes there, barely leaving a trace; and if one wanted to sketch a diagram of their movements during the spring and summer of 2001, it would have looked like a huge sheet of superimposed sewing patterns. Nineteen suicide hijackers who were involved in organizing the largest attack on the world's superpower remained invisible to the CIA, the FBI, and the police. Nearly invisible.

Fort Lauderdale, April 26, 2001

Inverrary Boulevard is a two-lane highway under the jurisdiction of the Broward County sheriff in Fort Lauderdale.

Shortly before 11 P.M. Deputy Sheriff Josh Strambaugh overtook the driver of a 1986 red Pontiac, near Forest Trace, a housing development. The vehicle's operator was driving a little erratically. Strambaugh switched on the siren and decided to carry out a routine check. The Pontiac's driver was Mohamed Atta.

Atta must have been scared out of his wits when Strambaugh, in white shirt and blue uniform pants, knocked on the window and asked to see his license and registration. Atta did not have his Egyptian driver's license with him— or didn't want to show it. The officer looked over the car and noted stickers written in Arabic. He questioned Atta, who remained collected and answered politely.

Luckily for Atta, Officer Strambaugh works for county Road Control, not Traffic Enforcement, a motorcycle brigade whose job it is to issue as many high-penalty tickets as possible. Besides, Strambaugh's tour of duty had just started; the night shift lasts from 10.45 P.M. to 6:45 A.M.

Strambaugh settled for some paternalistic advice and an admonition. He also instructed Atta to appear thirty days later in County West Satellite Courthouse at precisely 8:45 A.M. to present his driver's license. Should he—against expectation—not show, an arrest warrant would be issued, valid in all of Florida. A serious look of warning, a dutiful assurance from Atta—and the encounter must have ended.

Atta did not show up for his end-of-May court appearance, although on May 2 he had obtained a Florida driver's license, number A300540-68-321-0.

Now his name was entered into the computer for all Florida police precincts. In theory, "Mohamad Atta" was now stored in the computer memory of every police department in the state's sixty-six counties.

Delray Beach, July 5, 2001

Initially a warrant is just a matter of routine: No posse was about to fan out to arrest a certain Mr. Atta for his misdemeanor. Yet everything might have collapsed when the police again stopped Atta, this time for speeding.

It occurred in neighboring Palm Beach County, near the small city of Delray Beach, about eighty miles from Broward County. The police officer's name was Scott Gregory. But this time, of course, Atta could produce a license.

Adhering to normal procedure, Gregory counterchecked the personal data. For mysterious reasons, the computer withheld from Officer Gregory the fact that Atta was wanted in Broward County. Atta got off with a simple fine. "There is maybe a very small percent chance of the computer being out of order at such a moment," stated John Williams of the Broward County Police Department. He added, "Damn it, in a way we already had him."

Falls Church, Virginia, August 1, 2001

In the Washington, D.C., suburb of Falls Church, Virginia, a car drove into a parking lot next to a twenty-four-hour convenience store. Sitting inside the car were Hani Hanjour, pilot, and Khalid al-Mihdhar, logistics man. They had not come to buy cookies, chips, or bottled water. A service was offered in the parking lot that helped illegal immigrants obtain identity papers. Here Luis Martinez-Flores, himself an illegal immigrant, from El Salvador, waited for his customers.

To acquire an official identity in Virginia one needs nothing more than a sponsor willing to affirm, with his or her signature, that one has a permanent address in the state. Martinez-Flores offers this service for $50. Martinez-Flores drove the two men to a government building where they took care of the formalities.

The next day, Hanjour and al-Mihdhar made use of their new identity papers to become sponsors of "logistics men" Majed Moqed and Alhamzi. The other hijackers procured new identification papers the same way.

These papers were a further critical component of the

terrorists' plans. Without them, anyone on September 11 who didn't have an American driver's license would have had to show, upon check-in, his Arabic passport. The airlines' personnel might have wondered about the multitude of Arabic passports and asked unpleasant questions.

Warrick's Rent-a-Car, Pompano Beach, Florida, August 6, 2001

After presenting their Florida driver's licenses, Atta and al-Shehhi, rented, respectively, a white 1995 Ford Escort and a blue 1996 Chevy Corsica from Warrick's Rent-a-Car in Pompano Beach. They would put 3,204 miles on the odometers in three stages. Perhaps in this final phase they no longer trusted telephones and every arrangement had to be made in person.

The decision to attack on September 11 probably occurred shortly after Atta's and al-Shehhi's rental pick-up at Warrick's. On August 8 logistics men al-Mihdhar and Moqed attempted for the first time to purchase American Airlines tickets for the September 11 flights. They were out of luck: The software could not verify some of the information provided.

Al-Mihdhar and Moqed would not buy their tickets until September 5, at Baltimore-Washington International Airport. They paid in cash.

Las Vegas, August 13, 2001

When Mohamed Atta arrived by plane in Las Vegas, he rented a car and drove to the EconoLodge on Las Vegas Boulevard South. He paid $107.92 cash for Room 122 for one night. Atta unlocked the door and hung the "Do Not Disturb" sign on the doorknob.

"Do Not Disturb": the summit meeting of the four pilots. Now that the decision had been made, the terrorists needed to fine-tune the last details of their plans.

Now and again Atta would go to the Cyber Zone café. He would check his E-mail. A computer war game titled "Unreal" was a favorite of the café's patrons. Throughout its rooms you could hear the heavy explosions of bombs.

Las Vegas is a city of luxury, addiction, and sin. It is difficult to find a place where America celebrates itself and its way of life more uninhibitedly than here, in the desert of Nevada. Possibly that is why Atta traveled here. He had stayed at the EconoLodge in Las Vegas before, for two days starting June 29, in Room 22.

After one year in the land of the infidels, a year in which he ate breakfast with them, waited in traffic jams with them, and stood in line with them at supermarket checkout counters, here at the EconoLodge at the south end of Las Vegas Boulevard, surrounded by porno emporiums, pawnshops, and strip joints, he could survey America in its full grandiose depravity. An ascetic Muslim like Atta must have hated this Mecca of the godless.

Ziad Jarrah, suspected pilot of the plane that would crash in Pennsylvania, was not interested in the modest Econo-Lodge. He preferred the Circus Circus on Las Vegas Boulevard, a hotel that spares no effort to deepen its guests' belief that a life without fun is no life at all.

Like Jarrah, pilot Marwan al-Shehhi hated Las Vegas but also savored it, paying visits to the Olympic Garden Topless Club.

Toward 2 A.M. the club can be considered a worldly reproduction of the paradise promised to Islamic suicide bombers as a reward for their deeds. Here, however, instead of seventy-two virgins, there await, behind the two heavy double doors, a couple hundred women whose job is to remove their clothes and dangle their breasts in front of the men's noses.

The Olympic Garden is about as large as a gymnasium and, when really crowded—when four to five hundred men sit in dim corners with about as many women turning their hips in circles above their heads—it reeks of sweat.

The women sport names like Valerie, Samantha, and

Cindy. Some will say they're here because they have to feed and raise a child, or because otherwise they can't pay for college, or because they hope that this is how they'll meet the love of their life.

"Karen" talks that way too. She danced that night for pilot al-Shehhi. She wore a tight stretch dress, blond hair, and a twenty-dollar smile. "The guy looked pretty cheap." She doesn't regret he's dead: "He gave me a really shitty tip."

Panther Motel, Deerfield Beach, Florida, August 26, 2001

The Panther Motel on A1A, the shore road through Deerfield Beach, became the last stop for some of the hijackers. Marwan al-Shehhi and Mohald Alshehri moved into Room 12 on the first floor; the brothers Wail and Waleed Alshehri and Satam al-Süqami—all of them "strongmen"—took Room 10, located across from a small oval swimming pool.

Owners Diane and Richard Surma are Polish immigrants who achieved a modest standard of living thanks to diligence and hard work. Sixty-one-year-old Richard Surma grows oranges, preferably Honeybells, and collects odds and ends of all kinds: imitation African masks and Arab hookahs. He is not above finding collectibles by sorting through the trash left by motel guests.

The Surmas make an effort to create a friendly atmosphere in their motel. They are devout Catholics but also know that sometimes in business life you have to look the other way, such as when you rent a room for an hourly rate to young couples who don't yet have their own home, or to businesspeople for office-hour liaisons.

There is one kind of behavior for which Diane Surma has no tolerance, however: when more people stay in a room than are paid for. Hardly had the brothers Alshehri moved into their room when she noticed Mohamed Atta drive up and lock himself into the room with them. Immediately she

27

knocked at the door furiously to read her guests the rules of the house.

Atta interrupted her lecture almost at once: "Calm down, lady, I'm just a visitor."

Cold, penetrating, and somehow disdainful is how she later described to her husband the gaze of the visitor. Diane Surma, who is otherwise not a timid woman, got goose-bumps. She stammered, even excused herself to Atta for the disruption. A little later al-Shehhi went to see her: His friend was rather off-putting, he knew, she was the boss around here, no doubt about it—he wanted her to know they would not cause any further problems.

Only once was Richard Surma taken aback by his Arab guests: when he noticed that they had covered with towels two oil paintings hanging on the wall. The paintings were as erotically harmless as they were artistically insignificant: an impressionistic portrait of a girl in a slip in front of a jukebox, two girls at the beach.

Surma was surprised. He tried to engage al-Shehhi, whom he had no difficulty identifying as the leader of the group, in conversation. Please understand, he told him, that it would be no problem to take the paintings down if they bothered him and his friends. Was it perhaps for religious reasons? No, no, al-Shehhi warded off the motel owner, smiling. A technical conversation about hookahs with the young Arab was no more successful. In the end, Surma accepted that his guests were not interested in small talk. Since they paid in cash—$610, including tax—Surma did not worry about them anymore. The next day he saw that the towels covering the pictures had been taken down.

Shuckum's, Hollywood, Florida, September 7, 2001

For fifteen months the conspirators had done everything to blend in. Now suddenly they drew attention to themselves. Now they picked quarrels.

At Shuckum's, for example, located at 1814 Harrison

Street in Hollywood. Shuckum's is a dimly lit bar that specializes in slippery oyster dishes and dolphin sandwiches for $6.95. Ceiling fans sweep lazily above; rubber sharks and plastic swordfish adorn the walls. Atta, al-Shehhi, and a third man from the team killed about four hours here on the evening of September 7. Al-Shehhi and the third man together downed five vodkas with orange juice and five "Capt. Morgan" cocktails—a mixture of spices, Coke, and one and a half ounces of Puerto Rican rum of the same name.

Atta meanwhile drank cranberry juice and spent nearly the whole time playing "Golden Tee '97," a video game housed in a huge, dusty box located on the way to the bathrooms. One game of simulated golf cost fifty cents.

Hardly any of the guests who usually come to Shuckum's ever stood in front of the gadget, but Atta played for hours on end intently, doggedly. Star players could inscribe their initials into a Golden Tee ranking. As a matter of fact, the person entered as seventh-ranked chose as his abbreviation "Abu," which in Arabic means something akin to "father" or "leader."

When her shift was up, their waitress, thirty-eight-year-old Patricia Ingriss, presented the men with the bill: $48, tip not included.

The three hijackers became enraged. The bill was too high. Ingriss called her manager, Tony Amos. He tried to appease the excited men. Was it that they didn't have enough money on them, the manager asked?

At this Atta became truly enraged. "You think we cannot pay?" he screamed. "Who do you think we are? We are American Airlines pilots!" Atta pulled out of his pocket a wad of bills, fifties and hundreds, slapped a fifty and a single on the polished wood counter, and the trio took off.

Six days earlier, something similar had happened at the 251 Sunrise in Palm Beach. Pilot al-Shehhi and an unidentified man were drinking champagne and whiskey with three girls from West Palm Beach. In the end, the bill amounted to $1,100. "Fraud!" screamed al-Shehhi. He took off his glasses and showed every intention of getting into a fight with the bouncers.

But here again the aggression dissipated suddenly. Al-Shehhi threw a bundle of bills on the table, added a $25 tip, and the group disappeared like phantoms.

A day later, al-Shehhi turned up at a strip bar in Daytona Beach called the Pink Pony, again with an unidentified companion. They ordered several beers, slipped some bills under the strippers' garter belts, stared at them as if hypnotized, and left after about an hour.

They appeared to have stopped worrying about being discovered. They felt invulnerable, powerful. They were challenging America head-on and no one knew it.

Minneapolis, August 2001

And indeed, for the most part, the CIA, National Security Agency, and FBI suspected nothing. For fifteen months, Islamic terrorists planned the largest attack in history on the United States of America and no one noticed it. This was because "God's Pilots" attacked not from the outside but from within. Everything they needed they learned or bought on site.

Three weeks before the attack the FBI had a last chance to learn about what was happening. It was then that a French-Algerian named Habib Zacarias Moussaoui booked hours on a flight simulator at an aviation school in Minneapolis. He wanted to learn, in a hurry, how to fly a jet—landing procedures didn't matter—and he paid for everything in cash. The flight instructor became suspicious and informed the police. The French secret service had already issued a warning about Moussaoui; his home had been searched, his computer confiscated though not yet analyzed. Only after September 11 did it become clear that he had contacts to the Hamburg terrorist group around Atta and had received money transfers from Hamburg. Moussaoui may have been supposed to steer a fifth plane into the White

House, or been on the pirated jet that had four instead of five hijackers on board.

The ignorance of officials seems all the more incomprehensible since they had known since the 1993 attack on the World Trade Center that a worldwide net of Islamic fundamentalists was trying to attack America. In the earlier attempt, one tower was supposed to have crashed into the other, bringing forty thousand people down to certain death, but the terrorists, who were caught later, had miscalculated the amount of explosives needed.

In June 1993 two traffic tunnels, the United Nations Building, and the New York offices of the FBI were supposed to have been blown up simultaneously, except that the Islamic fundamentalists were arrested beforehand. A year later, twelve American jumbo jets on their way from the Far East to the United States mainland were supposed to have been blown up over a period of forty-eight hours, but the "Manila Air" plot was discovered in time. 1995: attack on United States troops in Riyadh. 1998: the bombing of American embassies in Kenya (253 killed) and Tanzania (10 killed). New Year's Eve, 1999: aborted attack on Los Angeles International Airport. January 2000: planned attack on the United States warship *The Sullivans* in Aden harbor. October 2000: successful attack on the United States destroyer *Cole* in Aden.

All of these attacks had a common goal: the mass murder of Americans. The hijackers centered around Atta combined the World Trade Center plan of 1993 with the Manila Air plan of 1994: to explode simultaneously a pair of jumbo jets. Possibly they had originally planned to fill small crop dusters with fuel and use them as flying bombs. Moussaoui had shown interest in such planes over the Internet, and Atta's unusual interest in the spring of 2001 for pest-control planes in Belle Glade, Florida, also stands out as unusual.

He and the other hijackers did not come to the attention of government officials because most of them did not fit the profile of "the enemy" developed by the thirty-billion-dollar-budget American agencies. They were not professional terrorists; they were beginners. They approached their task cautiously, worked by trial and error, improvised—in short, learned by doing.

The 180-page Al Qaeda handbook for terrorists contains a random mix of warlike phrases aimed at cave fighters, imagining from their base in Afghanistan how to terrorize the world. Atta and company would have found little of use to them here; they figured out by themselves how to use Internet cafés inconspicuously to exchange E-mail, or to get an overview of the best flight-training schools.

Their interest in the West and its way of learning and living wasn't feigned. The pilot leaders especially—Atta, al-Shehhi, and Jarrah—left for the West in the early nineties to learn "how this so-called First World saw us and how it behaved toward our Third World"—the reason Atta gave for wanting to study, in Germany, the politics of developing countries. These Muslims, hungry for knowledge and attracted to the West, became, in the West, warriors driven by hatred of the West. They were not sleepers; they were schoolboys who drew the wrong conclusions from what they saw and learned. And turned their conclusions into action, without apparent anxiety.

All western civilizations that enjoy power are very weak in their core. A phrase from Atta's "primer."

They were not robots of death after all, bombs on two legs waiting only for Osama bin Laden to set them off by remote control. They worked their way slowly toward the fateful day, small planes flying under the radar.

Between August 26 and September 5, the hijackers bought their tickets. With cool calculation they chose their flights. They were early flights, scheduled to depart between 7:45 and 8:14 A.M. from Boston, Newark, and Washington, D.C. The aircraft were Boeing 757s or 767s with nearly identical cockpits—something that had simplified the terrorists' training. They were headed for the West Coast, guaranteeing large quantities of fuel on board and therefore the strongest possible explosive force.

Panther Motel, Deerfield Beach, Florida, September 9, 2001

Around 10 A.M. pilot al-Shehhi and the strongmen checked out of the Panther Motel. They were picked up by about six other men, men the motel owners, the Surmas, can no longer remember. Atta was not among them.

They left behind two plastic bags with garbage. Following his old habit, Richard Surma rummaged through the garbage and found a box cutter, maps, a German-English dictionary, an instrument that pilots or flight engineers use to examine the quality of fuel, and, finally, video cassettes and a video cable. The tapes Surma found were unused, though others had apparently been used—Surma found the wrappings. The motel manager dragged the loot into Room 17A, his storage room. For a moment he wondered about the tapes: What sort of thing had his strange guests recorded?

Their last will and testament, possibly, suspects the CIA. A few last words to other God's warriors around the world—and an exhortation to follow their example?

Shortly before checking out, Waleed Alshehri went to the motel office to return the room key to Diane Surma. She was in a hurry because she still had rooms to clean but wished them a good trip. He fumbled around for a few moments, then took her hand and said in English with a guttural accent, "Thank you, it was good knowing you. You are a very good person."

Boston, September 11, About 6:00 A.M.

Strongmen Waleed and Wail Alshehri moved out of Room 432 at the Park Inn, 160 Boylston Street in Newton, an inner suburb of Boston about twenty miles west of Logan Airport. In their pockets were tickets for American Airlines Flight 11 to Los Angeles, bought on August 26 with a SunTrust

Visa debit card, using as address a shared post office box in Hollywood, Florida, paid for with two different Visa credit cards.

Check your weapon before your trip because you will need it for the execution of your act.

Strongmen Ahmed and Hamza Alghamdi checked out of the Days Hotel, 1234 Soldiers Field Road in the Brighton section of Boston. They paid for the pornographic film they had ordered. They had bought their one-way tickets to LA for United Airlines Flight 175, $1,760 apiece, on August 29, giving as address a shared post office box in Delray Beach.

Everyone should be ready to do his part, and your deed shall be endorsed by the will of God.

Strongman Satam al-Süquami went out onto Charles Street at the edge of the theater district in downtown Boston. Behind him were the wrought-iron fire escape and the red awning of the old Milner Hotel. Al-Süqami would be on American Flight 11; the ticket was paid for.

You will not return to earth and you will plant fear into the hearts of the infidels.

Pilot al-Shehhi, who had just phoned Jarrah, also left the Milner with his strongmen Fayez Ahmed and Mohald Alshehri, with nearly no luggage. On August 27 Alshehri and Ahmed had booked first-class, one-way tickets to Los Angeles on United Airlines Flight 175, at a cost per ticket of $4,500. As contact address they had given a post office box in Delray Beach. On August 28 al-Shehhi had paid $1,600 in cash for his ticket at the United ticket counter in Miami. The day had now come.

In the end, you will be the victor.

Boston, Logan Airport, 6:50 A.M.

Atta and Alomari's flight from Portland, Maine, landed on time, despite the delayed departure. The prop plane navigated to the low-numbered gates of Terminal B, unloaded its passengers: "Thank you for flying US Airways." People plucked their bags from the overhead luggage compartments. Atta and Alomari did, too, hurriedly; they had no time to spare. The gate for the connecting flight was at the far end of the terminal. Please, no more surprises.

The end is near and the heavenly promise within reach.

Atta and his strongman hustled quickly through Terminal B, past the still-closed franchise for Legal Seafood, past the blue neon of Auntie Anne's Pretzels, past Hudson News. In their pockets were business-class tickets for American Airlines Flight 11, booked via the Internet on August 28 and credited to Atta's frequent flyer account, number 6H26L04, opened three days before. The daily flight was supposed to depart at 7:45 A.M., with scheduled arrival in Los Angeles at 10:59 A.M. Expected flight time: six hours fourteen minutes, barring unforeseen circumstances. Atta's cell phone rang. He was being called from a telephone booth in Terminal C, the departure area for United Airlines. The conspirators made their final arrangements.

It was 7:25 A.M. when Atta and Alomari reached Gate 26. Several eyewitnesses believe they saw them run. But it turned out that they were not, as they had worried they would be, too late. Boarding had not even begun. Passengers were called ten minutes later—ten minutes before departure. In America you boarded planes the way you board buses in other parts of the world.

But Atta's second bag, checked through from Portland to Los Angeles, got left behind. They couldn't unload it quickly enough from the Beech 1900 to make it onto the Boeing 767. So Atta's last will went rolling about the landing strips of Logan Airport, along with a primer for Islamic suicide attackers—documents that after the fact would disclose a good deal about the perpetrators' thinking.

Remember your luggage, your clothes, the knife and the things you need.

At the gate, Atta and Alomari approached their second security check of the day. The metal detectors did not go off. The X-ray images of their suitcases did not show anything to worry security personnel. Not even knives with blades over four inches long were considered risky by the then-valid security regulations, and were permitted. Atta and Alomari got through. "Have a good flight."

Gate 26. They had to wait three to four minutes. Flight attendants in the blue-and-red uniforms of American Airlines sorted papers and checked computer lists. To them Flight 11 was an "F9C19Y53" flight—nine passengers in first class, nineteen in business, fifty-three in economy. The lists of the flight attendants show 8D next to Atta's name, 8G next to Abdulaziz Alomari, 2A for Wail Alshehri, 2B for Waleed Alshehri, 10B for Satam al-Süqami. The conspirators must have already seen each other at the gate. The team was complete. They had made it.

Meanwhile in Terminal C, a similar scenario took place. Here the team assembled, unremarked, around al-Shehhi. They would take over United Airlines Flight 175, sparsely occupied this morning with eleven crew members, fifty-six passengers, and five hijackers, a Boeing 767-222, built in 1983, with 66,647 flight hours to its credit.

Don't give the impression of being confused, instead be strong and happy with confidence and an open heart because you are engaged in work that pleases God.

God's servants went to work. Not only in Boston, but also amid the cement landscapes of Newark Airport and Dulles Airport outside Washington, D.C., the conspirators of September 11 mixed with the crowd of business travelers and vacationers. The world would learn a great deal this morning. Though as yet no one suspected anything, soon everyone would memorize the numbers of these flights and grasp what they represented.

Boston, September 11, 7:30 A.M.

Passengers for American Airlines Flight 11 assembled at Gate 26. Eighty-one people with purses, carry-on luggage, newspapers. They finished their last-minute phone calls, sent their last text messages, sipped weak coffee from paper cups. Thelma Cuccinello, seventy-one, a grandmother of ten from Wilmot, New Hampshire, had arrived in Boston by bus; her daughter Cheryl had dropped her at the station very early that morning. She planned to visit a sister in California.

Berry Berenson, the widow of actor Anthony Perkins, was on board. She had been visiting the East Coast and was flying home. Jeffrey Coombs was off on a business trip to Los Angeles for Compaq. A full day lay ahead of him; behind him were the good-byes from his wife, Christie, and their children: Meagan, ten; Julia, seven; and Matt, twelve.

Mary Wahlstrom, seventy-five, and her daughter Carolyn Beug, forty-eight, waited to begin their trip home. The thirty-year-old Tara Creamer, married, mother of Colin, four, and Nora, one, also waited. Brian Dale, forty-three, from Warren, New Jersey, waited. Alberto Dominguez, sixty-six, from Sydney, Australia, the father of four, waited. Robert and Jacqueline Norton, eighty-two and sixty, a retired couple from Maine planning a vacation in the American West, waited.

Tie your laces very tight and wear socks, so that the shoes fit snugly on your feet.

Finally they were being boarded. Atta followed the others in line through the passenger loading ramp and into the plane. He was in charge. On September 9 Jarrah had called him "Boss Atta" in a cell-phone message.

It was 7:36 A.M. The flight was going to be slightly delayed; estimates were by fourteen minutes, at 7:59 A.M.

In the plane, as soon as you get on, you should pray to God, because you do this for God, and everyone who prays to God shall prevail.

Atta used the phone. While the plane headed toward runway 4R/22L, he dialed, for the last time, the number of al-Shehhi's cell phone. They were connected for a minute or two, maybe three. Long enough to say things along the lines of, Everyone there? We've done it! We're on board. Allah is great. Paradise awaits.

Atta and al-Shehhi had known each other for a long time.

They had said good-bye to each other face-to-face on September 10. They had spent September 9 together in Boston, where they took care of final business. That evening they phoned the call center of Western Union, entered the appropriate numbers on the phone keypad to transfer $15,000, presumably to a recipient in the United Arab Emirates. The day before, Atta had sent back $7,860; a day later, the tenth, al-Shehhi transferred another $5,400 to the United Arab Emirates to Mustafa Ahmed Alhawsawi, a financial accomplice of bin Laden.

At this moment on this Tuesday morning, Atta and al-Shehhi could nearly see each other in their respective planes. Al-Shehhi and his team had also taken their seats. Just before 8 A.M. their flight rolled along a Logan runway and into the takeoff line behind American Airlines Flight 11. United Airlines Flight 175 would take off just after American Flight 11, at 8:14 A.M.

When the airplane moves, start praying the prayers of traveling Muslims, because you travel in order to meet God and to enjoy the journey.

Atta's American Airlines Flight 11 reached the near end of the takeoff runway and stopped to await control tower clearance. Across the aisle sat David Angell, fifty-four-year-old TV producer, and his wife, Lynn. People loved his sitcoms. Would Angell become the first victim of September 11, murdered with a box cutter?

In the cockpit the pilots pushed full steam on the General Electric turbines, and the plane raced down the 2,500-yard runway toward the northwest at a speed of 180 miles an hour, lifting off at exactly 7:59 A.M.

Pray for yourself and your Muslim brothers for the final victory and fear not, for soon you will encounter God.

World Trade Center, North Tower, 8:00 A.M.

Window washer Jan Demczur was on plan. 77th floor. He began to clean the door of Martin Progressive LCC. He had begun at 6:10 A.M. on the 48th floor at Dai-Ichi Kangyo, the Japanese bank.

Included in Tuesday's cleaning of the floor occupied by Martin Progressive were twelve doors and three large glass-partition walls. The job took Jan Demczur one hour. Shortly after 7 A.M. he would take the elevator up to Carr Futures on the 92nd floor. Like every day, he had to wash the large glass entrance door; this took him about fifteen minutes. Afterward he would go up to the 93rd floor, where he cleaned the entrance door and a glass wall at Fred Alger Management, a brokerage firm. At 8:30 Jan Demczur was done with the company door of Martin Progressive.

It was time for breakfast.

He took an escalator to the 78th floor, location of one of the two "sky lobbies." People who worked on the upper stories changed elevators here. Twelve large elevators shot up from the ground-floor lobby without stopping to the 78th floor, where you could choose among many smaller elevators to get to the higher stories. There were ninety-seven passenger and six freight elevators in each of the two skyscrapers. They were housed together with the utility ducts used for water and sewage and air-conditioning in the heart of the towers, which were built according to tubular principle in order to maximize office footage. As in the old factories in SoHo, which now house boutiques and lofts, there were in the World Trade Center almost no visible supporting columns and relatively thin flooring between each story. The utility shafts were covered with Sheetrock, so that any company moving in had quick and easy access to everything. Almost half the building's total weight was supported by two outer sheaths of steel. This construction was much lighter, more flexible, and more efficient than that used in older New York skyscrapers, such as the Empire State Building.

In the Boston Air Traffic Control Center, a windowless building some thirty-five miles northwest of the city, they were printing the first "flight progress strip" for American Flight 11. The paper strip consisted of seven columns that contained important information, such as flight code, altitude, duration, and position. The air traffic controller recorded the Boeing's takeoff from Boston in Zulu Time— Universal Coordinated Time—and reviewed the flight information on a high-resolution twenty-seven-inch Sony monitor. This morning he was monitoring a total of fourteen long-distance flights as they traversed American airspace.

At 8:15 he began to notice that something wasn't quite right. American 11 was turning slightly to the north over Worcester, Massachusetts, when it should in fact have been turning south.

At 8:20 the cockpit ignored the controller's request to climb to a cruising altitude of thirty-one thousand feet.

At 8:21 the dispatcher in charge of the flight—his name is unknown—began repeating the following radio message: "American 11, this is Boston Center, how do you read?" which essentially means, "Please respond." He expected at any second to receive the four-digit emergency code that pilots transmit in the event of a hijacking. But it didn't come.

As of 8:22 the Boeing's transponder, a type of tracking device for aircraft, stopped emitting signals; it seemed to have gone dead. Flight altitude could no longer be determined. With only a radar image of the aircraft on their screens, the air traffic controllers in Nashua could do little more than watch, with growing alarm, the plane proceed on its incorrect path.

At 8:23 American Flight 11, heading northwest, crossed the southern tip of the Green Mountains, which is where Massachusetts, Vermont, and New York intersect; then, breaking its flight path, it turned toward the Albany-Schenectady-Troy triangle and crossed the northern edge of the city of Amsterdam, south of Great Sacandaga Lake. "American 11, how do you read? This is Boston Center. How do you read?"

At American Airlines System Operations Control center, Craig Marquis, who was on duty this morning, heard the reservations supervisor in Reservations take flight attendant Betty Ong's emergency telephone call. She demanded to be connected to the operations center. Screaming and gasping for air, she reported that two flight attendants had been stabbed and another was being given oxygen. One passenger's throat had been cut; she believed the man dead. Hijackers had forced their way into the cockpit, she said.

Marquis had been working at American Airlines Traffic Control Center for twenty-two years. He was experienced in all kinds of emergencies. He had to make split-second decisions that could cost American Airlines millions: canceling flights because of storms, or deciding whether a threat was a hoax or real.

He grabbed the crew list for American Flight 11 and saw that Betty Ong was, in fact, on board the aircraft. She had made the call from one of the seatback phones and had been connected directly to Reservations when she pressed #8.

Flight 11 had taken off from Boston at 7:59 A.M.

The flight equipment was a Boeing 767-223ER, a special version of their 767-200 series, outfitted especially for American Airlines, one of Boeing's major customers. ER stands for Extended Range. This meant that the model, with a fuel tank capacity of twenty-four thousand gallons, was used mostly for long-distance flights. It was a two-engine aircraft with two aisles and a maximum range of 6,675 nautical miles.

The aircraft was owned by a leasing company and its call

letters were N334AA. It was powered by two General Electric CF6-80-A2 engines, had been built in 1987 and, as of September 11, had completed just under fifty-nine thousand flight hours and 11,789 takeoffs and landings.

Marquis asked that Betty Ong's personnel file be brought to him and asked her for her employee number and nickname. She told him. The call was not a false alarm.

The four hijackers, Ong told him, were seated in first-class seats 2A, 2B, 9A, and 9B. The injured passenger was in seat 10B. The hijackers had attacked the passengers and crew with a spray. Nutmeg or pepper spray, the FBI now suspects. She said her eyes were burning and that she was having trouble breathing.

"Is there a doctor on board?" asked Marquis.

"No. No doctor," said Ong.

Marquis wanted to know whether the aircraft was descending. "We're starting to descend," replied Ong.

Nashua, New Hampshire, Air Traffic Control Center, 8:28 A.M.

The aircraft banked sharply to the south, a 210-degree turn; it seemed as though the pilot were looking for the Hudson River Valley. At the mouth of the Hudson lies New York City. "American 11, how do you read?"

At 8:29 air traffic controllers began to receive radio snippets from the cockpit. The voice of someone with a strong accent could be heard at one point, saying, "Don't try to make any stupid moves! Just stay quiet and you'll be okay." And later: "We have some planes. We have other planes. We are returning to the airport."

Nashua Air Traffic Control Center is responsible for northeastern United States airspace up to an altitude of sixty thousand feet. At 8:29 A.M. it notified the Federal Aviation Administration that American Flight 11, with ninety-two people on board, appeared to be under the control of hijackers.

The center continued to receive bits of radio transmissions, unclear and meaningless, until 8:38. After that, an ominous silence prevailed.

World Trade Center, North Tower, 8:34 A.M.

By now the 78th floor was full of people. Rush hour had begun at the World Trade Center.

Jan Demczur took the elevator down to the 44th floor, home of the second sky lobby. Here people who worked between the 44th and 77th floors changed elevators. Demczur set down his tool bucket next to the elevator bank for floors 67 to 74. From here he would take another elevator up to the 74th floor and his next cleaning job, at Geiger & Geiger, Hyundai Securities Corporation. There was a small bench in the lobby near the elevators where he always stopped to drink his coffee and eat his doughnut. Demczur took the escalator to the cafeteria on the 43rd floor. It wasn't very busy. He paid for his breakfast and returned to the elevator. There were five men in the elevator next to his bucket, and the doors were about to close. They held it open for a second while Demczur got on; the doors closed.

Demczur had been in America since the summer of 1980, when an aunt who married an American invited him to visit her in New York. Demczur was given a tourist visa, something that still surprises him. The American uncle couldn't understand why Demczur would ever want to return home. He was an American and believed that everyone in Poland would be shot sooner or later. It was the era of strikes and the Solidarity movement; there was no work for brigades of plumbers, no work for Demczur. For the time being, Demczur stayed in New York. He wanted to save a little money and wait until things in Poland settled down. He had never been a union man. He just wanted to work. He found a job with a construction company. After sleeping on his aunt's couch for six months, he rented a room of his own in the East Village.

At some point he stopped wanting to return to Poland.

He became an American citizen, but, since his parents were originally from the Ukraine, he sent his two daughters to a Ukrainian Sunday school. He took his children to visit their grandparents in Slubsk, Poland, four or five times. The grandparents lived in the country. It's nice there, he told them. But his kids didn't like Polish food, and they missed their computers, so he bought them a house in America. It had a small yard, and the girls had their own rooms. There was a double garage, though Demczur owns only one car.

The faces in the elevator this morning were vaguely familiar, but he saw hundreds of people every day riding the elevators. He couldn't really place anyone. The older, dark-skinned man with glasses and headed for the 69th floor looked the most familiar to him. He was carrying two cups and two bags. The others were also returning from breakfast. The only one just coming in from outdoors was a beefy man who was wearing what looked like an expensive suit and carrying a laptop.

The elevator started up. All according to Demczur's schedule.

Nashua, New Hampshire, Air Traffic Control Center, 8:38 A.M.

The Boeing moved across the radar screen, a silent dot. Who was piloting the aircraft? Was it the captain, John Ogonowski, a fifty-two-year-old Vietnam veteran and pumpkin farmer from Massachusetts? Had he been the one trying to signal the center by pressing the microphone key on the control wheel in a rapid rhythm? Had he been driven from the pilot's seat at 8:38— until then he had probably thought that this was a traditional hijacking—and then realized the plane was being forced down in New York?

Or had Ogonowski been removed from the pilot's seat as early as 8:28, when the Boeing made a sudden and sharp turn south to hurtle along the Hudson toward New York City?

Or had it been a hijacker pressing the microphone button,

thinking he'd been addressing the passengers? "Don't try to make any stupid moves! We are returning to the airport." The words could have been directed at the pilots, but they also sounded like an attempt to calm the passengers.

Whatever the case, as of 8:40, John Ogonowski was no longer at the controls of the airplane. The Boeing 767 quickly descended to an altitude of nine hundred feet and screamed down toward the tips of skyscrapers and the streets of Manhattan, emitting a shrill sound. At this moment, when it was already much too late to do anything, the official chain of telephone calls comes to an end. Breathlessly, an FAA official informed NORAD—North American Air Defense Command—about the hijacking of American Flight 11.

At 8:41 the crew of United Flight 175, still unaware that it, too, was carrying five terrorists, responded to an inquiry from Nashua Control Center about American Airlines Flight 11 being out of control.

Two minutes before his own aircraft was hijacked by Marwan al-Shehhi and his strongmen, Captain Victor Saracini, a fifty-one-year-old navy veteran, reported that yes, they had been able to intercept something from American Flight 11, a strange transmission shortly after takeoff that sounded "like someone keyed the mike and said, 'Everyone stay in your seats!'"

Soon the transponder of this Boeing 767 also became silent. The presumed hijacking of United Airlines 175 was reported at 8:43. At the same moment two F-15 interceptors took off from Otis Air National Guard Base in Falmouth, Cape Cod—a routine procedure in cases of catastrophe.

On Board American Airlines Flight 11, 8:42 A.M.

As the Boeing hijacked by Atta's group rushed down the island of Manhattan, Madeleine Sweeney, a thirty-five-year-old flight attendant with twelve years' experience who lived in Acton, Massachusetts, called ground control from on board the American Airlines jet. On either a cell phone or an AirFone taken from a seat back, she reached Michael Woodward, one of the managers.

Sweeney calmly and collectedly reported on the situation. "This plane has been hijacked," she said. Two of her co-workers had been stabbed by the terrorists and were lying in the aisle.

Hit very hard in the neck, in the knowledge that Heaven awaits.

They had slit the throat of a passenger in business class. "He appears to be dead," she reported.

Kill and do not think of the possessions of those you will kill.

World Trade Center, North Tower, 8:43 A.M.:

Chuck Allen was sitting at his desk on the 83rd floor when he looked down for a moment at the Hudson River. He saw a small dot in the distance, just above the George Washington Bridge. An airplane. He noticed it because he had never before seen an airplane in that location. It was flying low. Probably approaching Newark.

Allen turned back to his computer screen.

Allen had received his pilot's license a few years ago. He knew exactly what it sounded like when a pilot shoved the gas lever forward to achieve maximum engine thrust. "You can control the altitude of an aircraft simply by modifying engine thrust. The nose of a jet rises when you push the throttles fully forward and full thrust is applied." That was the noise Chuck Allen was hearing at his back at exactly this moment.

Allen was in charge of computer operations at Lava Trading. At 7:15 that morning he had switched on Lava Trading's computers. He was responsible for processing stock exchange data and sending it in real time to his customers, the major Wall Street firms. For some time he had been developing a data backup plan for emergencies. "Just in case a plane crashes into the tower," he once said to his boss, adding quickly that the probability of this happening was next to zero.

On Board American Airlines Flight 11, 8:44 A.M.

Just before her conversation with ground control ended, flight attendant Madeleine Sweeney mentioned the seat number of one of the terrorists. Woodward asked where the hijacked plane was and got the following response: "I see water and buildings. . . . Oh, my God, oh, my God!"

Atta sat in the pilot seat of the cockpit. Through the narrow windows, the Twin Towers at the tip of Manhattan suddenly took on enormous proportions, within fractions of a second, as if through a zoom lens.

The last thing to do is to remember God, and your last words should be that there is no God but Allah and that Mohamed is His prophet.

You will notice that the plane will stop and then start flying again. This is the hour in which you will meet God.

Angels are calling your name.

Boston, 8:44 A.M.

The American Airlines executives had gathered at the Command Crisis Center. Flight 11 was isolated on the screen that shows the positions of all aircraft currently in the air. All eyes followed the movement of a small dot on the screen. The path of Flight 11 became a little shaky after making a turn over Albany, but then it stabilized again.

At 8:45 the radar dot on the screen suddenly stopped moving. For a split second Flight 11 seemed to come to a halt over New York. Then the aircraft disappeared from the screen.

Chuck Allen heard a muffled, sucking, unbearably loud noise at his back. Like the sound of two high-speed trains crossing in close proximity to each other. Allan heard the voice of his programmer, Liz Porter, yelling from the office intercom: "What the hell was that?"

American Flight 11, with ninety-two people on board, crashed into the North Tower of the World Trade Center at a speed of 378 miles an hour.

Chuck yelled back: "A jet-helicopter hit the building, I think." Debris was falling outside the window. Paper floated in the air. Liquid was flowing down the windowpanes. And the tower was leaning to the side. Allan knew that a skyscraper has give. He knew that his floor could swing about five yards in either direction in hurricane-force winds. But this wasn't swinging anymore. The building was simply leaning massively to one side.

Throughout the tower people began to scream, clinging to chairs and desks. Furniture slid around. Pens and file cabinets fell to the floor. Telephone calls ended in midsentence. Computer screens went black.

The Boeing 767 crashed into the north side of the building at about the level of the 96th floor. Floors 94 to 99 were destroyed immediately. The plane hit the center, its wings almost completely horizontal.

A fireball erupted from the west and east sides of the tower, as well as from the hole on the north side created by the plane's impact. The south side was also substantially damaged, with debris spewing out.

With its wingspan of 156 feet, the Boeing 767 had cut through about thirty-five exterior girders upon impact— more than half. Because they were so close together and so firmly interconnected, the remaining exterior columns took on the building's additional weight, thus preventing immediate collapse.

The columns were built so close together only because of a quirk on the part of the building's creator. Minoru Yamasaki, the architect of the World Trade Center, had vertigo. The prospect of standing one thousand three hundred feet above the streets of Manhattan and being separated from the abyss by nothing but a pane of glass made him anxious. Yamasaki believed that skyscrapers of this size should have something solid on their outside walls, something that would give people who live or work in such buildings an impression of safety.

Because there were no supporting columns or walls between the exterior girders and the core of the building, the aircraft encountered almost no resistance as it plowed through offices.

After about six-tenths of a second the heavy parts of the Boeing—the engines, for example—came to a halt in the core of the building, where they destroyed or critically damaged up to half the supports. Fragments also cut through stairwells, severed elevator cables, and displaced entire stairway sections. For everyone above the point of impact at this moment, the tower had become a death trap.

Impact and explosion had ripped the aluminum wings and the fuselage of the aircraft into parts the size of a human fist.

North Tower, 83rd Floor

Through Chuck Allen's office windows the horizon looked skewed. In the walls you could hear a grinding and squeaking. The tension was tearing at the bolts, making a noise he had never heard before, not even in the fiercest of storms. Then the tower came back. Its nearly three hundred thousand tons swung back and forth—four times, five times. Then it was quiet. Completely still. No fire alarm, no announcements. Nothing. Chuck tried to call his wife. He got a dial tone but was unable to make a call. He wife is Palestinian.

Sabah Allen-Hassounah reads the Arab newspapers every day and receives Al-Jazeera, the Arabic-language news channel. The Middle East is not that far away from her house on a hill. Sabah knows many of the leaders of the Arab world personally. She is also familiar with that dubious organization Al Qaeda, and she knew that the Egyptian pediatrician Ayman al-Zawahiri was the true head of the group, that bin Laden was really only its front man.

When Chuck called, his wife was still at an early morning PTA meeting. He looked out the windows and thought about what he should do next. A fire was burning in the hallway and wisps of smoke were seeping in through cracks under the door. There had never been a fire drill.

The Boeing 767 had been carrying enough fuel for a transcontinental flight from Boston to Los Angeles. At impact there were still some nine thousand gallons of fuel on board, most of it in the wing tanks.

On impact the aluminum tanks had ripped apart. Jet fuel shot out with the speed of flight. Its droplets atomized in the air. A combustible mixture formed within fractions of a second.

This mixture exploded on impact, ignited by the enormous heat of friction, by sparks from pieces of steel, by hot engine parts, and most of all by short circuits in the wiring of the North Tower.

The blast wave from the explosion shot through the girders but left them in place. The force of the explosion was so great that parts of the aircraft hurled out of the other side of the tower. After impact, bewildered passersby on a street near the World Trade Center stood around a huge cylinder of bent metal. It took a while before they realized they were looking at an aircraft engine.

The jet fuel was not completely consumed during the explosion. Substantial amounts shot out of the bursting tanks and poured down over lower floors, a petroleum froth that sprayed a film of fuel over stairwells, offices, and elevator shafts at a rate of more than a hundred miles an hour. Curtains, upholstery, and carpets soaked up the fuel like wicks.

Death came in fractions of seconds to people on the floors immediately affected by impact. The fire simply vaporized them.

North Tower, Cantor Fitzgerald Offices

The offices of Cantor Fitzgerald were on the 101st to 105th floors. The company deals primarily in fixed-interest securities, especially government bonds. Governments throughout the world finance their budget deficits with these types of securities.

Twice in its history—most recently in the late 1990s—Cantor Fitzgerald had developed electronic methods to bring this market's sellers and buyers closer together.

Although Cantor Fitzgerald was able to use this technology to secure a substantial market share, it also put some of its own brokers out of business. Thus a recent drop in company morale. Many employees were worried about their jobs. Worldwide, Cantor Fitzgerald employed twenty-one hundred people prior to September 11, of whom one thousand were located in the World Trade Center.

Michael Wittenstein, a broker at Cantor Fitzgerald, was in the middle of a conversation with a customer when the aircraft hit. Shortly after, he called back and apologized, telling the customer, "We are evacuating. I believe there was an explosion in the boiler room." Wittenstein did not make it.

When the airplane hit, a Cantor Fitzgerald auditor was in the elevator. Virginia DiChiara was on her way from the Sky Lobby on the 78th floor to her office on the 101st. Virginia DiChiara is an energetic, active forty-four-year-old with a powerful voice. She wears her hair long. She had left her house in Bloomfield, New Jersey, later than usual that Tuesday. Her two dogs, Remy and Sydney, had wanted to romp outside longer because the weather was so nice.

The express elevator in which she was standing was delayed because a man squeezed in at the last minute. The elevator doors opened again and then slowly began to close. As the gap narrowed to about fifteen inches, the tower suddenly shook. Immediately the doors stopped and the lights in the elevator went out. Two cables in the elevator's ceiling had snapped and were swinging back and forth, spraying sparks. Everyone screamed.

DiChiara saw a blue, iridescent light through the gap in the door. Burning jet fuel was dripping down through the elevator shaft. The man in front of her forced his body through the gap and disappeared into the Sky Lobby. DiChiara thought for a moment. For one second, two seconds, three seconds. The fuel dripped more heavily. She covered her face with her hands and pushed against the doors with her elbows. That was how she got out.

She felt the fuel dripping onto her shoulders. Her hair and her blouse were on fire. She extinguished her burning hair with her hands and then rolled on the ground until the fire stopped burning on her body. She crawled over to a wall and sat down.

She saw that her hands and arms were completely burned. She knew that her face and back were also burned. She felt no pain. She was alone in the Sky Lobby and didn't know what to do. Pieces of marble had broken off the walls. Big chunks were scattered on the floor. Smoke was everywhere.

Then she saw a man with a briefcase walking through the Sky Lobby. She knew him. He also worked for Cantor Fitzgerald, on the 101st floor. She called out. The man came over to her.

"Virginia?" he said.

"I think I'm a little burned," she said.

He tried to help her, but he didn't know how. He knocked on one of the doors on the 78th floor. A man opened. They took Virginia and poured water over her burns. She fainted.

When she returned to consciousness, her colleague said to her, "Virginia, there are two options. We can wait here for someone to come and save us. Or we can walk down, if you think you can make it."

She knew that no one was about to come up to the 78th floor to save her.

"Let's go," she said.

She saw that large pieces of her skin were peeling away from her arms and hands. She saw large blisters forming. She couldn't stand to be touched. She stood up on her own and followed her colleague and a stranger back to the Sky Lobby. Smoke was still everywhere.

The elevator she had been in had disappeared. "A big, black hole," says DiChiara. She had not seen anyone else leave the elevator after she did. Four people had been in it.

The two men led her to the stairwell. They walked down the stairs ahead of her, so that they could catch her if she fell. She had to walk carefully, the burns on her hands kept her from holding onto the stair rail. People got out of the way to let her pass. They stared at her in horror. One woman screamed when she saw her face.

"Don't worry," she said. "I'll be okay again soon."

DiChiara didn't want anyone to panic on her account. A panic in the stairwell would have made it even more difficult for her to escape.

She was very concerned about her face. She saw how bad her hands looked and was afraid that her face was just as severely burned. She asked her colleague.

"Virginia," he replied, "your face isn't nearly as badly burned as your hands."

But she kept running into people who stared at her in horror. Their descent continued smoothly until they reached the 28th floor, where they were held up by firefighters coming up the stairs.

One of the firefighters asked DiChiara if she was okay.

"I'm okay," she said.

On the 21st floor, she stopped when someone handed her a cup of water. She poured some over her arms and drank some. She felt a strong urge to sit down but was afraid she wouldn't be able to get up again. "I'm someone who needs to be active," says DiChiara. She kept going. She wasn't thinking anything.

At least she couldn't remember thinking anything. In retrospect, she says that she probably thought about her brother and the fire she had experienced once before in her life.

She was six and her brother was nine. He was playing with matches. Suddenly both he and the room went up in flames. Little Virginia ran downstairs to get her parents. Her father ran upstairs and grabbed his son, whose skin was already 90 percent burned. The boy died.

North Tower, 83rd Floor

Chuck Allen's programmer, Liz Porter, was standing in her office. She had closed the door to the hallway. For a second she thought, *If worse comes to worst, I'll break the window. At least there's air outside and I can live a few seconds longer. I'd rather jump than burn to death.* Then someone yelled that he'd found a stairwell where it was safe. Only the elevator was burning.

Chuck Allen thought, *They probably won't let me back in the office this afternoon. I'd better get my car keys.* He went back into his office to grab his shoulder bag and the keys. He left his laptop and $1,800 in cash he had just withdrawn from an ATM to pay the electrician. Parts of the building were still falling outside his window.

Allen had experienced car bombs in the Middle East. He had been in Israel when Iraq fired Scuds at the country. He and Sabah were living right behind the American embassy in Beirut when it was blown up in 1983.

Chuck Allen left the 83rd floor of the North Tower at about 9:05 A.M. He was Lava Trading's last employee to leave the office. It didn't really occur to him to see whether anyone was left in the other offices. He had no idea that the employees of General Telecommunications had remained in their cubicles on the same floor, waiting to be rescued.

The stairwell on the building's east side was full of people. The air was still relatively breathable. The four people from Lava Trading stuck together. They were all trying to make calls on their cell phones. Chuck had a reputation among his coworkers for being a little eccentric. In addition to being an amateur pilot, he was an amateur radio operator. He was carrying a two-meter handheld transceiver in his shoulder bag.

Allen transmitted a Mayday signal on various frequencies. As soon as he had established contact he was thrown off the air: "All traffic has been cleared off to keep frequencies clear for emergency calls. Get off the frequency." They thought he was playing around. From the bits of conversation he was able to gather that an American Airlines jet had hit the towers. He didn't get it. "Okay. Planes crash, let's face it. But why into the towers? The pilot had the whole Hudson River, for God's sake. What was wrong with this guy?"

The fire door on the 77th floor was locked. The group had to climb back up the stairs and run back through the tower to find another stairwell. It didn't look good in Stairwell Y. It was filled with smoke and the sickening stench of jet fuel. It made the eyes burn. For the first time, Allen realized that not everyone would make it.

Now they were moving incredibly slowly, step by step. For some reason, a heavyset blond man was holding in his hand the September issue of *Esquire*, with Tom Hanks and Steven Spielberg on the cover in Prada suits. The man holding the *Esquire* was Michael Wright, chief accountant at Network Plus, on the 81st floor. He had been sitting on the toilet reading the Tom Hanks story when the plane hit. When he opened the door of the men's room, there was a three-story gash where there had once been a hallway.

Allen was not particularly religious. He had become something of a fatalist while living in the Middle East. When it's time to go, it's time to go. His colleague Keith started getting nervous. Suddenly he lost his nerve. "I can't breathe! I can't stand this!" he screamed, forcing his way past the others.

They ran into firemen on the 25th floor. They were completely exhausted from climbing the stairs. The firemen told the group, "Keep going. It gets better. It's safe downstairs." But they, too, were afraid. You could see it in their faces.

The air improved when they reached the 20th floor. There was still no fire alarm or announcement on the PA system. At 9:40 Chuck Allen managed to reach his wife, Sabah. She was just about to call a doctor on her cell phone. She was worried about becoming hysterical. She was convinced that Chuck's office had been hit. "Allah," she prayed, "don't let him suffer long." Then her phone rang and Chuck's number appeared on the screen. He told her, "We're still in the building, but we're almost outside." He had to shout to be heard. She could hear people yelling in the background.

North Tower, 106th Floor

Windows on the World was situated on the 106th and 107th floors—one of the best restaurant locations in the, well, world. Anyone who wanted his or her bacon and eggs here had to be a club member. On clear days you could see for fifty miles: the Ferris wheel on Coney Island, the Control Tower at Kennedy Airport. Now you could see nothing but smoke.

Jan Maciejewski worked in the kitchen. He came from Poland. During the day he installed software; at night he worked at Windows on the World. Today, however, he'd put in for the early shift—he needed the money because he wanted to treat his wife, Mary, to a cruise.

After the plane hit, Maciejewski called Mary. He couldn't get down, because all four stairwells had been destroyed. He had to wait for a helicopter. On the phone he seemed calm. He told his wife that he wanted to give her a cruise as a present. She told him to hold a wet towel in front of his face. Then Mary heard the fear in her husband's voice. She had to break off the conversation: Her own building was being evacuated too. She worked on Water Street, only six blocks away from the towers. "I love you, Jan."

"I love you too. Get out now."

When Windows opened in 1976 the city was nearly bankrupt. In the meantime Windows became the highest-grossing restaurant in the United States. It symbolized the rebirth of downtown Manhattan; whoever worked here had more than just a job.

The seventy-nine waitresses, cooks, cleaning staff, vegetable scrubbers, and wine stewards came from more than thirty different countries.

The sixty-three-year-old ladies' lounge attendant, Lucille, was from Barbados. Her boss had told her to come in late this morning. "Get a good rest," she had said. "Come in at nine instead of seven." Lucille, however, came half an hour early as usual, even though she'd been to the hairdresser's the night before.

Victor Kwarkye worked next door in the men's lounge. He came from Ghana and was such a recent arrival in New York that he still bowed to anyone he did not know. The British financial publisher Risk Waters had planned a conference beginning at 9 A.M. in the Banquet Room on the 106th floor. Eighty-seven participants of the conference had already signed in. Some had flown in for the event from Canada or England, and Windows had hired extra waiters to handle the occasion—among them Mohamed Chowdhury, a Muslim from Bangladesh, who had wanted to work today so he could be off tomorrow. His wife was expected to deliver the next day.

Doris Eng, Windows' dining room manager, spent the last minutes of her life calling the central switchboard of the New York Fire Department, six times all told. Each time she asked, "What are we supposed to do?" She got no answer. The stairwells were destroyed, and helicopters were unable to land on the roof because of the thick clouds of smoke.

A man is photographed leaping from the 106th floor. He is Norberto Hernandez, a pastry chief, father of three and grandfather of two. His eyes are closed and he looks calm, as if sleeping.

Two hundred and six people died in these minutes. None

of the seventy-nine employees of Windows on the World survived.

North Tower, 67th Floor

American Flight 11 with Mohamed Atta in the cockpit hit thirty floors above Jan Demczur's elevator, destroying most of the windows Demczur had just cleaned that morning. It killed sixty-nine employees of Fred Alger Management on the 93rd floor, where he had been cleaning between 7:35 and 7:55, and employees of Carr Futures on the 92nd floor whom he'd just seen an hour and a half earlier. The six men in the elevator—which could hold twelve—were being rocked back and forth as it swayed, stopped for a second, swayed again, then started sliding downward. The men pulled themselves together.

An elderly man standing near the door yelled, "Press the STOP button! Press the goddamn STOP button!" Nobody reacted, so he pressed it himself. The elevator stopped and the others stared at him. He was calm.

For five years Al Smith had worked at the post office of the Port Authority, which regulates affairs between the states of New York and New Jersey. It manages the bridges, tunnels, and ferries that link the two states. It also once owned the Twin Towers. Two thousand of the Port Authority's eight thousand employees worked in the World Trade Center. Smith is sixty-one years old, single, and lives in a small apartment next to the subway line in the Bushwick section of Brooklyn. He has held all kinds of jobs; in the 1960s he spent a year and a half in prison for burglary. In prison, someone cut his throat with a razor blade; he still carries a large scar from the experience. He has become calmer with age. He makes sculptures out of wood and cardboard, sells them at flea markets, and would love to be able to support himself that way. He looks younger than sixty-one. He was the smallest man in the elevator.

As on every morning, Smith had just picked up breakfast

for himself and Janet, his handicapped coworker. He always did this on his way to work. First he went to the cafeteria, then to the post office. He was ten minutes late this morning because he had missed his subway train.

It was 8:48 A.M., still quiet, and there was a smell of something burning. Jan Demczur pressed the emergency call button. The emergency call center was located in Lower Level Three of the North Tower. They waited. A calm male voice answered half a minute later. It said that there was a problem on the 91st floor, an explosion or something. Then it fell silent. Demczur pressed the button again, and so did George S. Phoenix III, a Port Authority engineer who worked on the 74th floor. He had been in the building since 8 A.M.; in his left hand he was carrying a small cardboard tray with coffee, milk, and a doughnut. There was no response. Two minutes later, smoke began seeping into the cabin. Black smoke, the kind of smoke you get from burning jet fuel. It started to get warm.

"We have to get out of here," yelled Phoenix.

A stocky man in a nice suit pulled a cell phone out of his jacket pocket but couldn't get a dial tone. Phoenix also tried his. Jan Demczur didn't own a cell phone, and he wouldn't have known whom to call anyway. He tried to open the elevator door. The stocky man in the good suit helped him. His name was John Paczkowski, and he was acting director of the Port Authority. An important job. Paczkowski pulled to the left and Demczur to the right. Luckily it was one of those elevator doors that close in the middle. They got it open. They were looking at a gray wall. Another man in the elevator, Colin Richardson, groaned quietly. The door snapped shut again. Paczkowski and Demczur pulled it open again and jammed the handle of Demczur's squeegee into the door. Once again, they were facing a wall. They were stuck somewhere between the 44th and 74th floors. There were no elevator banks here, just the long elevator shaft and a blank wall.

Demczur ran his hand over the gray surface. It looked like drywall. Paczkowski kicked the wall, but it didn't yield.

Phoenix also gave it a try. Nothing happened. The smoke got worse. Phoenix dipped one of the paper napkins from the cafeteria into his milk and held the napkin over his face. Al Smith, Colin Richardson, and the sixth man, Shivam Iver, did the same thing.

"Anyone have a knife?" Demczur asked. They searched through their pockets, but all they could find were ballpoint pens. Demczur pulled another squeegee from his bucket. He removed the rubber strip from the upper piece and pulled off the handle. Now they had two tools. Demczur started hacking away at the wall with the thin upper piece, which was about fifteen inches long, and handed the short, triangular handle to John Paczkowski. About eight minutes had passed since impact as they began scratching into the wall. It was drywall, not concrete.

The two men with Polish names had taken charge. Richardson and Shivam Iver seemed traumatized. They were silent and groaned quietly from time to time. Al Smith talked to the two men working on the wall, encouraging them. At thirty-six, George Phoenix was the youngest man in the elevator. He wanted to do something, but he didn't know what. He climbed onto the handrail and tried to push open the ceiling, something he'd seen people do in many movies. But the ceiling didn't yield. There didn't seem to be any joints or anything; it was as if it were welded to the walls of the elevator cabin. Phoenix pounded on the ceiling with his fists for several minutes.

Phoenix kept on hammering. Demczur and Paczkowski went on working persistently.

After five more minutes, the two men had scratched inch-deep indentations into the wall. Phoenix, the engineer, suggested making longer gashes to destabilize the drywall surface. They followed his advice. Soon the indentations were more than two inches deep. There were clearly several sheets of drywall, held together by a steel frame.

Someone blamed Al Smith for having pressed the STOP button.

Smith said nothing.

"There's no point talking about it," said the acting director of the Port Authority. He was sweating, glad that they had a task they could concentrate on, anything that moved them forward, kept them together.

Paczkowski and Phoenix took turns. But Demczur wouldn't let go of his tool. He had a plan again and he could get to work. He scratched and scratched, until his hand started to swell and bleed. When they reached the third layer, the metal strip slipped out of his hand and fell exactly into the gap between the door and shaft. Now they had only one tool left. Richardson cursed silently.

By 9:20 A.M. they had been able to scratch a four-inch hole into the wall and the air improved a little. Phoenix grabbed hold of the handrail on the rear wall of the elevator and, with his back to the wall, kicked like a horse at the drywall. The wall cracked. Demczur and the powerfully built Paczkowski, who was a former Marine, joined in too. The edges started to give way and the hole quickly grew. About six inches behind the first wall was a second wall. Fortunately it was much thinner, and Phoenix was able to kick through it on his first try. Now there was a noticeable improvement in the air quality.

During the next few seconds they realized there was a room on the other side of the wall. By 9:30 the hole was big enough for Al Smith, the smallest of the group, to squeeze through.

Smith emerged into the men's room on the 50th floor. He fell onto the tiled floor. The air was good and it was light. He yelled into the hole that he was going to get help.

"I'll be right back," he yelled as he ran away across the tiles. The men in the elevator didn't believe him or didn't want to take the chance. They kept working on the hole. Paczkowski was about twice as big as Smith.

Smith ran across the empty hallway. As he passed the elevator bank, one of the doors opened, and he was standing in front of an open elevator. He knew that he was not really supposed to get in, but he got in any way and took the elevator to the 44th floor sky lobby. It was the same spot they had left forty minutes earlier. His plan worked. When the door opened he found himself in a different world, a catastrophic world of police and firemen running this way and that. Al Smith stopped one of the firefighters and explained his problem. They got back into the elevator and took it up to the 50th floor. By now it was 9:35. When they reached the men's room, the last man, John Paczkowski, was just climbing out of the hole. The men hugged each other briefly.

For the first time that day they introduced themselves. Jan Demczur no longer pronounced his first name the Polish way, and the others thought his name was John. Demczur wrote four telephone numbers onto the small piece of cardboard he used for his schedule. It was 9:40. For the first time, George Phoenix reached his wife on the cell phone.

They all ran into the nearest stairwell, which was completely empty. Demczur also thought about his wife. She worked as a bookkeeper six blocks away. He had met her in a Ukrainian church fifteen years ago. He thought about asking George Phoenix if he could use his cell phone but then decided he could talk to his wife later. The six men stayed together until they reached the 44th floor lobby, where they lost each other in the chaos.

The men from the elevator were together for an entire hour, but now each of them again had to fend for himself. They were in different stairwells, they forgot about each other, so many new things were happening. Most of the people they met were coming from upper floors. For the first time, Demczur learned that an airplane had hit the North Tower.

ATTACK FROM THE SOUTH

World Trade Center, South Tower, 8:12 A.M.

Steve Miller was four minutes late. He pulled his security pass out of his brown leather briefcase and slid it through the electronic reader at the metal gate in the lobby of the South Tower. The traders at Fuji Bank on the 80th floor started their day at 8:20 A.M., and Miller had to have finished checking out their computers by then. Recently the bank had merged with other banks to form Mizuho Holdings, but employees still called it "Fuji."

Being late was no way to start the day. Besides, his new brown boots were pinching him. His wife had talked him into wearing the damn things because she thought they made him look like a cowboy.

By 8:20 A.M. all the computers were working properly and Miller could finally take off the boots. He walked over to the window and gazed out at the Brooklyn Bridge. The air was so crisp this morning that he could even see his apartment in Brooklyn.

Miller had studied religion, history, and literature. He had lived with an Indian tribe for two years, and collected old books, though up here at the bank nobody cared about that stuff. Miller did know his way around computers, however, and that made him one of the most important people on the floor. If monitors went on the blink, Fuji Bank traders could lose millions of dollars within a matter of minutes.

An average trader has as many as six screens lined up on his desk. Together they can transform information from all over the world into money. A little knowledge picked up in the course of a morning—about the falling cost of steel in Indonesia, the rise in interest rates in Russia, the threat of a recession in Brazil—might earn a trader enough money by evening to buy his wife a small token of affection. Say, a Jeep Cherokee.

Miller was not a trader; he was more like a caretaker. All day long, the traders yelled into their phones, but when one of the monitors went down, they all shouted "Smiller!"— his E-mail user name.

It seemed like another one of those days when nothing much would happen. A few traders would stop by, stare out the window at the water, and prattle on about the sailboats they were going to acquire some day.

On Board United Airlines Flight 175, 8:37 A.M.

The skyline of Manhattan was still shimmering in the early-morning light of this late-summer day when the urgent inquiries from Nashua Air Traffic Control Center reached cockpits across New England. Where was American Flight 11? Had anyone sighted the plane? The pilot was no longer responding. Air Traffic Control was not yet sure—beyond all doubt—that the plane had been hijacked. For a good twenty minutes it had been flying off course and now was heading south toward New York City. For eight more minutes it would still be just another Tuesday.

In the cockpit of United Flight 175 pilots heard an air traffic controller request that they look out for the now-silent Flight 11. At 8:38 A.M. Captain Victor Saracini reported, "Yes, we've spotted him . . . seems at about twenty . . . ah . . . twenty-nine thousand, twenty-eight thousand feet." At this moment his own Boeing crossed the Hudson Valley heading west. They had been looking to the left, south, when they saw Flight 11.

Back among the passengers on Flight 175 Ruth McCourt, forty-five, was enjoying her four-year-old daughter Juliana's excited anticipation as they began their getaway. The girl had been promised a visit to Disneyland. Dwarfed by the huge airplane seat, "Miss J" nervously awaited her meeting with Mickey, Goofy, and Uncle Scrooge.

In California they planned to meet up again with Paige Farley-Heckel, forty-six, Ruth McCourt's best friend. The two women had known each other for six years. They shared a love of reading, cooking, and traveling, and generally a gusto for living. Farley-Heckel had booked on American so she could cash in her frequent flier miles. On a normal day, this decision would not have amounted to much. On September 11, however, it meant that Farley-Heckel was sitting in a hijacked airplane and would die eighteen minutes before her best friend Ruth McCourt.

World Trade Center, South Tower, 80th Floor, 8:39 A.M.

Smiller looked around. All in all, he reflected, the World Trade Center was pretty run down. Considering the millions of dollars traders around here earned, it looked kind of pitiful. It smelled of dust, stale coffee, and old food—probably because nearly no one went out for lunch; at lunch hour the elevators took an eternity. The millionaires sat at their desks and ate Big Macs and french fries out of boxes. When a computer crashed and Smiller had to start rummaging through the garbage to find the right cable, he'd first have to comb through old plastic forks, fries, and wadded-up napkins. Disgusting. And why did one of the richest banks in the world choose mud green for the color of the wall-to-wall carpet? Maybe because you couldn't see the dirt on it. Someone around here should do a real cleaning job, not just empty wastepaper baskets at night.

Smiller was paid well for what he did: $120,000 a year,

and as a "bonus" he got the gift of free time. About three-fourths of the time the computer system ran like a well-oiled machine. During long stretches no one was looking over Smiller's shoulder, and he was free to pursue his real interests: searching for old books on eBay, deciding whether tonight he'd bring his wife red peppers or basil and tomatoes, and best of all, working on his magazine. The magazine, titled *Good Bye,* consisted exclusively of stories about the dead. An empty casket adorned the front page. Smiller wrote obituaries of punk rock stars like Joey Ramone, or of a cow in Thailand that had been kicked to death by a professional kick boxer, whom the cow had apparently trampled; the boxer was sentenced to a year in jail. Smiller was a sort of global gravedigger, the negative pole to the traders' positive.

But sometimes Smiller wondered if all this was really worth the money. He sometimes thought he should have become a librarian somewhere rural. And he wouldn't mind losing sixty pounds.

On Board United Airlines Flight 175, 8:40 A.M.

The air traffic controller in Chicago ordered Captain Saracini to change course: "United 175, move thirty degrees to the right. I want you out of that traffic." At 8:41 A.M. Saracini reported having heard that suspicious radio message from American Flight 11 right after takeoff, when a voice told everyone to stay in their seats. These were the last words transmitted. At 8:43 A.M. radio contact with United Flight 175 broke off forever.

The pilots, crew, Ruth McCourt and daughter, and all the other passengers were in the hands of the hijackers. Instants earlier the terrorists must have jumped out of their seats in first and business class—Marwan al-Shehhi in 6C, Hamza and Ahmed Alghamdi in 9C and 9D, Fayez Ahmed and Mohald Alshehri in 2A and 2B—and herded passengers and crew into the last rows. They killed at least one flight attendant. And at least one of the hijackers disappeared into the cockpit: Marwan al-Shehhi.

Smiller's mood got a lift when he read an article over the Internet about rich American women who had gotten it into their heads to conquer Mount Everest. The expedition cost $70,000, but even so—according to this article, anyway—they usually only succeeded in falling in love with the sherpa hired to get them to the top, because sherpas were so unaffected and lovable. One or two married their guides and brought them back home. Afterward they couldn't understand why their rich friends looked at them as if they'd lost their minds.

It was 8:45 A.M., a calm day. If none of the computers crashed, Smiller could bury a few more corpses.

Suddenly he seemed to feel his desk tremble. A gust of wind hissed past his window. *Strange,* Smiller thought, *a thunderstorm on a day like this?* Or was it simply the automatic window-washing machine on its quarterly cleaning run?

Smiller went to the window to see what had happened. Tens of thousands of bits of paper were sailing through the air, like a tickertape parade when the Yankees won another World Series. Where was it coming from? Since when did anyone throw tickertape off the top of the World Trade Center?

Ten seconds later Mr. Keigi, one of the Japanese directors of the bank, ran past Smiller's desk. Mr. Keigi seemed very upset. He made wild gestures with his arms. "Get out of here!" he yelled. "A bomb, a bomb in the North Tower of the World Trade Center!"

Smiller remembered that the directors of the bank always speculated that next someone would steal a nuclear bomb from Russian stockpiles and set it off in the harbor. *Oh, well,* Smiller thought to himself. He put on his boots and went out. He'd have to wear them down eighty flights.

He dashed into the stairwell, ran down three flights of stairs, and started sweating terribly. This wouldn't do. He looked around. The serious expressions of the others stirred a sense of anxiety in him. This calm, "just-don't-panic-now" panic was nearly as bad as real panic.

Otis Air National Guard Base, Cape Cod, 8:52 A.M.

Two F-15 fighter jets took off from Otis Air Force Base on Cape Cod in pursuit of the hijacked airplane.

The jets were twenty-four years old. Still, they were equipped with heat-sensitive, radar-guided rockets. They had missed stopping the first hijacked passenger plane and now they were late for the second. No one had really thought about the possibility of being attacked from the air. On the day that four commercial airplanes fell from the sky like weapons of war, the United States had on standby, to defend an area of nearly four million square miles, exactly fourteen fighter jets.

After the terrorists had taken control of Flight 175, the Boeing raced across southeastern New York at 500 mph and into New Jersey, flew over Newton, veered sharply east at the level of New Brunswick, then north again across Staten Island and upper New York Harbor, describing a wide arc aimed toward downtown Manhattan.

On Board United Airlines Flight 175, 8:54 A.M.

Ruth McCourt could not have known that during these very minutes her brother, Ron Clifford, a businessman from New Jersey, was walking through the lobby of the Marriott Hotel at the foot of the North Tower. She could not have known that during the same minutes a badly burned woman was staggering out of the tower and into his arms. But she may well have started to suspect by now that she herself would die in this plane. So would her daughter. And everyone else.

Sentenced to death with her in the rear of the Boeing were three Germans, the entire administrative leadership of BCT Software of Baden-Württemberg: Heinrich Kimming, president of the Board of Directors; Klaus Bothe, director of development; and Wolfgang Menzel, director of personnel.

Among the rows in the milky light of the cabin, Brian Sweeney, a thirty-eight-year-old business consultant from Barnstable, Cape Cod, held a mobile phone in his hand and left a last message for his wife Julie on the answering machine.

"Hi, Jules, it's Brian. I'm in a plane being hijacked and it does not look good. I just wanted to let you know that I love you and that I hope to see you again."

Calmly, as if without fear, he added, "If I don't, please have fun in life and live your life the best you can."

World Trade Center, South Tower, 8:59 A.M.

United Flight 175 approached Manhattan from the southeast, descending. At the helm, presumably, was Marwan al-Shehhi, his field of vision focused on the goal, the world passing by under the belly of the Boeing as it dropped its nose and crashed into the South Tower.

Angels are calling out your name.

South Tower, 9:00 A.M.

Smiller had reached something like the 65th floor when he heard an announcement: "The fire," said a voice over the loudspeaker system, "is only in Tower One. You may return to your seats and resume your work." *What the fuck,* thought Smiller. He looked for an elevator and jumped in. About ten others stood around him waiting for the elevator to start moving. Smiller felt packed in. He was sweating. *What the fuck*, he thought again, jumped out, and went back to the stairwell. Mr. Keigi and three of Smiller's other bosses rode back up to the 80th floor. They wouldn't survive.

Two minutes later, Smiller left the stairwell again. Traffic jam. He went in search of a phone. He wanted to tell his wife that they were being evacuated but that he was fine. He heard that people in the other tower were jumping. *Now that's fucked up*, he thought. *I don't want to see that.* He looked down and there was a loud explosion.

South Tower, 9:03 A.M.

The United Boeing 767 pierced the tower at the southeast corner and blew up on the opposite side. Most likely, the force of impact destroyed at least four floors, perhaps even six; a huge fireball burst from the tower in two directions.

Images shot by an amateur filmmaker from the vantage point of Battery Park at the southern tip of Manhattan show that the plane was in a sharp turn when it hit the South Tower. Apparently, the hijackers nearly missed their goal and had to crank the plane around in the last minute.

The Boeing had two Pratt-Whitney JT9D-7R4D engines; upon impact the plane weighed about 112 tons. The force with which it slammed into the tower was enormous, but the tower was sunk more than two hundred feet below-ground; it took about six-tenths of a second until the plane, or whatever remained of it, stopped moving. According to experts' calculations the force of impact was probably about 32,600 kilonewtons. The building had been designed to withstand much more: A hurricane-force wind raging against its broad side might amount to as much as 58,400 kilonewtons.

Looked at from above, the World Trade Center towers consisted of two rectangular tubes: a nearly square outer tube and a rectangular core in the center. The inside core of the building contained the eight shafts for the elevators and the three stairwells.

Loaded with about 9,500 gallons of jet fuel for the flight from Boston to Los Angeles, Flight 175 probably hit the tower with roughly 8,200 gallons of fuel left.

Unlike the plane that went into the North Tower, the plane that plowed into the South Tower was stopped in its course not by the whole rectangular core of the tower but by one of its corners. The Boeing demolished or sheered many girders and almost completely destroyed the drywall lining of the insulating shell that protected the steel columns against fire.

In any case at least one stairwell in the building's central core remained intact—the reason that in the South Tower some people from floors above the impact survived.

South Tower, 9:03 A.M.

The ground shook as if in an earthquake. Fuji Bank's computer whiz threw himself on the carpet, hands shielding his head. Smiller got up again after two seconds. *What the fuck?* He went back to the stairwell. People were still standing around. Smiller had to go to the bathroom. Nice and clean, he thought as he sat down in the stall.

South Tower, 81st Floor, 9:03 A.M.

Twenty floors higher and twenty minutes earlier, Smiller had been sitting peacefully thinking up new obituaries. Now, Smiller's colleague Stanley Praimnath had to throw himself under his desk to keep Flight 175 from picking him off. Praimnath, computer expert in the Loans Department, had just reassured a colleague in Chicago: No, the fire was in the tower next door. Security had sent them back to their offices. "Everything here's okay." Then, looking out the window at New York Harbor and the Statue of Liberty, he suddenly saw a huge red *U* and an *A,* and the massive gray body of an airplane speeding directly toward him—no, not

71

speeding, because at that moment Stanley Praimnath's world went into slow motion. The roar of the turbines was the most horrible sound he'd ever experienced. He thought, *Oh, Lord, You take over. I can't help myself here.* He saw, right before impact, how the right wing of the plane lifted up slightly. He threw himself under the desk.

Because of the slight turn before impact, the Boeing 767 hit above Praimnath's office. He cowered under his desk, the sound of torn steel lingering in his ears. He had heard no explosion. The ceiling collapsed, part of the floor disappeared; he was covered with debris, but unharmed. He waited for the explosion. He cried and prayed, "Oh, Lord, I still have so much to do. Please let me see my family again. Please, Lord, let me out of here."

Stanley Praimnath is very religious. He's happiest on Sundays while leading Bible class at Bethel Assembly of God in Elmont, Long Island. Every morning in the shower he prays: "Lord, cover me and all my loved ones under Your precious blood." Since the death of his father, he has felt he has a direct connection to God. In his words, "I call Him, and He responds."

The explosion never came. Once Praimnath was able to free himself from the debris and get back on his feet, he could see, no more than thirty feet away through a doorframe at the end of a hallway, the tip of an airplane wing, burning. Electric cables dangled, sparks flew; it was dark from all the dust. The air reeked.

Praimnath crawled on his belly from the Loans Department into what had once been the lounge. Next, into Telecommunications, where the door to Stairwell A should have been located. "Oh, Lord, help me, send me help." The exits, however, were blocked by debris. Then on a piece of ceiling he saw the reflection of a flashlight. He started pounding against the wall, screaming, "Please, don't let me die, wait for me. It's me, Stan, from the Loans Department."

United Airlines Flight 175 crashed only two or three stories below the offices of Euro Brokers but diagonally across from them. Nothing was left of his office when Brian Clark got back on his feet. It was like a dry explosion. No flames, no smoke, just total destruction of the dividing walls, dropped ceilings, computer terminals. Suddenly it went dark. Clark, the vice president of Euro Brokers, was fire marshall for his firm. Fifteen minutes earlier the fifty-four-year-old had been sitting at his desk when the plane crashed into the North Tower. No reason to start a panic in the South Tower. In his mind he had a picture of the Empire State Building in 1945, when an Air Force B-25 bomber had flown into it during a heavy fog.

Clark took out his flashlight and with five coworkers found the door to Stairway A. It was hot and sooty, and smelled of smoke. They made it down three flights. Through a crack in the wall of the stairwell Clark saw the shimmer of flames from the inner office spaces. On the 81st floor they ran into a heavyset women accompanied by a slender man. The woman was panting. She said it was safer to go up to the roof and wait for a helicopter.

Clark said—forcefully—that it was a better idea to start the descent. Then he heard someone banging against the wall. He heard a voice: "Help, help. I can't breathe anymore." Clark decided to leave the group behind and check it out.

His fellow worker Ron DiFrancesco was the only one who decided to continue down the stairs. The heavy woman convinced the others to help her get up to the roof. The last Clark ever heard from his people: "We'll make it. It'll all work out."

Clark followed the cries for help and saw in the midst of wreckage a relatively unharmed wall of Sheetrock. An open-

73

ing had been knocked out. A hand was reaching out of the gap. It was the hand of Stanley Praimnath.

"Who are you? Do you believe in Jesus Christ?" said the voice behind the wall. "Who sent you? You're my guardian angel." Later, Praimnath would not remember why he asked all these questions. He remembered only that he was convinced that he was supposed to die at that moment.

A piece of the ceiling broke off and fell onto Praimnath's other hand, pushing a nail into it. This was no time for theology. Clark answered, "My name's Brian. I go to church every Sunday. But if you're looking to save yourself, please try to climb over the wall."

"Let's pray together," Praimnath answered.

So it was that Stanley Praimnath and Brian Clark, separated by a wall of Sheetrock, kneeled down on the 81st floor of the burning South Tower and prayed together amid the ruins of Fuji Bank's Loans Department.

After that they enlarged the hole in the wall and Praimnath succeeded in squeezing through. He was weeping from exhaustion and fear. His shirt was gone, his undershirt looked as if it had gone through a shredder. Before him stood a stockbroker in his elegant if heavily dusted suit. They hugged each other. Clark said, "If we get out of here, we'll be brothers for life."

South Tower, 44th Floor

Anthony DeBlase, another trader for Euro Brokers, took a different course of action from that of his boss Brian Clark. When the Boeing 767 crashed into the neighboring tower at 8:45 A.M., he immediately proceeded to descend. His brother Jimmy worked over where the flames were.

It was burning fairly high up in the North Tower. He counted the floors. Then he phoned Cantor Fitzgerald where Jimmy worked. No answer.

Since the 1993 attack, Anthony DeBlase had not been able to shake the fear that the tower might fall over one day.

When they were kids, he and Jimmy once calculated how far the tower would fall if somebody cut it down. At least as far as Chinatown, they speculated.

"It must have been a small plane. It'll all work out," said Peter Ortale from the neighboring desk. He had been married only last May. "If everything's okay I'll be back in twenty minutes," said DeBlase and went out to the elevator. Ortale stayed behind. Except for Brian Clark and Ron DiFrancesco, so did the other sixty employees of Euro Brokers. Not one would survive the day.

As soon as Anthony had left the office, his mother Anita called from a polling station on the Lower East Side. The sixty-one-year-old was volunteering today—Primary Day for New York City's mayoral election. One of Anthony's colleagues, possibly Peter Ortale, answered the phone and said that Anthony had left already. Anita DeBlase was relieved.

She was glad that her youngest son Richard had walked off his job two years ago in order to be in the fashion business. Before that, his office had been all the way up beyond the 100th floor. She went out on the street and saw the plume of smoke from the North Tower from more than a mile away. She crossed herself. "God help those people."

Only when her husband walked into the polling center with a Pall Mall in his mouth and declared, "Jimmy-boy's in there," did she remember that her oldest son Jimmy had recently gone to work for Cantor as a bonds trader. At once she set off toward the towers. She had been only sixteen years old when Jimmy was born.

In their teens the three DeBlase brothers had sworn to kill anybody who killed one of them. Many of their friends either had wound up in jail or were heading that way. Not the three DeBlase brothers. They had all made it—one more broad-shouldered than the next, more ambitious than their father, who emigrated as a child from Italy and became a limousine driver.

Jimmy, Anthony, Richard. From the bumpy cobblestones and warehouses of downtown Manhattan's West Side they had struggled their way up those towers, which, since 1971, had been looming over them. Every morning that Anthony DeBlase walked to work at Euro Brokers he could recapitulate his life story: out of bed at 6:45, down Greenwich Street to the South Tower, and all the way up on the express elevator.

Anthony DeBlase had always been sure that Jimmy would outlive them all. Jimmy had all his ducks in a row. He was the exact opposite of his father, who spent the day smoking on his golden velvet couch, reading books with titles like *How to Make 10 Thousand Dollars in a Day for 30 Days*. Jimmy was six feet tall and weighed nearly three hundred pounds. He coached football and had three sons and a house in Manalapan, New Jersey. He was head of the family, the type who wears a bright red blazer and sings karaoke at dinner parties: bursting with self-assurance, sometimes overbearing.

At this moment, worry over his brother chased Anthony DeBlase down the stairs. People were jam-packed on the 66th floor. Anthony DeBlase was starting to get nervous. Behind a door he found a freight elevator that went to the 44th floor. Anthony still heard the announcement: "Everything's safe. You can return to your offices." Then, some twenty seconds after he and about ten others had got out of the elevator in the South Tower, he heard an explosion in the elevator shaft. It had caught up with his tower now—the second plane had hit.

On the 40th floor, Anthony met a nine-year-old boy who had gotten separated from his mother. "Do we have to die?" the boy asked him. "Sure, but not today," DeBlase answered. DeBlase started to crack jokes about the big woman in front of them: "Seen her butt?" He was trying to cheer up the boy—and also himself.

Later, Anthony DeBlase would learn that at that moment Jimmy DeBlase was calling his wife, Marion. "A plane hit the tower. We all have to get out."

The offices of Cantor Fitzgerald, the financial firm where Jimmy DeBlase worked, were located on the 101st to 105th floors of the North Tower. American Flight 11 had rammed into the floors just below. At 8:46 A.M. 677 of Cantor's roughly 1,000 employees were sitting at their desks, already at work.

The explosion tore them into pieces. They burned up. Or suffocated. Or jumped out the window in despair.

Deanna L. Galante. Secretary, thirty-two, planning to go on maternity leave in six weeks.

James J. Kelly. Mortgage broker, thirty-nine, got up early many a Sunday morning to make waffles and milkshakes for his four daughters.

Laurence Michael Polatsch. Stockbroker, thirty-two, on the fast track. Once he even talked to Julia Roberts at a newsstand and asked her out to dinner. She nearly accepted.

Lisa and Samantha Egan. Sisters who worked in the personnel office, thirty-one and thirty-four, who perished the way they lived their lives, together.

Ward Haynes. Broker, thirty-five, test-drove his new Porsche for the first time the weekend before.

Edward Mazzella. Vice president for sales, sixty-two, gone three days before he was supposed to retire.

Jonathan Connors. Another vice president, fifty-five. In a red box he kept souvenirs of that day in 1993 when the World Trade Center was attacked for the first time: a soot-smeared shirt, a Metrocard, and the cashmere scarf he'd used for a face mask.

Jacquelyn Sanchez. Secretary, twenty-three, called her mother a last time to say good-bye to her eleven-month-old son.

Joshua Rosenblum. Assistant broker, twenty-eight, planned to marry Gina Hawryluk, a Cantor colleague who had taken time off to prepare for the big day.

Jude Safi. Broker, twenty-four, knew all Elvis and Sinatra songs by heart.

Troy Nilsen. Computer expert, thirty-three. Three months after the attack, his autistic son Scott was still looking for Daddy.

Kaleen Pezzuti and Matthew Gryzmalski. Twenty-eight and thirty-four, they met on the 105th floor of the World Trade Center and grew to love each other.

Zuhtu Ibis. Computer expert, twenty-five, born in Turkey. He came to the United States when he was eighteen and worked himself up to the 103rd floor of the World Trade Center.

Fred Gabler. Broker, thirty, was supposed to become a father in October.

Jude Moussa. Bond trader, thirty-five, left his native Lebanon sixteen years ago because he was fed up with terrorist bombs.

All 677 people who worked that morning in the offices of Cantor Fitzgerald were dead. Including Jimmy DeBlase.

North Tower, 89th Floor

Cantor Fitzgerald was one of the eight really large companies spread across the 204 floors of the World Trade Center. But those two gleaming proud towers also contained many smaller companies that one might not expect to find there.

If there were such a thing as a typical floor in the World Trade Center, it might have been the 89th floor of the North Tower. It housed the downtown office of MetLife, a small insurance company, a public relations agency, a shipping company, two law firms, and a lot of empty office space—nearly a fourth of the entire floor.

This morning, Rafael Kava was sitting in the offices of Mutual International Forwarding, the floor's small shipping company. The eighty-year-old Kava did not lose his calm when the world exploded a few floors above his head. The building reared up, throwing him off his chair, the windows blew out of their frames, and fire poured from the ceiling. Kava slowly got up, took his briefcase and his hat—the kind that old men in France and Italy wear when they play boule or boccie—and proceeded without particular haste to leave the office of his small shipping company on the 89th floor of the North Tower.

It was hard to surprise him.

Rafael Kava's family had often had to escape. For as long as he remembered, actually. Kava's father was a Jew from Vienna who later worked as an Italian civil servant in Alexandria, Egypt, where Rafael Kava was born in 1921. Until 1956 he lived in Egypt. After that, he had lived in Milan. He had been a printer in small shops. In 1976 Kava emigrated to New York, where his nephew Albert Cohen had started a shipping company. Albert had fled from Egypt to America in 1962. The shipping company was a family affair—Cohen's wife, Cohen's son, and his son's wife worked there too.

Rafael Kava lived with his sister on Staten Island. He usually did not sleep well and woke up early, which is why he commuted to Manhattan earlier than the others. He was always the first person on the 89th floor. At 6:30 A.M. he would sit down at his small desk next to the entrance door and start to type lists on his electric typewriter. He did not want to get accustomed to a computer, and he would not get accustomed to English either. He was fluent in Italian, Arabic, and French, but his English was limited. Nobody would think of forcing him to learn: Kava was something like the soul of the shipping company.

The hall was filled with black smoke. At first Kava just stood there and tried to get oriented. He thought about where he should go, about whom else on the floor he knew. He had been on the floor for twenty years, but he hardly knew anyone. There was Walter, the bald man from the insurance company next door, and of course Theresa, the sweet secretary at Cosmos Services—he spoke Spanish with her. And then there was the black lady who worked for the lawyers at the other end of the floor. He did not know her name.

Kava stood next to the door, took two or three steps into the dark, to where he assumed Walter and Theresa might be, then he stepped back. He tried the other direction, toward the lawyers' office; again he couldn't see anything and stepped back. The air quality was getting worse and worse. Not so far away, he heard women screaming. He waited in front of his nephew's office. He did not want to forget anything.

He called for help, quietly.

Mutual International Forwarding was at the north end of the North Tower, almost exactly seven floors below where the plane hit. The shipping firm rented about seven hundred square feet, the smallest rented space on the 89th floor. But then Mutual International Shipping had been there the longest too. Two years before the inaugural festivities marking the official opening of the World Trade Center, the shipping company had moved into the North Tower. At that time the 89th floor did not even exist. Mutual International was the first company to rent space on the 19th floor; they were still working over their heads. They had occupied offices on the 89th since 1992. The World Trade Center meant a lot to Albert Cohen and his uncle Rafael Kava; it was a symbol of having arrived after being on the run for so long. They lived in New York, they worked in the World Trade Center.

It was important for small firms to have "World Trade Center" appear on their letterhead. It conveyed a sense of financial power, of being part of the global marketplace. In that way the World Trade Center was almost more valuable for its wrapping than for its contents. The two huge towers were the symbol and seal of concentrated wealth.

The World Trade Center had initially been conceived as a center for overseas trade, not as a financial center. In the early 1970s the first occupants were shipping companies like Cohen's and Kava's, ship insurance companies, and lawyers specializing in international trade.

When the cost of downtown real estate boomed in the early eighties, many of the maritime companies could no longer afford the rents. Stockbrokers in dark suits and button-down shirts replaced shipping agents wearing jeans. In the end the largest tenants were Morgan Stanley, Fuji Bank, and Cantor Fitzgerald, all financial services companies. Insurance companies such as Aon, Marsh & McLennan, and Guy Carpenter had also rented entire floors.

Walter Pilipiak's company was average in size: fourteen people, about two thousand eight hundred square feet on the north end of the tower, 89th floor. Right in the middle. On the right was Rafael Kava's shipping company, on the left an advertising agency. Pilipiak is forty-eight years old, a broad-shouldered, balding man who once played ice hockey. He grew up in Brooklyn, and you know it to hear him talk. He has sold insurance for the last thirty years and specializes in ships and harbors in Japan. For the last three years, he has been head of Cosmos, an offshoot of Itocha, the world's third-largest shipping firm.

Like Rafael Kava, Pilipiak knew hardly anyone on the floor, but as an insurance man he always greeted each and every person he met, including the Chinese lawyer who joined him this morning in the elevator from the 77th up to the 89th floor. Mr. Lin was thirty-one years old and worked with a secretary in an office on the west side of the building. Mr. Lin did not return the greeting. He never did, according to Pilipiak. Pilipiak saw the young Chinese man disappear into his office, which was right next to the elevator.

American Flight 11 hit just as Pilipiak was unlocking the steel door to his office. He and the door were hurled into the office. His hockey experience helped. Pilipiak twisted in midair; his shoulder slammed into a wall of Sheetrock. The building shook. Inside the office were his four coworkers—Theresa Moya, Okane Ito, Harold Martin, and Yoshi Movi. Pilipiak was afraid; he didn't know whether the tilting would end. After what seemed like an eternity, the motion stopped and the tower screeched back into position. Pilipiak heard steel ripping. He jumped up. His coworkers looked at him—he was the boss. Dense black smoke had begun seeping into the room through the open door. Pilipiak ran out. The small passage to the elevator that he had just walked through was filled with thick smoke and smelled of gasoline. *The same way it smells when you fill your tank on a warm summer day,* thought Pilipiak, *only one hundred times stronger.* Pilipiak walked a few steps. He heard women screaming. Then he spotted Rafael Kava.

The old man was standing in the hallway with his briefcase and hat, as if waiting for a train. The hat reminded Pilipiak of his father-in-law, who came from Italy and always wore the same kind. Pilipiak's roots are in Byelorussia.

"Come with me," he called out to Kava. He brought Kava with him into his office and closed the door. Inside, the air was still okay, especially compared with the hallway. It was strange that none of the windows had been destroyed, since the plane hit just above them, and next door, in Kava's office, all the windows had burst out of their frames. Pilipiak sat Kava down on an empty office chair. Theresa Moya, the secretary, brought the old man some water. She had known him for a long time. Pilipiak wondered about the whereabouts of all the other employees. Twenty people were supposed to be here. He stuffed his jacket into the opening under the door and called his wife, who worked three blocks north on Broadway. There was no answer. He called one of her colleagues and asked him to tell her that he was alive.

At that moment, someone outside banged at the door. Pilipiak opened up. A woman with blond hair, her face covered in soot, stood before him. She pointed down the hall, to the east, to where the communications company was located.

The woman's name was Lynn Simpson. She was director of Strategic Communications, the PR agency located in offices on the 89th floor's northeast side. The offices no longer existed.

Strategic Communications advises big financial firms on their advertising and publicity, and organizes their parties and conferences. It had leased about six thousand five hundred square feet on the northeast side of the tower. This morning, five of the company's twenty-four employees were in the office. At the reception desk, Sabrina Tirao waited for phone calls. Evan Frosch, a graphic designer, and Frances Ledesma, project coordinator, were working in the company's small library, leafing through material for an elaborate image campaign for a big New York bank that Strategic Communications would launch later in the week. That was why Lynn Simpson had been tied up in discussions with art director Thomas Haddad since 8 A.M.

Thomas Haddad did not see a shadow or hear the plane approaching. Everything happened simultaneously in his head: the approach and impact, the images and sound. It was light and noise all at the same time. Maybe more noise than light, incomprehensibly loud, and Haddad thought he saw two large sparks, two streaks of light behind him. Then he was thrown to the ground like everyone else.

When they looked up again, half of their offices were gone. The explosion had split the Strategic Communications offices in two. The only reason the five employees were alive was that they had been working on the right side, the western side. The eastern part was burning. The ceiling burst open, the windows exploded.

Lynn Simpson was lying in the middle of the conference room. She had been thrown a few feet and her face was bleeding. She looked around to see Haddad standing in front of open sky. Two of three windows had blown out. A small fire was burning in the conference room; liquid fire was dripping from the ceiling and accumulating on the conference table, like a puddle on fire. Lynn Simpson's office, in the rear, had been chopped off. She ran out into the hall. She stumbled through the darkness, heard screams, then turned back, got lost. Suddenly a door opened, a ray of light shot into the hall, then the door closed again. It was the moment when Walter Pilipiak was stuffing his jacket under the door. She went to the door, banged against it; Pilipiak, whom she didn't know, opened it. The air got better. She took three or four deep breaths and ran back to get her people.

Before Simpson got there she ran into them in the hall. They were holding hands like children. The office was burning behind them; Simpson saw the conference table go up in flames.

All of them proceeded to the Cosmos offices. They met people for the first time. The PR agency had been there for six years but had had no contact with other tenants. Now there were eleven of them in the insurance offices, five from Cosmos, five from Strategic Communications, and Rafael Kava, who was holding his hat in his lap. Cosmos was something of an island; it seemed to be the last place on the 89th where you could still breathe.

No one believed that anyone else on the floor had survived. They made phone calls. Haddad called his wife. He told her he wasn't sure he'd ever see her again. Frances Ledesma kept reminding a friend that she had life insurance. Until five minutes earlier, most of the people in this room had never exchanged a word. Now they were putting their affairs in order in front of each other. Kava was the only silent one.

Pilipiak went and got a radio from his office and placed it in the middle of the large room. The announcers were talking about a plane that had flown into the World Trade Center. They were joking about drunk pilots; it was one of those off-the-wall early-morning broadcasts. Art director Thomas Haddad couldn't stand it and switched to an all-news station.

It was at that moment that United Airlines Flight 175 hit the South Tower. They heard the dull sound of impact but couldn't see anything. Again the building swayed, but much less than the first time. The radio announcer sounded desperate. "We're being attacked!" he shouted. Outside the sky was still blue. They saw a police helicopter still in the air, facing them, looking in at them through the windows. Then it turned away, as the people inside knew they were helpless to do anything.

Three floors below, James Gartenberg and his secretary Patricia Puma were trapped in the ruins of their office. Gartenberg worked for Julien J. Studley, Inc., a real estate firm that scouted office space for large companies. The firm had plans to close this branch in November. Gartenberg had been given the option of moving to the main office in Midtown or to a branch in New Jersey. Neither move would have improved his position. He was thirty-six, and for some time now he'd had an offer from a competitor. September 11 would have been his last day of work at Julien J. Studley and in the World Trade Center.

Gartenberg and Puma were not able to open the door to the stairwell. Puma tried the phone on her desk. It worked. She called 911. No connection. She called home, though she knew that at that moment her husband was taking the kids to school. They had three children, the youngest sixteen months. Nobody was home. Gartenberg ran past her and out into the hall. He looked like he'd lost his mind. When he came back he said he couldn't open the door to the stairwell, it was blocked by debris. Fire was everywhere. They were trapped.

Puma tried again to reach home. Her husband had returned. He was sitting with their baby daughter. She was calm at first, then became hysterical during the course of the conversation, as if finally realizing what had happened. She began to scream and weep. She told her husband what she had seen. Fireballs erupted out of elevator doors, a wall had caved in.

When the plane slammed into the tower, Patricia Puma had been on the way back from the bathroom. The explosion caught her in the hall. A fireball completely destroyed the bathrooms on the 86th floor. Where moments before she had looked at herself in the mirror, now was a dark hole. The tower swayed, the steel frame screeched. Puma was thrown to the ground, stood up, started running again between the swaying walls of her office. Something behind her collapsed—it must have been a wall. If she had been were she was two seconds earlier she would have been buried in the wreckage, she told her husband.

"I love you. Stay calm. I'll call the police," said Kevin Puma.

She put down the receiver. The phone on Gartenberg's desk rang.

It was Adam Goldman, one of Gartenberg's friends from school. Goldman lived in Chicago. He had heard on TV that a plane had flown into the North Tower.

"Adam, we have a fire on the floor," Gartenberg screamed. "I'm shut in, I won't get out."

Goldman explained to his friend that it had been a plane crashing into the building.

"On TV it looks as if the smoke was up," he said, "so you're better off going down."

"We can't get out," said Gartenberg.

"Stay calm," said Goldman.

"I can't stay calm, Adam! I'm scared. Please come get me out."

Gartenberg hung up and called the company's main branch in Midtown. The receptionist didn't know anything about the accident. She connected him to the director of personnel, Margaret Luberda. Luberda had joined the company only a few months earlier. She did not know Gartenberg personally and had heard that he planned to leave the company. She didn't know about the attack, either. She was sitting in a windowless office on the fifth floor of a highrise on Park Avenue.

"Margaret, we are trapped!" yelled Gartenberg.

"What's happening?" Luberda asked calmly.

At that moment, a colleague tore open her door and told Luberda what had happened. It was 8:52 A.M. Everyone thought it had been a small plane or a sightseeing helicopter.

"Where are you?" asked Luberda.

"In the reception area. The glass is completely blown out. It's all gone."

Gartenberg saw Brooklyn, just as glorious as before. He saw blue sky and bits and pieces falling down from above, but he didn't see any smoke. The glass walls that had separated the reception area from the brokers' offices didn't exist anymore. Suite 8617 had become one giant office.

"So go find the emergency exit," Luberda said to Gartenberg.

"We can't."

"Why not?"

"Too much junk in front of the door. I can't get through."

"Try again."

"We can't get through. It's too heavy."

Luberda put Gartenberg on hold and called 911. The police connected her to the Fire Department. She told some man there that two company employees were trapped in Suite 8617 of One World Trade Center. The fireman sounded calm and trustworthy. She got back on Gartenberg's line.

"They'll get you out, Jim," she told Gartenberg.

He felt reassured. He got a call from another friend from New Jersey, Adam Rosen, a friend from school. Gartenberg had lots of friends from school. He was president of the Alumni Association of the University of Michigan.

Puma phoned a fellow employee, George Martin. She told him that the emergency exits were blocked. He reassured her.

Gartenberg's wife arrived at her office on the Upper East Side at 8:55 A.M. It took her about ten minutes to walk from their apartment to her office. She was three months pregnant and the mother of a two-year-old daughter. She worked as a speech therapist for children. There was a message on her answering machine. It had been recorded at 8:46 A.M. and came from her husband.

"Jill, there's a fire on our floor. I love you, Jill. Tell everyone that I love you. I don't know whether I can get out. Jill, I love you so much."

He had never sounded so desperate as he did then. None of it made sense. A beautiful walk through the Upper East Side, then this panicky voice. Jill Gartenberg stood in her office, staring. The phone rang. It was her husband. He was much calmer now.

He told her that help was on its way. He asked her to go see his mother, who lived not far from Jill's office. Jill promised that she would but was confused. She couldn't decide how serious it all was. Their daughter Nicole was at home with the baby-sitter. James was his mother's favorite. As Gartenberg hung up, the second plane crashed into the South Tower. Jill Gartenberg walked out into the street and saw the thick smoke spreading out over the lower tip of Manhattan.

It was now 9:05 A.M. Both towers were on fire. She started to cry and scream. She did not believe that anyone could escape from up there. She had visited her husband's office only once, but she knew that it was very high up. Jim Gartenberg did not care about the view. He often complained to her how long it took to get there on the elevators. He couldn't afford to waste any time.

Meanwhile Patricia Puma was talking to her husband for the second time. Kevin Puma worked for the Transit Authority and had just gotten home after working the night shift, which he did so that he could take care of the kids on the days his wife worked. He had the TV on but the sound turned off.

He saw the fireball burst out of the second tower. Over and over again, the TV reran footage of the impact. Kevin Puma and his wife repeated the conversation they'd already had twice. Patricia Puma told him again how she'd been in the bathroom, and how everything had collapsed. He told her again that she should get out. She said that Gartenberg had checked the emergency exits and they were blocked. He begged her to try anyway. He didn't think it was a good idea simply to wait. What he saw on the screen looked very dangerous.

At that moment Kevin Puma saw on the screen the name

"James Gartenberg," inserted beside the Twin Towers. He turned on the sound. They were on TV.

"You're on TV," he said to his wife.

Jim Gartenberg was giving a live interview to ABC News. The wife of a colleague named Robert Goodman had called ABC and given them Gartenberg's phone number. Later she said she had wanted to bring his situation to the attention of as many rescue crews as possible.

Gartenberg appeared calm as the announcers asked him questions. He described the air quality and the blocked exit. He said he was in good shape, given the circumstances. Twice he gave his location: "We're on the 86th floor, facing the East River." Rescue crews were on the way, he said. Gartenberg seemed certain that he'd soon be out. He was disconnected so the newscasters could announce that all bridges leading into Manhattan had been closed.

Gartenberg switched to the line where Margaret Luberda was waiting, still in her Midtown office. Colleagues were telling her that on TV, Gartenberg sounded brave and composed. She congratulated him on his TV appearance.

"Margaret, I didn't want to tell them how bad it really is," Gartenberg said. "I didn't want other families to panic."

"How's the air?" she asked.

"It's getting worse. Should I throw a chair through the window?"

"Let me clear it with the Fire Department," said Luberda. She asked a colleague to find out and continued her conversation with Gartenberg.

"Is the floor hot?" she asked.

"No."

"Is smoke coming through the floor?"

"No, only from outside, from the stairwell."

Now it was the Fire Department on the other end of the line. Under no circumstances should he break through the windows, they said. Again Luberda gave them Gartenberg's exact location. North Tower, 86th floor. Suite 8617. Then she returned to Gartenberg's line.

"They know now exactly where you are."

Three floors above Gartenberg and Puma, Pilipiak was tying an ice-hockey jersey around his head and running out of the office. The shirt had been hanging on his wall for good luck. The air was better out on the 89th floor. He ran along the narrow hallway toward the escalators. The gas fumes were gone; now it just smelled of dust and concrete. Pilipiak ran to the right, where the ladies' rooms used to be. They were destroyed. The offices in back, headquarters of Broad USA, Inc., looked as if no one there could have survived. Luckily, Broad had moved out about a month before.

Everything was black. He couldn't even make out the doors to Stairwell A. He ran to the left to Stairwell B, across from the men's rooms. Here the hallway looked better, but the door there couldn't be opened either; it seemed locked. Maybe this was a fire precaution, or else someone locked it. Pilipiak walked a few steps to the office where Mr. Lin, the lawyer who never said hello, had vanished this morning. A mountain of debris—no entrance, nothing. Lin must be dead. They had never once exchanged a word. Pilipiak remembered him as the man who always threw his tie over his shoulder when he stood at the urinal.

As Pilipiak was about to turn around and go back to the others, he saw a man wearing a double-breasted suit and red shoes. The man came toward him from the west. It was Bob Sibirium. He worked at MetLife. So others had survived as well. They weren't the only ones. Sibirium had also been selling insurance for the past thirty years.

They pulled at the door, but it wouldn't budge.

MetLife had been renting some ten thousand square feet in the southwest corner of the tower. From there they could look at the South Tower and the Hudson River. The southeast portion was burning; the core with the elevators and bathrooms looked as if it were bombed out. You could look through the ladies' rooms to the south.

This morning only thirteen of their roughly fifty employees were in the downtown offices in the North Tower. The others were out in the field. Sibirium was one of several department heads. The weather had been so exquisite that day that he had driven to work in his '82 Mercedes. The car was parked on Lower Level Two in the yellow area where MetLife department heads had reserved parking spaces. Later, Sibirium would briefly think about his car, which he loved. The parking area had been empty. The only time the offices were fully occupied was usually Monday mornings, since sales representatives rarely spent much time in the offices.

This morning, Sibirium had planned to talk with his assistant Camilla about an upcoming trip to a big account in Spain. She was seventy-seven and briefly lost consciousness when the plane hit, but she came to soon after. Here, too, ceiling tiles were falling like scales. Outside his windows, Sibirium saw a ball of fire shoot out of the building. The building swayed. A few walls collapsed, the lights went out.

The MetLife office was divided into two offices. Eleven people occupied the larger one; two others worked in the smaller one. The air quality in the large office quickly went sour. People were calm. They left their office and walked north between the elevators to the law offices of Drinker, Biddle & Reath. There the light was better and so was the air. A fire was burning in the center of the hall, at about the level of the elevators, but it was avoidable. Nobody seemed to notice that their two colleagues from the other MetLife office weren't with them.

Drinker, Biddle & Reath is a large law firm that rented about ten thousand square feet on the 89th floor. On this morning none of the lawyers had yet arrived; the only one there was the receptionist, Diane Davout. She lived in Bensonhurst, Brooklyn, and had been with the firm for ten years. She was friendly with Theresa Moya at Cosmos and also with Rafael Kava, who also always arrived early and who in truth really did secretarial work. It was the support staff that was there at this hour. Diane Davout liked Rafael Kava.

When the plane hit, she was thrown down like the others. She didn't really know what to do. She took off her heels and put her sneakers back on. At first she walked through all the offices. Seven windows were missing. Then she waited.

Ten minutes later people with blackened faces came running into the reception area—the MetLife people, led by Sibirium. Diane knew all the faces on the floor. She made a few calls. Her boyfriend wasn't home. She called her girlfriend Joanne, who worked in Brooklyn City Hall, and told her to switch on the TV. Then she waited again. She wondered whether she shouldn't just take off. She was wearing sneakers, after all. Nobody else was running away, so for now she stayed put.

Half an hour after American Flight 11 hit, Sibirium came back with a tall man wearing a helmet and holding a long flashlight. He said he was from the Port Authority and that they should follow him. Diane Davout immediately ran after him, he looked like a man who could be trusted—not some lawyer or insurance broker. He guided them to Stairwell B, opposite the men's rooms. A short man was waiting over there, also wearing a helmet and holding a flashlight. Both men had climbed up from the 88th floor, on which they had been trapped. They had knocked the door down with an ax, Sibirium said. At last there was a free passage for the prisoners of the 89th floor.

The eleven MetLife employees and Diane Davout went down the stairs while the tall man in the helmet walked around the hallways to look for others.

Walter Pilipiak and his colleagues, the five survivors of the PR agency, and Rafael Kava were waiting—making phone calls, surfing the Net, sending E-mails—when the door opened.

"Get out of here, quick!" the man with the helmet shouted. Theresa Moya held eighty-year-old Rafael Kava by the hand. At the open door, the other Port Authority man helped the last of the twenty-three survivors from the 89th through the door into the stairwell. Pilipiak brought up the rear. Pilipiak watched as his two saviors disappeared above him. They were going up to help others, they said.

The 89th floor was vacated—nearly vacated. Inside the smaller MetLife office two employees were trapped in the ruins. No one heard them. They telephoned for their lives and talked to family until the South Tower collapsed and the connection broke off. And from Mr. Lin, the lawyer who never said hello, there came no sign of life.

North Tower, 86th Floor

Three floors below the 89th, Gartenberg and his secretary were still stuck; they couldn't get out of their offices either. Gartenberg's friend Goldman called again from Chicago.

"The smoke's getting worse and worse, Adam," said Gartenberg.

Goldman decided not to tell him about the second plane.

The conversations became shorter; everything had been said.

Margaret Luberda wanted to talk to Patricia Puma.

"How are you doing?" Luberda asked. "Can you breathe?"

"Not too well," said Puma.

"Do you have water?"

"Yes."

"Dip your jackets in water and take deep breaths," Luberda said.

Gartenberg yelled out that debris was falling. The ceiling was collapsing.

"Look for shelter somewhere," said Luberda.

"We'll crawl under the reception desk," replied Gartenberg.

The two crawled under the desk, carrying the telephones with them.

Gartenberg talked to his mother and his wife. They were both sitting in his mother's home. They didn't know what was happening outside. Jill thought that her husband suddenly seemed calm. She didn't know what to say to him. Her mother-in-law was sitting next to her. All she said was, "Stay on the ground." He told her that wasn't easy. They wanted to avoid the smoke that was welling up from under the door, but they also wanted to be able to call out to the firemen when they came. They had to be arriving any minute.

Again Patricia Puma talked to her husband on the phone. He told her once more she should get out, but it didn't seem to get through to her.

"Try it at least, please!" he called to her.

She told him he should take good care of the children. She coughed. He told her he loved her, that help would come soon.

Gartenberg got another call from Chicago.

"I love you," Gartenberg said. "You are my best friend. I don't know whether I'll ever get out. Please take care of my family."

Goldman tried to encourage him. Gartenberg cried.

He called his wife once more.

"I love you," Gartenberg said.

Once more he got on the inside line with Margaret Luberda.

"It's really starting to be suffocating," he said. Then the connection broke off.

It was 9:45 A.M. Luberda looked at her watch; they'd been connected for exactly fifty-eight minutes.

Patricia Puma reached her husband one last time. He didn't try to convince her of anything anymore. The last sentence she spoke was, "I AM going to hang up. James Gartenberg says we have to save oxygen."

For an hour the telephone connection had led them to believe the situation was manageable. That was over now.

Rosen, Goldman, and Luberda tried again and again to reach the 86th floor in the North Tower. They no longer succeeded. Jill Gartenberg retreated into a room in her mother-in-law's apartment and closed the door. Kevin Puma watched the smoking towers on the silent screen in his living room.

North Tower, Inside the Stairwell

Pilipiak walked down past the 86th floor where James Gartenberg and Patricia Puma were trapped, following the voices in front of him. He turned around a few times but no one was behind him any longer. The escapees from the 89th met hardly anyone else from the upper floors on their way down. Pilipiak caught up with the rest. Lynn Simpson, director of the PR agency, mentioned that people in the stairwells were calling out the numbers of their floors to each other. She heard no "eighty-nines" and no higher numbers, either. As far as the 78th floor they proceeded down the stairs calmly, without problems. Then at the 78th-floor Sky Lobby they had to switch stairwells, and the floor was completely dark. Pilipiak used the light from his cell phone to guide the group. Most of them still remember how the man with the ice-hockey shirt wrapped around his head led them across the lobby with the light from his cell phone. It was during this moment of changing stairwells that the tenants of the 89th felt closer to one another than they ever felt before or after. The survivors of the 89th held tight to each other. In these few minutes some were seeing each other for the first and last time.

In front of two stairwells they met two men arguing over which was the right way down. The survivors of the 89th split up—once again they had to make choices. They lost touch with each other forever. The 89th floor had been destroyed and they no longer shared a common space where they might meet again.

Rafael Kava remains something of a symbol of this brief togetherness. They all remember him, even the people from the southwest end who saw him only briefly; later they would talk about the old man with the hat. Most of them remember helping him out. They all believed that he was dead—he could not have made it out.

Rafael Kava, however, was walking down the stairs holding on to Theresa Moya's hand, a refugee once more.

FAA Control Centers, Cleveland and Chicago, 9:28 A.M.

A day in the life of an air traffic controller can be rough. Rain, snow, sudden drops in temperatures, the dense air traffic over the American continent, tight takeoff and landing schedules—these are the origins of stress. But there had never been a day like this. From coast to coast, the alarm level was red in all twenty-two FAA control centers. For ten years not a single hijacking in American airspace—then suddenly four within one hour.

The last hijacking of the day started with strange sounds that culminated in the barking sound of a startled, almost featureless voice from the cockpit of United Airlines Flight 93.

"Hey, get outta here!"

One breath earlier you could hear a small sound like a *pling* or a *bling*, the sound that alerts the pilots inside the cockpit to an incoming text message, a kind of an E-mail they can see on a display, green on black.

A controller in Chicago had sent a message to every pilot then in the air, a warning: "Beware of cockpit intrusion." The cockpit crew of United 93 acknowledged receiving this message by typing in one word: "Confirmed."

Seconds later the hijackers had taken over the plane.

A controller in Cleveland now heard a new, heavily accented voice from the cockpit. It belonged neither to the captain nor to the copilot. The voice said, "There's a bomb on board. This is the captain speaking. Remain in your seat. Stay quiet. We are meeting their demands. We are returning to the airport."

Cockpit of United Airlines Flight 93, 9:35 A.M.

The Boeing 757-222 had taken off from Newark at 8:42
A.M. At this moment it was over Cleveland, Ohio. Ziad Jarrah was holding the microphone. Jarrah was the pilot and
leader. The cockpit voice recorder holds the proof. Starting
at 9:30 A.M. the machine recorded for half an hour. The tape
from the recorder also proves that for long stretches Jarrah
was not the only one in the cockpit. You can hear him
speaking in Arabic to an accomplice. You can hear them
say that they are going to let the plane crash if the passengers try to wrest the controls from them. You can hear Jarrah
and the other one pray.

*Pray for yourself and for your Muslim brothers and for
the final victory and fear not, for soon you will encounter
God.*

It was all in the terrorists' primer. Jarrah followed it word
for word. He prayed according to plan.

The day before, Jarrah, the fourth of the four pilot/leaders
group that included Atta, al-Shehhi, and Hanjour, had somehow found time to mail a good-bye letter to his girlfriend
back in Germany. Around 9 A.M. from the airplane on the
very day of the attack, he called her number in the city of
Bochum, located in the Ruhr Valley. Did he still sound "totally normal," as he had in the preceding weeks?

In the air above Cleveland, Jarrah pulled the Boeing up
to over forty thousand feet. He let the plane drop into a left
turn toward the south, then completed the turn back to the
east, toward Washington. The White House? The Capitol?
Camp David? Was Jarrah searching for *Air Force One*, the
president's plane?

World Trade Center, North Tower, 78th Floor, Inside the Stairwell

Mike Hingson and David Frank started on their way down,
but only after searching for and not finding the main switch

for their P3000, their main computer. They worked for Quantum Software, a company that sold data backup systems as security against catastrophic events. A sales presentation had been planned for this morning.

Hingson, who is blind, of course saw nothing of the explosion eight floors above, but he did hear a booming explosion and felt the building sway. Then everything seemed to be sinking. Maybe three feet, Hingson guessed. An earthquake? No, he thought, not an earthquake. He is from California; he knows what an earthquake feels like. Besides, he could smell fumes. David Frank thought a natural gas line had exploded. Nonsense: There weren't any natural gas lines up there. Besides, it was much too strong for that.

An attack? Immediately Hingson rejected the possibility. *It doesn't make sense to put a bomb that high up,* he thought. It had to be some sort of gas blast.

"We've got to get out of here, we've got to get out of here," his friend David kept repeating. Hingson tried to calm his friend down. He thought David might be more upset than he was because he could see what was going on. Hingson had learned to focus on what was really important. He had learned how to deal with danger. Every day on the streets he was face-to-face with danger. There was Roselle, his Seeing Eye golden retriever. If Roselle were going to work well, she had to stay calm; she got nervous when her master got nervous. So stay calm Mike, stay calm David, stay calm Roselle.

People running into the stairwell were holding scarves over their mouths. During the first attack on the World Trade Center in 1993 it became clear that the stairwells were too dark and the ventilation systems overtaxed; many people had spent hours in the elevators or in overcrowded stairwells. Not long after, a new alarm system was installed. The stairwells were supplied with battery-powered emergency lights and the walls were painted in glowing fluorescent colors. Security guards regularly checked the escape routes.

However, these security measures provided protection only in the case of normal fires. An evacuation through the stairwells was possible only if it took the fire two or three hours to work through the plaster boards.

David Frank noticed that the dark-green strips of inlay detail that bordered the elevators were bulging and cracking: The building had obviously received a serious structural blow. Nobody would be coming up here again for a long time, he thought.

The first flights of stairs were easy. Nobody was ahead of them. Frank walked ahead, with Mike Hingson and Roselle behind. Roselle was working hard. She panted a lot, but that was because she was thirsty. Occasionally people passed them. They did not know the whereabouts of their other colleagues.

Frank is a Buddhist. He believes there's a hidden meaning behind everything that happens. He had got the impression that "this is supposed to tell us something." He didn't know what kind of message it could be. His experience of Buddhism had taught him humility; he could understand how some people might not like the United States. If this was supposed to be a message, we should listen.

Hingson brushed against every door he passed. Was it hot? Could it be opened? None of them felt warm, and only about every third door opened.

A little below the 70th floor the stairwell began to fill up—a traffic jam, hundreds of heads on the stairs beneath them. Somebody spotted the blind man and asked the others to make room for both men and the dog. Nobody complained. Everybody moved to the side.

It was thoughtful, but Hingson didn't really want special treatment. He liked to prove that even a blind man could get along in life—especially, of course, at work. He owns a talking computer and handles his job as an ATL territory manager. But what can you do? This wasn't the moment for a discussion, though it really didn't help that people let him pass on the left—when Roselle wasn't on his left side he couldn't make use of her.

On about the 40th floor they heard screaming from behind: "Move to the side! Burn victims coming through!"

Frank moved aside. First he could see them on the stairs above: a woman in her late twenties or early thirties. Once more he experienced a moment of clarity and promised himself to look very closely. She walked like a zombie, eyes straight ahead, no expression. Her clothes were half burned off, skin was peeling off her arms, neck, and face. Her hair, which he assumed had once been blond, looked like baked-on gray phlegm. The woman was in shock but walking. When all is said and done, Frank found himself thinking that shock could be a pretty useful thing.

Soon the next burn victim passed by. Strangely, she was about the same age, same height, had the same hair. She looked just as burned and was also in shock.

The fumes got stronger below the 40th floor—they crept into your lungs, coated your taste buds, fogged up your head. From below, they were handing out small water bottles. That provided some release, even for Roselle. She was only three and a half years old and had been with Hingson for only the past nine and a half months, but he knew she was competent. She took the turns in a way Hingson could follow and stopped where she had to. She was responsible and could maintain focus.

North Tower, 61st Floor, Inside the Stairwell

Nobody could touch Manu Dhingra or he would go crazy with pain. A coworker walked ahead of him, another behind. That's how they descended the stairs from the 83rd floor. Disaster had struck Dhingra as he exited the elevator on the 83rd floor of the North Tower at 8:45 A.M. His body had been scorched, not by fire but by an enormous wave of intense heat hitting his face, arms, and entire torso. Behind him, the elevator was incinerated the moment after he stepped out, with people still in it.

Let me die quickly, prayed Manu Dhingra, *let it be over with quickly.* Actually he had always thought himself lucky. He had always managed to scrape by, to stay a step ahead of bad luck. He'd come so far, from India as a child, with his family. He'd gone to college and become an options broker for Andover Brokerage, a day trading company. He liked his colleagues in the World Trade Center; there was a Ping-Pong table in the office and a view spanning all of New York City. He was twenty-seven years old.

Surrender yourself. You are the weaker one. Let it go. For one long, very peaceful moment he thought like this. Then he thought of his mother, and that it wasn't acceptable that she be left grieving for her son. He forced himself to move ahead. "Nobody will rescue you up here," one of his two colleagues said. "You have to walk. Are you able?"

Of course not, but he had to.

He did not want anybody to stay up here on his account. He was going to try. He didn't expect to make it down eighty-three flights. He hoped that on the way down someone would come to help.

Manu Dhingra couldn't see much; his eyes were nearly shut.

"How much farther to go?"

"We'll get there in a minute."

"How much farther?"

"Not much farther."

"Where are we?"

"On the tenth floor."

In truth they were only on the 61st, but the lies helped. He couldn't sit down, his friends wouldn't allow it. Once in a while there was water. Then he could open his eyes just a bit, see the fright in the eyes of strangers.

"How do I look?" he asked.

"You look great. You'll be okay again in a week."

Normal, healthy-looking people were walking down the stairs. *Why me?* he thought. *What did I do wrong? Am I being punished?*

He was already familiar with the pain that would be with him for weeks on end, but he didn't know yet how he was going to look when it was all over. He didn't yet know that the doctors would say how lucky he was after all that the skin on his face had been so smoothly peeled off. Just like after three chemical peels, they would later tease him. "Look, you've got no more wrinkles."

Now all he knew was that his skin was flaking off in shreds, that there was horror on the face of each person who looked at him, that he had to hold out. He held out until the very first rescue worker he saw. Then he fainted.

On Board United Airlines Flight 93, About 9:45 A.M.

In the passenger cabin strongmen Ahmed al-Haznawi, Saeed Alghamdi, and Ahmed Alnami took turns keeping the thirty-seven passengers and five flight attendants in check. They had been divided into two groups. About a dozen people were being held up front in first class, curtains drawn. The rest in economy class, near the tail.

Terrorist rule was not strict. They not only allowed their hostages to make phone calls, they encouraged them to contact their families. Flight attendant Sandy Bradshaw, thirty-eight, went unnoticed as she boiled water in the flight kitchen—for possible use as a weapon, she told her husband over the phone. Many of the victims made phone calls.

Thomas Burnett, thirty-eight, manager of a medical technology firm, called four times. He was on his way home to San Ramon, California. When he first called at 9:40 A.M. he told his wife, Deena, who was at home in the kitchen and watching the burning towers in New York, "No, I'm not okay. I'm on the airplane, United ninety-three, and it's been hijacked. They knifed a man and they've got a bomb. Call the authorities." He hung up.

On the second call, Tom Burnett said the hijackers were in the cockpit. He asked his wife: That business at the World Trade Center, was it a passenger plane? She told him she didn't know. "Okay," he said and hung up.

The third time he called, Tom Burnett wanted to know the news. He pumped her for information, his wife said later. She told him about the Pentagon. Burnett hung up.

When he called the fourth time, he said, "Okay, there's a group of us and we're going to do something." His wife kept interrupting: "No." She had learned what fear was this morning. No, she screamed, stay put, don't do anything. But he said, "If they're going to drive this plane into the ground then we've got to do something." After that, he hung up. Forever.

World Trade Center, North Tower, 40th Floor, Inside the Stairwell

David Frank announced the floors. He and Mike Hingson were on the 40th floor when the first firefighters reached them. Frank was surprised to see what a load of equipment they were carrying with them: hatchets, pickaxes, shovels, protective suits, oxygen tanks. More than sixty pounds' worth, he guessed. They seemed exhausted. People in the stairwell burst into applause.

Almost every firefighter looked at the blind man, his dog, and his friend, and asked whether everything was all right. Always the same exchange:

"Are you okay?"

Hingson: "I'm just fine, thank you."

To Frank: "Are you with him?"

Frank: "Yes, I'm with him. We're fine, thanks."

At about 9:35 A.M. they reached the 2nd floor. The floor was wet and slippery, but it did not smell like fuel. Roselle slurped greedily. It was water. They went down the last flight of stairs. Frank surveyed the chaos: building parts, pieces of walls, ceiling tiles lying all over. Water everywhere.

On the ground you could see police and WTC personnel. "Keep moving, keep moving." They took the east exit, the one that led into the shopping passage. One last time a few steps up, then down again through a small dark passage. At the end there was light: the sky.

At least three men were now saying the Lord's Prayer. Todd Beamer, thirty-two, a businessman from New Jersey, was praying. Since 9:47, when he had not been able to reach his family, he had been talking over the phone to Lisa Jefferson, a supervisor at GTE, the telephone company. He told this stranger about his children—about David, who was three; and about Andrew, who was one. He asked Jefferson to call his wife with last greetings and a pledge of love.

Beamer also talked about some passengers' plan to mount an attack on the hijackers. The pilot and copilot were lying in the aisle up front, injured and possibly dead. It was close to 9:58 A.M. and he was putting his affairs in order: "Our Father who art in heaven, hallowed be Thy name . . ."

After the prayer, which Lisa Jefferson repeated in unison with Beamer, he was off the receiver. The phone, however, was still connected. She heard someone say, "Ready, guys?" Then, "Let's roll."

Nobody knows what happened during the next seven minutes. The telephones that were still live alternated periods of silence, shrieking, the sound of wind, then silence.

Starting at 10:01 A.M. the cockpit voice recorder recorded curses and screams in English and Arabic, sounds of a fight, uproar.

Pilot Jarrah was well prepared for such a fight. He had learned everything he needed about man-to-man combat at the US-1 Fitness Center in Dania, Florida. He had starting going on May 1, and went for the last time on September 7, four days before the hijacking: ninety-six training sessions over four months. His trainer was Bert Rodriguez, master of several Asian martial arts and a trainer for antidrug officers of the DEA.

During his first lesson in the ring, Rodriguez had tested his new student. He put his fist in front of Jarrah's face. The fist was covered with a blue boxing glove. Jarrah didn't know what to make of it. He danced a few steps from side to side, lifted his arms, and asked himself how to get past the blue glove. Rodriguez said, "Don't think while fighting," and pushed his fist into his face. Jarrah stopped thinking and smiled in embarrassment. Smiling doesn't fit with fighting, Rodriguez said, and this time he didn't push his fist into Jarrah's face but punched him. Jarrah stopped smiling and tried to knock Rodriguez's fist to the side. "That's right," said Rodriguez and pushed his other fist into Jarrah's face. Jarrah lost control and bounced off Rodriguez's raised fists. Rodriguez hit once more. Jarrah went down. Rodriguez said, "I love to fight. You learn really quickly what kind of guy the other person is."

Rodriguez taught Jarrah that there were only two types of blow: straight and circular. There were also only two types of kicks: straight and circular. Whether you used your fists, elbows, knees, or feet you were always aimed at the same points: eyes, nose, larynx, liver, testicles, and all joints. Among other places.

Rodriguez explained that there were certain spots on the body that were particularly pain-sensitive. One such spot was above the elbow. If you found it and pressed with only the tip of your finger, you could bring an opponent to his knees. It was most efficient if you hit this point with a knuckle-duster or a blade.

Rodriguez also explained to Jarrah that during a fight it made sense to have a knife at hand. "It's always good policy to bleed your opponent," Rodriguez said with his soft voice. "Try to cut him so that he sees where he's cut. If you have a choice, cut under the arm. The underside's softer and right under the skin there's lots of blood."

If a group attacked you it was smart to finish off the biggest and scariest guy first, instructed Rodriguez. That scared off the others. Here too it was smart to make wounds or break a limb so that the bones poked out from the muscle. Next the two would go at each other for a while. As Jarrah tried to translate what he'd learned into blows and kicks, Rodriguez knocked him to the ground again.

Over time Jarrah made progress. At the end of twenty lessons it hardly fazed him when Rodriguez pounced on him with a baseball bat. All the while Jarrah kept asking questions. At times it seemed to Rodriguez as if Jarrah were passing his newfound know-how on to students of his own.

Jarrah, however, was defeated in his last fight. United Flight 93 went down shortly after 10 A.M. The plane quickly lost altitude. Eyewitnesses saw it flutter, shift, and shake to the left and right until it bored a thirty-foot-deep ditch into a field near Shanksville in western Pennsylvania. The plane, the people, and everything else burst into pieces no larger than a phone book.

Was United Flight 93 the only one of the four flying bombs to be shot down by fighter jets? Did a rocket hit the Boeing? Parts of the plane were found as far as five miles from the area of impact. A nameless passenger who called 911 from the phone in the bathroom screamed into the ear of an operator just before the end that he had heard an explosion and that he saw white smoke. It was the only statement of this kind. Officials deny downing the plane.

What about the claims made by the hijackers of having a bomb on board? An empty threat? Or were they able to set off some kind of explosive? Perhaps at the point that the passengers decided to end the nightmare?

By 10:06 A.M. the skies over America were empty. Air traffic had been almost completely grounded. The nation was paralyzed.

World Trade Center, North Tower, 4th Floor, Inside the Stairwell, Shortly After 10 A.M.

Jan Demczur ran into bad congestion in the stairwell. It was on the 4th floor. He had been going down for more than an hour, after he and the other men had managed to get out of the elevator by cutting through the wall of the elevator shaft with his cleaning equipment.

When Demczur and others reached the 4th floor, a policewoman ordered them back up. "The stairwell ends here," she yelled. Slowly people started walking back up. When they came to the 6th floor, the policewoman shouted, "Shit, let's try it," and ran down again. Demczur followed her. The 3rd floor was black from thick smoke. The stairs ended. They all held hands and walked across a hallway. Demczur recognized changing rooms. He lost his orientation. They entered another stairwell that was half blocked by rubble. They crawled through and reached a huge space that was filled with twisted steel and wreckage. Demczur thought they had gone too far, that they were somewhere in the basement. On the other hand he could see daylight. Then he noticed the time clock, the very one through which earlier this morning he swiped his identity card. The clock was sticking outward and looked as if it would never work again.

Only then did Jan Demczur grasp that his big plan was in serious jeopardy. Up to now his whole life had been one big plan: the day, the month, and the year were all divided into surfaces of glass that he would clean. That had been his plan.

Now he was on ground level. He exited the building going west. It was 10:20 A.M. He sat down next to an ambulance on the West Side Highway. Somebody gave him oxygen. Briefly he thought about Rako Cami, the man who operated the window-washing machine on the roof. Then he saw parts of the North Tower falling. He put the oxygen mask to the side and slipped away without the rescue worker noticing. There was no more plan.

Plaza in Front of the World Trade Center

After an exhausting descent, Chuck Allen's group reached the plaza in front of the North Tower. Allen had led a group of coworkers down the stairs from the 83rd floor. He loved the plaza with the huge bronze globe and caryatid in the center, the benches and fountain. He walked through the glass door. There was nothing to remind him of the plaza as it had been that morning. It was strewn with large pieces of debris. He saw people.

"Don't look over there," he said to Liz Porter, his programmer, covering her eyes.

"Look where?" she asked, brushing his hand to the side.

There were twenty, thirty, maybe forty dead bodies. It was hard to say because they were parts of bodies.

They saw a torso with a belt around its hip, a second, a third, a fourth. They were all wearing the same kind of wide black belt. It took Allen a moment before he comprehended that they had all been passengers. Those were passengers lying there. Those were the shredded bodies of people who not long ago had put on their seat belts at the captain's signal. There was no blood. There was no layer of dust covering the ruins yet. Everything could be seen with clarity. Policemen were standing around.

"Don't look over there," they said. "Move over to the escalators. Turn off your cell phones!" Everyone was looking there. Everyone was trying to use his or her cell phone.

In the underground shopping mall the water was ankle-deep. There were sprinklers. The revolving doors were bent out of shape and broken. Allen passed Border's Bookstore and went out onto Church Street.

"We believe this was intentional," a policeman said.

Allen called his wife. "What really happened?" he asked Sabah. Then he walked north. Somewhere, almost in Midtown, he wanted to make note of the phone number of another survivor. He asked a Pakistani who was standing next to his fruit stand whether he could borrow a pen. Chuck Allen had lived in Islamic countries for many years. He is convinced he can read the facial expressions of foreigners. He had a sense of what would happen now, but he wanted to know for sure. "Isn't it horrible?" he asked the fruit man. The man turned his head to the side and didn't say anything. Allen thought, *He cannot say that he sympathizes with those who did this, but he does.*

North Tower, North Entrance

Virginia DiChiara left the building through the north entrance. Though badly burned, she had made it to ground level. It had taken an enormous effort of will. They guided her to Church Street where ambulances were lined up. A few people were sitting on the curb, injured people. DiChiara saw a lot of blood and knew that she would not be able to sit over there. She couldn't tolerate the sight of blood and was afraid she'd faint. An emergency worker guided her into the ambulance. The coworker who had accompanied her on her way down was still with her.

She asked for water but received little. She did not understand why they wouldn't take her to a hospital. Slowly she felt the pain. She looked at her hands: They were red, no skin. She waited and waited. Her colleague called DiChiara's parents and told them their daughter was okay.

Half an hour later they drove her to St. Vincent's Hospital in Greenwich Village. The hospital was prepared for an onslaught of injured people. Dozens of doctors and nurses were waiting outside. Stretchers stood ready in long rows. Apart from Virginia DiChiara, hardly anyone arrived.

South Tower, Main Lobby

At some time or other Steve Miller—Smiller—reached the last step. His new cowboy boots were torturing him. An army of employees streamed out the doors into the open. He walked home toward Brooklyn. When he turned back he saw, way up, where his office once was, nothing but black smoke. The plane had smashed exactly into his floor.

As Smiller walked across the Brooklyn Bridge he tried not to think about his feet, or the other horrors. He decided his life should change. He would become a librarian somewhere in the countryside. He couldn't help but think of the old Chinese proverb, "May you live in exciting times." What the Chinese wished on their enemies.

South Tower, Plaza

Brian Clark and Stanley Praimnath reached the plaza level of the World Trade Center at 9:50 A.M. The surface of the moon. The only people running around were police, firefighters, and ambulance personnel. "Better run now," one of them shouted and told them not to look up. Parts of the building were coming down with more frequency.

"Let's go," said Clark, and both men ran hand in hand across the burning open plaza over to Church Street.

Clark thought, *War zone.* After two blocks they came to the wrought-iron gates of Trinity Church. A minister said the church was open, they could go in. Praimnath, totally out of breath, held on to the gate. He was afraid the whole tower would collapse. "No way, it's a steel structure," said Clark. He was an engineer, after all.

South Tower, Plaza, Shortly After 10 A.M.

When Anthony DeBlase finally arrived at plaza level, he saw corpses. He saw a man decapitated by a falling body part. He saw a head bursting like a melon. He saw a burning leg. He saw things he thought could never exist in his world.

He howled. He ran west, with the others. A woman was walking against the crowd, she ran toward him and embraced him: Anita, his mother.

"Jimmy," his mother said. "We have to find Jimmy."

Anthony looked up to where the sky was filled with dust and smoke and said, "God, give me my brother back. What do you want him for? He'll snipe at you and nag you and lecture you till you lose your mind." That's how Jimmy was. How Jimmy used to be.

Had he been crushed? Had he jumped? Had he suffocated? Had he been pulverized?

A few weeks later the first eight body parts found were identified with the help of DNA tests. Among them were those of James DeBlase.

SEARCH AND RESCUE

Dan Potter hated the buzz of the alarm clock. Jean knew her husband's aversion, so every morning she was faster than the alarm clock and kissed him awake. In a year and a half of marriage the alarm clock had hardly ever caught them by surprise.

Jean worked on the 81st floor of the North Tower, in the offices of the Bank of America, where she was an assistant to the head of trading. Dan and Jean had met through an ad in the *New York Post*. His first marriage had broken up; his eighteen-year-old son had moved into Dan's small apartment after living with his mother became impossible.

Dan Potter had yet a third family: the New York Fire Department. He had been a firefighter for twenty-three years. He never complained, but he was beginning to feel that Manhattan was wearing him down. "You have to be young in Manhattan," he says. To carry one hundred pounds of gear up stairs, sometimes as far the fiftieth floor, because a sprinkler had gotten set off by accident. "You feel like a cat chasing its tail."

The only thing worse than a false alarm is a real alarm. In an instant a skyscraper can be transformed into a huge, blazing furnace or a labyrinth of black smoke from which you have to grope your way out. You damn well have to

112

love your own city and the people in it to endure this kind of work. Potter is that kind of guy.

The catch: He's forty-four years old. That's why he decided to find himself an easier position—as a fireman in the Bronx. Working there is a picnic compared to Manhattan. The buildings are seldom taller than four stories and, best of all, you rarely have to go in. You park the engine on the street and aim the hose full blast. "A great job," says Dan Potter. Even if it means going back to school.

That's why he left home on September 11 in civvies: jeans, knit shirt, penny loafers. A couple of weeks earlier he'd started his course work on Staten Island, and at the end of it all he'd be a lieutenant—in the Bronx.

Canal Street, Manhattan, 8:47 A.M.

Chief Joe Pfeiffer of the First Battalion was examining a leaky gas pipe when he saw a passenger plane hit the North Tower.

He radioed a dispatcher with words like "a direct hit" and "huge jet." In an instant, Pfeiffer set off a level-three alarm. A level-three alarm means that nineteen FDNY trucks are immediately set into motion.

Metro-Tech in Brooklyn also received an emergency message: "BLDG EXPLOSION." The case number for the event: 0727.

8:48:03 A.M.: "Caller states explosion at top of WTC," an employee at the emergency center typed into the computer.

8:48:07 A.M.: "Plane into top of building," a caller states.

8:50:12 A.M.: "Male caller states: Plane just flew into WTC—possibly commercial airplane."

8:50:22 A.M.: "Female caller states, WTC exploded."

8:52:53 A.M.: "Female caller states big hole in right side."

8:53:28 A.M.: "Male caller states someone falling off building."

At 8:55 A.M. a 10-60 alarm was announced, signaling a larger disaster.

At 8:59 A.M. a level-five alarm was declared, the maximum level of alarm provided for in New York City emergency regulations.

American Airlines Flight 11 hit the World Trade Center just as New York's firefighting units were in the middle of changing shifts. Throughout the city's firehouses, men from the day shift were arriving to take over. Firefighters from both shifts stood together drinking coffee while mechanics cleaned equipment. Within thirty minutes of the first alarm, more than one hundred fire trucks had raced to Lower Manhattan.

Many thought a private plane had flown into the tower. Some probably had in the back of their minds the accident of July 28, 1945, when a twelve-ton American B-25 bomber crashed into the Empire State Building. The collision occurred shortly before 10 A.M. in a dense fog, between the 78th and 79th floors, at a height of about eight hundred feet. The plane had been going about 200 mph and tore a hole roughly twenty feet wide and eighteen feet high into the front of the building. The B-25 was carrying about eight hundred gallons of gasoline. The firefighters were able to take the elevators up to the 60th floor, and the fire was extinguished within thirty-five minutes. Putting out the fire in the Empire State Building had since become part of the training for all New York City firefighters in leading positions.

The dimensions of the disaster of September 11, however, were on an altogether different order: the Boeing 767 weighed more than 120 tons and was carrying close to nine thousand gallons of jet fuel, not gasoline.

A fire was now raging that would soon reach a temperature of over 2,000° Fahrenheit. The thin layer of fireproofing on the steel trusses of the stories that were hit had been jarred loose. These trusses were now exposed, without protection, to enormous heat.

The core of the building was considered a fireproof zone,

with emergency stairwells and hydrants. Fireproof doors, sprinklers, and the firewalls between the floors were supposed to contain any fire until firefighters arrived. Building materials and fire protection measures had been so conceived that the World Trade Center would hold up for at least three hours—enough time to evacuate everyone from the towers.

Nobody considered the possibility that a plane might discharge several tons of jet fuel into the building.

The fire was further nourished by an enormous quantity of paper from the offices. Worse, apparently none of the fire extinguishing systems worked: sprinkler heads were ripped off by plane wreckage, and water pipes in the core of the building were destroyed.

Training Center for Firefighters, Staten Island

Dan Potter was working on the sixty questions of a test when the cell phone of the person sitting next to him rang. For a split second Dan was annoyed. Then his neighbor shouted, "A plane flew into the World Trade Center." Dan ran to a window. It was true. Thick black smoke was pouring out of the north tower. *I have to call my wife*, he thought and looked for a pay phone. He dialed her office number. Her phone rang. He heard her voice: "This is Jean Potter. I am not at my desk right now. Please leave a message."

"Are you there? Please answer."

Nothing. Potter ran to his car and hit the accelerator— 70 to 75 mph in the left lane, wheel in one hand, FDNY badge in the other. He could have skipped the badge. The streets were empty.

World Trade Center, North Tower, 81st Floor, Bank of America Offices

To many American men, Jean Potter might be considered a trophy wife: a cascade of red hair fit for a shampoo ad, the figure of a model, dazzling brown eyes. Jean could have married a lawyer or a doctor. She wasn't interested. She didn't want an egomaniac with high-flying career plans; she wanted someone she could rely on; someone who would protect her against life's uncertainties and imponderables; someone who wouldn't discard her when five years later another trophy walked past the glass door of his office.

Dan had thought over the idea of using the personals for a long time. Firefighters usually meet their wives in a bar, or while saving lives in a burning building, or at another fireman's wedding, or at baptisms or barbecues. A sister, a cousin, the sister-in-law of a fellow firefighter—this was acceptable, but not someone from a want ad. Ads were for the vulnerable, the shy, those who get blown through life like leaves. Problem was: Dan Potter was the shy type.

Jean was the first to respond to the ad. The two made plans to get together at a pub in Greenwich Village, met a few times, and realized before too long that they were in love. Not the way young people are when they dance the night away at Jimmy's Bronx Café or some other "in" spot, but in a quiet, more touching way.

Since then, Jean had worn a silver chain around her neck engraved with 10617, the number on Dan's badge. It had been a Christmas present. They were more than a couple; they were a team that didn't need an alarm clock when they woke up mornings in Jean's apartment in Battery Park City. The first thing Jean used to see every morning as she got out of bed was the Twin Towers.

Jean never particularly cared for the World Trade Center, and on September 11 it was no different. She hated the elevator that in a matter of seconds catapulted her to the 78th floor, where she had to switch to a small elevator for the ride to her office on the 81st. Nor was she thrilled by the view of the Brooklyn Bridge and Manhattan Bridge. It unsettled her to look down instead of up at passing helicopters. On September 11, she was wearing a lavender pants suit and black shoes with flat heels.

Driving across the Verrazano Bridge, which connects Staten Island with Brooklyn, Dan started to count the floors. Did the plane hit below Jean or above? Her phone line was still working. She wasn't in the thick of it. He was driving 75 mph. He counted, messed up, counted again from the beginning. It was torture. Dan, who was supposed to protect his wife for the rest of his life, was taking a class while she burned to death! He counted again and thought about what he always preached about emergencies: "Take the stairs down, never the elevator. In case you're above it, take the stairs up. Wait on the roof until the helicopter arrives."

He counted again. The result: his wife was above the fire. He felt some relief as he raced across the Verrazano Bridge. He believed his wife was waiting for the helicopters on the roof of the North Tower.

FDNY Emergency Message Center

8:56:44 A.M.: "Male caller states he is on the 87th floor: Says four persons with him."

8:56:57 A.M.: "Female caller on 47th floor states: Building shaking, gas odors."

8:57:26 A.M.: "People screaming in background—caller states cannot breathe—smoke coming through door—103rd floor—possibly trapped."

8:59:17 A.M.: "Male caller: the 86th floor collapsing."

World Trade Center, Base of the North Tower

Fireman John Ottrando was one of the first to park his truck in front of the North Tower, at the corner of Vesey and West streets. Ottrando was the driver for Engine Company

24's five-man team. They came from a Greenwich Village firehouse at Houston Street and Sixth Avenue.

Ottrando, forty-four, is an Italian American who lives on Staten Island. When the first alarm sounded, Ottrando was standing in the garage raving about the New York Giants. His day shift was supposed to begin at 9 A.M. His buddy Louie Arena had brought in his broken lawn mower. They were counting on a quiet day, the kind of day on which you repair lawn mowers in the firehouse garage.

Ottrando's Greenwich Village firehouse was responsible for the World Trade Center, and no one was particularly thrilled about the assignment. There was always something: a broken sprinkler, a nicotine addict. The men from Greenwich Village always raced off, lights flashing, one hundred pounds of equipment on their backs. Every time they came home miffed. The World Trade Center was grating. So it was no surprise that Ottrando did not even look up at the glistening facades when he shot onto Sixth Avenue with his truck at 8:56 A.M.

When Ottrando got out, he saw the giant hole and the thick black smoke pouring out. "Holy shit!" he cried. An engine company specializes in entering a burning building to extinguish the fire. The parts of an engine company are: the man who holds the hose that spouts five hundred gallons of water a minute—about equal to the power of a wild horse, which is why a backup man has to stand directly behind the hose man in order to control the water pressure; a so-called control man, who counts and adds up the length of the hoses; the officer, who directs the whole scene; and the driver, who stays down on the street and works the pumps. For Engine 24 the driver was John Ottrando.

Every engine company teams up with a ladder company, a second fire truck. The men from the ladder company are not supposed to extinguish fires; they break open doors and windows, fight the smoke, and take care of the victims.

Ottrando followed the four men of Engine 24 and the eight men of Ladder 5 into the lobby of the North Tower. He climbed over pieces of marble and steel supports; he saw people pouring out of stairwells and smoke blowing out of elevator shafts. Ottrando had heard nothing about a passenger plane, or about nine thousand gallons of jet fuel. He didn't know that the plane had cut the steel cables of some elevators when it plowed through the tower, causing the cabins to plunge to the ground. But he saw what happened to the people who must have been standing in those elevators. They were charred and lying on the marble floor—nothing but burnt flesh, hair, clothes, scorched by flames and hurled out of the crashing cabins. Ottrando ran back to his truck to get covers for the burned.

His buddies rammed their axes through the windows to let out smoke. Then they got going, toward the 90th floor, while Ottrando stayed down with the hoses. Ladder 5 took Stairwell C, Engine 24 disappeared into Stairwell B.

Marcel Claes was Engine 24's backup hose man. Claes is the son of a Belgian immigrant. The father of three, he once worked as a nurse and had been with FDNY for eleven years. His biggest fire ever had been the one six years before at the empty St. George Hotel. Back then, ten stories had fallen and not a single person was killed.

Fear is something firefighters train themselves out of, and that's why Claes climbed the stairs, step by step. It was his job to climb up ninety flights to help others. After a dozen flights Claes struggled for air. He had to stop a minute. In addition to his heavy boots, helmet, and bunker gear, he was carrying an oxygen tank that weighed more than thirty pounds and a hose that weighed nearly as much. An orderly procession of office workers streamed past him in the opposite direction. Some patted him on the shoulder, some cheered him on, some offered him a blessing. Claes saw burnt hands and faces, bleeding heads. He moved on.

North Tower, 60th Floor

By now exhaustion had overtaken Jean Potter's legs, but still they went down step by step. People were trying to maintain order among the lines of the fleeing. Nobody thought it conceivable that the tower might collapse. People were in a hurry but they didn't push. As soon as the first tower shook it had smelled like a gas station. For a fraction of a second, Jean had been confused. Then somebody grabbed her by the hand. It was Ben, from the next desk over.

"We're going down the stairwell," he said. "Now."

Jean was fire warden for the 81st floor. They had regularly practiced for this kind of situation, and actually she was supposed to call the security desk to ask for instructions. She did nothing of the kind. Jean had no idea what had happened; she knew only that there had been a disaster. She looked down the stairs and prayed. Two things consoled her on her way down: one, that her husband was not on duty at his home firehouse on Liberty Street opposite the World Trade Center; and two, that she was wearing shoes with flat heels.

Base of the North Tower, 9:03 A.M.

Downstairs in front of the World Trade Center, firefighter Ottrando bent over the hose he was supposed to connect. While crouching on the ground, he saw a gigantic fireball falling from the sky. United Airlines Flight 175, with Marwan al-Shehhi in the cockpit, had smashed into the South Tower. He had to get the stupid hose from the hydrant to the truck and from there to the North Tower. The World Trade Center was supposed to have connections for hoses on every floor, but on what could you count on a day like this?

More and bigger pieces of steel and glass were crashing onto the street. Some things that fell were still moving. It took Ottrando a while to realize that these were people. He did not want to look but he had to—in order not to be killed. They were falling at a crazy speed; the ties of the men seemed to stand straight up in the air.

9:03:11 A.M.: "Male caller. Wants to know how to get out of the building."

9:04:14 A.M.: "Male caller states: People trapped on 104th floor, back room, 35 to 40 people."

9:04:24 A.M.: "Male caller states: Trapped on 22nd floor—hole in the floor—smoke coming in, can't breathe—male caller states he will smash window."

9:04:50 A.M.: "Male caller states 103rd floor: Can't get out—floor on fire—people getting sick."

9:05:03 A.M.: "Police helicopter reports: Air Sea No. 14—people falling out of building."

9:06:41 A.M.: "Air Sea No. 14—not possible to land on roof."

9:07:40 A.M.: "Call from 130rd floor, Room 130—about 30 people—lots of smoke—female caller is pregnant."

9:07:51 A.M.: "Second plane hit second building . . . unknown extent of injuries."

9:08:02 A.M.: "Female caller, screaming."

9:08:15 A.M. "Female caller states WTC in flames—states fire department has to put it out."

9:08:22 A.M.: "Elevator stuck on 104th floor—people in elevator."

9:09:14 A.M.: "Male caller states from the second tower that people are jumping out a huge hole in the side of the building—probably no one catching them."

9:09:43 A.M.: "104th floor—male caller states that his wife is stuck on the 91st floor—all stairwells blocked—says he is concerned about his wife."

9:11:30 A.M.: "Female caller states woman presumably in wheelchair on the 68th floor, possibly by herself."

9:12:18 A.M.: "Male caller states on 106th floor about one hundred people in room—needs directions on how to stay alive."

More and more fire companies had arrived at the World Trade Center over the last fifteen minutes. Peter Hayden, commander of the First Division, had set up a central command station in the lobby of the North Tower. Hayden and the other FDNY officials believed there was no way to extinguish this fire. He and his colleagues hoped it would burn out in the upper stories, but they were afraid that these might collapse after a couple of hours. The most important thing now was to free the people trapped on cut-off floors, as well as anyone trapped in the ninety-seven passenger elevators or the eight freight elevators.

Every firefighter in the North Tower was getting his or her orders from Hayden, including Ottrando and Claes, the men from Engine 24, as well as Rick Picciotto, FDNY Battalion Commander.

Once he saw the second plane crash into the South Tower, Rick Picciotto could no longer bear staying at headquarters. Picciotto had been with the fire department twenty-eight years. He had a warm smile and a large gap between his teeth. He was also in shape. Every day, he rode thirty miles on his bicycle or sweated an hour on his StairMaster; he had brought the exercise equipment to the firehouse. Picciotto was smart and ambitious, and had gradually risen through FDNY hierarchy. In his wallet he was carrying graduation pictures of his son and daughter.

As soon as he entered the North Tower lobby with his crew, Picciotto headed straight for Hayden.

"Pete, how can I help?" he asked.

"Employees are trapped on the 21st and on the 25th," Hayden replied. "Go up and see what you can do."

Picciotto saw the destruction in the lobby. The burned bodies. Steel struts were crashing onto the plaza. But he switched off his sense of horror as if clicking a remote. He was here to help, not have the jitters. He had to get to the trapped people, then go up to the 90th. Thanks to his exercise on the StairMaster, he should be up there in about a half hour, he guessed. One hour of StairMaster was the equivalent of 220 floors—the two towers of the World Trade Center combined.

FDNY Emergency Message Center

9:14:52 A.M.: "Female caller states from the 100th floor—unable to speak."

9:15:34 A.M.: "Several people jump from windows of the WTC."

9:17:20 A.M.: "Male caller states he can't get out."

9:17:39 A.M.: "Male caller states on 105th floor . . . stairs collapse."

9:21:31 A.M.: "Female caller states they are in Stairwell C on 82nd floor. Doors are locked. Caller states they need someone to open doors."

9:23:05 A.M.: "Male caller states he is on the 84th floor, Tower Number 2, can't breathe—call cut off."

9:24:54 A.M.: "Male caller states stairwell on 105th floor collapsing."

World Trade Center, North Tower Lobby, 9:24 A.M.

Hayden heard over his radio that a third plane was approaching the WTC. He ordered his people to evacuate, also by radio. The equipment malfunctioned. Nobody could hear him. He stayed in the lobby.

FDNY Emergency Message Center

9:25:28 A.M.: "Male caller states that he is locked in on the 105th floor. States doors are hot."

Shortly before 9:30 A.M. the last call came from Windows on the World. Within the next minutes 206 people died. Pastry chef Norberto Hernandez was photographed jumping from the 106th floor. Hernandez was the father of three daughters and grandfather of two.

9:36:33 A.M.: "Female caller states they are trapped in elevator . . . explains they are dying."

9:39:40 A.M.: "Female caller states floor is very hot—no doors—states she will die—still on phone—would like to call mother."

9:40:45 A.M.: "Male caller states people passing out."

9:42:04 A.M.: "People still jumping from tower."

Sarasota, Florida, 9:30 A.M.

During his first televised appearance since the news came, President George W. Bush, visibly moved, spoke of a "national tragedy." The two crashes were, he said, an apparent terrorist attack on America. The short statement lasted hardly a minute and was broadcast from a room in Emma E. Booker Elementary School, where since 9 A.M. President Bush had been visiting a classroom. While being welcomed, his adviser Karl Rove had whispered in his ear the news that a plane had flown into the World Trade Center.

Immediately Bush asked to be connected to the White House. During a brief phone conversation, his security adviser Condoleezza Rice informed him of the incident. He took counsel with Chief of Staff Andrew H. Card, Jr., and decided to proceed with the program. He walked into the classroom to practice reading with the seven-year-olds who had been waiting for two hours for the president, in anticipation of presenting the story of a goat they had practiced for this day.

While Bush was listening to the children in the classroom, outside his advisers learned that the second tower had been hit. Immediately they switched on the TV. Chief of Staff Andy Card whispered into Bush's right ear that a second plane had just flown into the WTC: "America's under attack."

Bush turned visibly pale. Still, he continued his visit for another six minutes, praising the children as he listened. Only then did he get up. "This is a difficult moment for America," he said before leaving.

His first call went to Vice President Dick Cheney in Washington, and after that to FBI Chief Robert Mueller. Then he turned to his escort and said, "We're at war."

He sketched the text for a brief statement in front of the TV cameras with a black felt-tip pen on a yellow note pad. Bush declared that he wanted to return to Washington that instant.

Washington, D.C., Air Traffic Control, Dulles Airport, 9:33 A.M.

More than an hour after American Airlines Flight 77's departure, controllers at its airport of origin registered a signal that they could not identify. It was on the radar screen moving quickly east, toward Washington—toward the no-fly zone over the White House, the Washington Monument, and the Capitol.

There had been indications that Flight 77 was out of control since 9 A.M. Immediately following the first crash into the World Trade Center, a controller had unsuccessfully tried to raise the Boeing's cockpit. But Flight 77 remained silent. It had taken off late from Washington-Dulles, at 8:20 A.M. A control point in Indianapolis radioed with increasing desperation: "American 77, Indy, radio check, how do you read?" The transponder had been turned off, as had happened with the three other hijacked planes. Cockpit: silent. Position: uncertain. At 9:24 A.M. NORAD sent an alarm to Langley Air Force Base in Hampton, Virginia. At 9:30 A.M. two F-16 fighter jets took off. They were to intercept American Flight 77.

On board Flight 77, Barbara Olsen conducted a final conversation with her husband Theodore. Olson was forty-five, a TV commentator, and an icon to American conservatives. She reported that crew and passengers had been herded to the back of the plane. What was she supposed to tell the pilot?

Was the pilot sitting next to her? Did the hijackers drive him out of the cockpit and put him with the passengers?

World Trade Center, North Tower, 24th Floor, 9:25 A.M.

From her office on the 81st floor, Jean Potter had gotten to a floor in the twenties. She prayed. And gave thanks again to her flat-heeled shoes. She ran into firemen going the other way. She recognized some of them—they were buddies of her husband. Jean Potter did not know whether she should be happy or sad. On the 6th floor, daylight streamed into the stairwell. She'd made it. Then, suddenly, everything came to a halt. People were pressing against her. She felt squeezed in. Jean Potter did the forbidden: She shouted out hysterically, "Let's go." Nothing moved.

Manhattan, West Street

To Dan Potter it felt like evening. The streets of Lower Manhattan lay in deep shadow as he parked his silver pickup on West Street; black clouds of smoke darkened the sun. He ran across the street to the firehouse where his bunker gear was hanging. He had to get his wife off the roof, and you couldn't do that in penny loafers. There was an ambulance, and a few EMS workers were standing around. A Japanese man lay on the ground with a broken leg. Potter put on his suit and saw a familiar face next to him. It belonged to Peter Bielfield, an old friend of his from the Bronx.

"Hey, Pete, how's it going?"

Pete pulled up his pants and answered, "We're going into the burning towers, Dan. What else?"

Dan put on his helmet. He was about to leave with Pete when he realized that he needed to get his ax and crowbar.

"I'll just go now," said Pete.

Dan would never see him again.

The White House, Washington, D.C., 9:38 A.M.

At 9:38 A.M. American Airlines Flight 77, after a skillfully executed downward spiral, thundered low over the streets of Washington, shearing off trees and streetlights, then bore into the west side of the Pentagon, welling up as a huge, black-veined fireball. Five hijackers around leader Hani Hanjour, six crew members, and fifty-three passengers died on board. One hundred and twenty-five persons died inside the Pentagon.

The F-16s from Langley were 105 miles, or twelve flight minutes, away. They now circled over the city.

In Washington, most officials assumed that the plane had been heading for the White House. Vice President Cheney, Condoleezza Rice, and other members of the staff had been hastily brought down to the Presidential Emergency Operations Center, a tubelike bunker built to survive an atomic bomb.

At around 9:40 A.M., as hijacked United Flight 93 also seemed headed toward Washington, Cheney recommended and Bush ordered that if the passenger plane approached the city it could, in an emergency situation, be shot down.

At 9:45 A.M. President Bush, who by this time was aboard *Air Force One,* learned that a plane had crashed into the Pentagon. He asked whether his wife and daughters were safe.

Meanwhile the fourth plane to have been hijacked that morning, United Airlines Flight 93, with Ziad Jarrah at the controls, was still in the air. Soon some passengers would revolt and lead a last hopeless fight. The plane went down at 10:10 A.M., with four hijackers, seven crew members, and thirty-four passengers on board.

"Stay calm," said a voice from the loudspeaker. "Stay inside. It is now safer inside than outside."

Mark Oettinger went to the window. He saw three bodies fall on the grass directly in front of him.

"Let's go," he said to his five coworkers. "We'll take the passage through the basement to the South Tower." He knew his way around the World Trade Center. He was proud of that.

Mark Oettinger is a carpenter. He builds furniture and sets up panels and desks. He had already worked in the famous Dakota apartment building, in huge buildings on Times Square, and often in the World Trade Center. He loves wood and old stone. On September 11 he and his five coworkers were supposed to remodel floors and to expand work areas at the Bank of America.

Now, in the hour of disaster, Oettinger was afraid, of course, but he also felt something else, something exciting: He was needed. He was young, only thirty-five, and in good shape. Whatever was happening out there was dangerous, but he knew what he was doing. He knew about danger, about bombs and explosions. Before he'd become a carpenter he'd been in the army. To be honest, he'd never seen combat, only been on maneuvers. This here was for real.

They were all depending on him, he thought. Not just his coworkers, but the bank employees too. First he needed to get a hold on the situation. The women first—he had to help the women. He hurried the people down ten stories. That part wasn't so difficult: His charges were pretty calm. Except when they were in the lobby and in front of them lay a figure, broken glass, blood everywhere. She was dead.

Ruins everywhere. More dead bodies. The explosion had hurled them from high above. They didn't look like the dead bodies you saw on TV. On TV when someone plunges from a roof he just lies there with a little blood around him. These looked exploded, thought Oettinger, exploded on impact.

There was a dull odor, a little like ammonia, and it left an unsettling taste that stayed in your mouth. A hospital smell that can't be erased no matter how much you try to get rid of it. The smell of death.

Oettinger believed he knew some of the dead. He had worked for lots of companies in the building. It wasn't unlikely one of them was someone he spoke with yesterday or the day before. He knew lots of people, and lots of people knew him. Often somebody would slap him on the shoulder. "Hey, remember me? You redid my office." He thought of Chris, Pat, Brian, of people from his shop who were on a job somewhere higher up in the tower. *Don't think now. Keep going.*

It was hard to get the women past the bloodbath. They wouldn't move.

"Don't look down and don't look to the side," he said. "Look over there at the exit sign. It's beautiful outside. Get out."

He sent them out onto Cortlandt Street, then went back in, climbed up past the 10th floor this time, looking for more women to get out.

They needed water. On TV you always see people with wet towels over their faces when there's a fire. He needed little towels, but there were only paper towels. He tore them off, wet them, and handed them to the women, who were having trouble breathing.

"Take deep breaths—but not constantly or the towel will go dry." He must have been on the 17th floor—no, 18th. He found more scared people.

"Come on, I'll get you out."

He came out of the stairwell with four women.

"We'll take it from here," he heard a fireman tell him. "We'll take over now."

He couldn't leave. As if mesmerized, he drifted about in the lobby looking for people to save, guiding them to the exits, constantly perking up his ears for someone crying somewhere—that sound told him where he had to go.

Finally he left the North Tower. For a minute he sat down in a small park. No birds. No people. He sat on some steps and cried.

North Tower, 44th Floor, Inside the Stairwell

"Don't worry, the fire's far above you," Jan Khan heard the firemen say. He squeezed against the wall to let them pass. They took up a lot of room with all their heavy equipment. They were sweating, panting.

"I still see their faces as they climbed past," says Kahn.

Khan was sweating too. The stairwell was narrow and hot and in his legs he already felt the thirty-seven flights they'd come dome. With him were Larissa and Chris, colleagues from the New York Metropolitan Transportation Council, an agency whose main responsibility was traffic routing.

Jan Khan has black hair, a black beard, a full face. He emigrated in 1992 from what was once British Guyana to the United States. He is a calm, thoughtful man not prone to big talk. He was born a Muslim but doesn't have much of a connection to religion.

His office in the World Trade Center was on the 82nd floor. His first thought on hearing the detonation at 8:45 A.M. was "a rocket." The second thought: "Get out."

He took his briefcase because his cell phone was in it. He ran to the office entrance, about fifty feet away. A dozen or so people were already there, but they didn't leave. The hallway was nothing but dark, thick black smoke. Khan heard screams for a second time. Here he was standing around with his fellow employees. How were they supposed to find the staircase in all this smoke?

His colleague Tony said he would go look. He groped his way out and was immediately swallowed up by smoke. The others looked at each other in silence. *I want to go home,* thought Khan. *I have to go home, my family's at home, that's where I belong.* On the outside he was calm. Then came Tony's voice.

"I've found the stairwell. Come on, follow my voice. Over here, over here, over here, over here."

Khan felt his way ahead, reached the staircase after a few steps, and started the descent.

Ever since the firefighters had started up the stairwell there'd been continual tie-ups. Sometimes Khan waited on a step for two, three minutes. He talked reassuringly to Larissa. Her husband worked in the South Tower and she knew that a plane had also exploded into it. She was crying. Khan said her husband was probably fine. *I want to go home, home, home,* he thought.

He took the cell phone from his briefcase and tried to call his wife but didn't get through. He saw cracks in the stairwell walls.

After the 10th floor things proceeded more smoothly. The air improved. Then the exit: Khan left the stairwell.

I will get home, he thought. *I'll get there soon.*

FDNY Emergency Message Center

9:47:15 A.M.: "Female caller states 2 World Trade Center—Floor 105—states floor underneath her—collapse."

9:47:23 A.M.: "Man waving jacket—man just jumped."

9:49:21 A.M.: "Twenty people on top waving—they are alive—please send help."

9:54:36 A.M.: "Male caller hears people crying."

9:55:28 A.M.: "2 World Trade Center—106th and 105th floors collapsing."

World Trade Center, North Tower, Ground Floor, 10:00 A.M.

Jan Khan had arrived on the concourse, the underground level that connected the two towers. This was also home to the Twin Towers' shopping center. Sprinklers were spraying water from the ceilings. Immediately Khan was soaking wet. He waded through and walked through a revolving door and past Banana Republic. Chris and Larissa were still with him.

All of a sudden as he was passing a coffee cart he heard a loud crash. "The sound of a gigantic explosion, as if something was collapsing behind us." Khan spun round to see the revolving door he had just used being folded top to bottom like an accordion. Same with the elevator doors. Entrance doors and shop windows burst from their frames and came flying toward them. Next a strong wind blasted through the shopping passage "like a hurricane."

"We'll die now," Khan said to Chris and Larissa, and reached out for their hands. The wind pushed Khan and Larissa to their knees, into the water and onto the broken glass. Chris threw his arms around a column and held on.

The gust of wind picked up Khan and Larissa and swept them across the ground. They came to rest in front of a pile of rubble. *I won't die, I can't die, I've got to go home, home, home.*

Suddenly all was quiet. All sounds, all wind, had ceased. Khan had lost his glasses. He was very worried he couldn't see anything anymore, everything around him was dark and black. Khan thought that maybe he'd been blinded. He was hardly able to breathe. He felt as if the air were a solid mass. He did not know that the South Tower had just collapsed.

"Larissa?"

"I'm okay," said Larissa.

"Chris?"

"I'm okay." Chris was still holding on to the column.

"I can't see anything anymore," Khan called out.

"Me neither," Chris replied.

"Me neither," said Larissa.

Khan knew now that he was not blind. It was the dust that had made everything so black.

"Over here, over here, over here, over here," Chris called. Larissa and Khan tapped their way toward him. Other voices rose out of the darkness. Soon, ten to twelve people had gathered. Khan was afraid "for the first time in my life." *I'll die after all,* he thought. And next: *No, I'll go home, I have to go home, that's where my family is.*

Liberty Street Firehouse

Dan Potter was still in the firehouse, a few minutes from the World Trade Center, when he heard a noise as though a freight train were coming straight at him. He saw a man standing at the front of the station house, his arms open wide, exclaiming, "Holy shit, it's coming down."

Glass, dust, and steel flew into the firehouse as if whipped by a dark tornado. Dan believed he would suffocate. "It felt as if someone was stuffing your body with black cotton balls."

World Trade Center, Base of the North Tower

Jean Potter had the descent behind her and had been running through the lobby of the North Tower, wet through and through from the sprinklers, when something rumbled behind her. She turned around and saw the South Tower, 110 floors, nearly one-third of a mile of glass and steel, falling toward her. People were screaming. The black cloud descended, Jean surrendered. She had walked for an hour, and this was the end. There was no point trying to run. The black colossus would bury her.

A policeman grabbed her and dragged her down into a subway entrance. The colossus was coming after them. They went farther down, as if into their own grave. *Thank God Dan's attending class on Staten Island,* she thought. *I have to call him. He will think that I am dead.*

North Tower, 35th Floor

Rick Picciotto stopped for a moment in the stairwell of the North Tower when he heard a sound such as he had never before heard, despite twenty-eight years as a firefighter. "As if a tractor trailer was rolling through your living room," is how Marcel Claes, the backup man for Engine 24, would later describe it. Picciotto thought that an elevator's cables might have been severed and shot down the shaft. It took fifteen seconds. Then there was nothing, nothing but silence. Just like after an earthquake. "Deafening silence," Picciotto says.

His firefighters looked at him. "What was that?" Picciotto radioed. Nothing but static on his unit's channel.

A few seconds later Picciotto learned from another channel that the South Tower had collapsed. Picciotto held his two-way radio and bellowed into it over and over, "What tower? What tower? What tower?"

No answer. He started to scream. "The TV antenna on the North Tower, a water tower, what tower?"

The response was full of static but clear: "The entire South Tower."

Picciotto could not grasp it. Nobody could grasp it, not on the 35th floor and not outside either, where John Ottrando, the driver for Engine 24, was running for his life, just like his colleagues from FDNY, the NYPD, and the Port Authority Police. Ottrando sprang after a jeep and was completely covered by a cloud of steel, glass, dust, and concrete. But he survived. Every firefighter heading up the stairs of the South Tower was dead.

Nobody in FDNY had expected that either of the monumental towers might completely collapse. Not so soon— less than one hour after the attack.

The South Tower was hit second but collapsed first. The point of collision was lower and thus a bigger load was pressing down on supporting columns that had also been damaged on the floors that were hit. Experts also think it possible that the core of the South Tower suffered more serious damage than that of the North Tower.

Steel columns bear their burden only when supported from the side. The columns in the tower cores, as well as those on the outside, received support exclusively from the floor trusses. These consisted of steel rods slightly over an inch in diameter holding a steel plate covered with four to five inches of reinforced concrete. The narrowly spaced steel columns on the four aluminum faces of each tower lost their side support once the floor connections broke and the first stories crashed down, taking one or two others down with them. The steel columns buckled under the load of the higher floors.

According to another theory, the light steel rods of the floor trusses heated up first. During the twenty to thirty minutes after impact, the floors between the inner and outer support columns began to sag. Without the support of these cross connections and softened by the heat, the outer columns buckled or broke like matches under the weight of the floors above the area of impact—an estimated 45,000 tons in the North Tower and about 110,000 tons in the South Tower. At soon as the fire-stressed outer columns lost their support from the cross trusses, the tower was doomed: The complete top of the building crashed down upon the flooring structure and the vertical impact continued, like dominoes, downward.

The uppermost floors crashed to the ground with an estimated speed of about 125 mph, close to the speed of free fall. In no more than fifteen seconds the whole building was down.

After the South Tower's collapse the firefighters' task changed radically. FDNY works under extremely risky conditions, but there has to be at least a slim chance for rescue. None now existed. FDNY is not a club for forlorn suicidal types, nor was Picciotto any such man. Trying to get from the 35th to the 92nd floor at this point would have been committing suicide.

New York firefighters are in a league of their own, a brotherhood with its own laws, its own code of honor, and its own history. Irish and Italian immigrants who couldn't get a job anywhere else in the New World devoted their lives to putting out fires. It was their chance to become part of the American dream, to find a home in the land of the "free and brave," their chance to move from worker to hero.

New York City has more tall buildings than any other city of the world, and the stairwells are like endless tubes. Whoever dares enter these burning traps day in and day out is revered. Even in a fast and tough city like New York. If for that reason alone, New York's firemen have earned the title "New York's Bravest."

Grandmothers wave when they pass. Wall Street bankers salute with red cheeks. Preschoolers learn their songs. Pretty girls push for dates. Not bad for a group whose average entry-level salary is $29,973 a year.

On Board *Air Force One,* 10:05 A.M.

Air Force One had taken off at 9:55 A.M. from Sarasota. Once aloft and flying north at a very high altitude, the passengers on board could see on the TV screen what was happening in New York—what was happening in America. President Bush talked with Secretary of Defense Donald Rumsfeld and National Security Adviser Rice over the phone.

"We are going to take care of this. When we find out who did this, they are not going to like me as president. Somebody is going to pay," he said to Cheney.

At this point the passengers on *Air Force One* did not know where the plane was heading. A call had been received at the White House, claiming that "*Air Force One* is next." The caller was apparently familiar with details of the president's travel routines. He also used secret codes, the one for the president's plane, among others. Security personnel considered the threat credible.

The news situation on board *Air Force One* was also confusing. There were reports of a car bomb in front of the Pentagon or State Department, of a mysterious Korean Airlines plane supposed to be coming in from the Pacific, of a plane said to have been hijacked in Amsterdam.

Liberty Street Firehouse

Not long after 10 A.M. the smoke in front of Dan Potter's firehouse lifted. From his distant corner he could see that the rest of the building had collapsed. No firefighters were to be seen. Potter decided to make his way to command headquarters on West Street, at the north end of the World Trade Center. On his way: debris, burning cars, and fire trucks. No people. It seemed to him as if he were the only survivor on the streets of New York. Since debris and bodies were still pouring down, Potter decided to make his way through buildings that were still intact.

He walked through the emptied halls of a branch of Deutsche Bank. Drawings by four-year-olds were hanging on the walls of a kindergarten. He remained the only survivor in New York.

He looked out a window and up. He saw no World Trade Center anymore, only blue sky. *Holy shit, the South Tower is gone.* Then he looked north. Okay, it was still standing. Up there on the roof, Jean was waiting. *Dan, you've got to get her down from there, the helicopter is not going to come.*

Church Street

Better to die up there than down here. Jean Potter turned around and left the subway station the policeman had pulled her into when the South Tower collapsed. Aboveground, the cloud had lightened some. Silence. As she walked along the street, whitewashed figures called out to her to cover her mouth with a handkerchief. The cloud was toxic. Wet and covered in dust, Jean Potter could only make out shapes. She walked like a robot, north, looking for some piece of peace amid this inferno. Other people might look for a church under these circumstances, but Jean Potter was searching for a firehouse. Maybe one of Dan's buddies could explain why the world had come to an end on a sunny Tuesday morning in September.

World Trade Center, North Tower, Lobby

The group around Jan Khan was debating how to get out from under all this rubble. They stood there talking. "We were too afraid to move," says Khan. Most of all they were afraid of falling into subway tunnels through holes in the ground.

They could not stay where they were, however. They couldn't see anything, but they could hear the building groaning and crunching.

"Let's form a human chain," someone said. They agreed this was a good idea. Chris went first, followed by Larissa, then Khan, then another woman. They clung to each other, Chris testing the ground with his feet. The building grumbled. They knew a subway station had to be close by. They groped their way over to it but soon realized nothing was left of it. They proceeded at snail's pace, a caravan of fear. They had been on the move for about twenty minutes when they heard a voice from a great distance: "Somebody there?"

"Yes!" Khan and the others called back. "Who's there?"

"I'm a firefighter. Can you see the flashlight?"

"No. Please keep calling. We'll follow your voice."

"Over here, over here, over here, over here, over here, over here."

Soon Khan recognized the beam of a flashlight, then the firefighter himself. The man led the group to other firefighters. They suggested sending the group out through the station. "No fucking way!" said the first firefighter. He led them on, until suddenly they saw a ray of light. It grew bigger and stronger until they found themselves on Vesey Street, north of the World Trade Center.

"Don't look up! Don't look back!" policemen were screaming. "Run for it, run for it, run for it!"

Khan ran as fast as he could, past destroyed cars, past

debris, across Vesey Street, onto Church Street, north. After two blocks he stopped and turned around. He had reached safety. He started to cry.

North Tower, 35th Floor

Nearly all civilians below the area of impact on the 96th floor had left the tower. Hundreds of firefighters, however, were still in the stairwells. *High time to get the guys out,* thought Rick Picciotto. Without waiting for word from higher up, he took his bullhorn and shouted, "Time to evacuate, drop everything, get out!"

The backup man from Engine 24, Marcel Claes, threw down his hose and started to run down the stairs. He kept his oxygen tank—you never knew. Dozens followed him. Last was Picciotto, who checked every floor. Over and over again he kept yelling the same two words into the bullhorn: "Get out!"

The evacuation ran smoothly until the 16th floor, where there was a traffic jam. Rubble from the South Tower had destroyed parts of Stairwells A and C in the North Tower. Picciotto ordered his men to use only Stairwell B.

Down they went, floor by floor, until Picciotto opened a door on the 12th floor and saw some fifty to seventy people sitting in an office. He stood there. He couldn't believe his eyes. What were they doing here?

"Come on, guys, let's go!"

Only then did he see the crutches and wheelchairs. Picciotto ordered his men to help the handicapped.

Marcel Claes reached the lobby and ran through a broken window to freedom. Seconds later, Picciotto once more heard the piercing rumble, the horrifying clamor. Picciotto was on the 5th floor and if the North Tower collapsed as quickly as the South Tower had, he would have exactly twelve more seconds to live.

Dear Lord, Picciotto thought, *do me one favor and let me die quick.* Picciotto thought of his wife, of his children in their graduation hats. Then he said a prayer.

The North Tower collapsed in an almost absurdly controlled way, as if following a master plan for its demolition. The first thing Picciotto noticed about the stories collapsing above him was the wind—not a wind so much as a hurricane, hurling him down the steps and turning day to night.

Picciotto saw nothing. He couldn't tell whether he was dead or alive, dreaming or thinking, trapped somewhere in Lower Manhattan or on his way to the other world. Minutes passed until Picciotto heard a cough, then he heard another one. Whichever pile of dirt he was in, Picciotto did what he had learned to do when civilization had still existed. He introduced himself.

Base of the North Tower, 10:40 A.M.

Shortly before the second freight train bore down upon Dan Potter he met a friend he had last seen twenty years ago—Fire Marshall Mel Hazel. Potter prepared himself to die. "You can be lucky once, but not twice." He was consoled by the thought that he did not have to be alone at the end of his life. His friend Mel Hazel crouched next to him, pressed against the wall, hands folded over his head. *If we have to go, at least we go together*, Potter said to himself.

For several minutes the two were lying buried in dust and debris, unharmed. Potter tried to switch on his flashlight, but it was useless: He was too weak, he was trembling. The two crawled like blind beetles through the debris, until Potter said, "Mel, I think we're on the street."

"Nonsense," answered Mel.

"But look," Potter said and dug into the debris until he hit something that looked like pavement. He got up.

"My wife," he said, "was on the 81st floor. She went to the roof. I have to find her."

Church Street

Jean Potter did not turn around when the second tower collapsed, carrying with it her desk and handbag from the 81st floor. She continued marching on in her lavender pants suit. It must have looked as if her own ghost were walking through Lower Manhattan, a dead person on vacation. People handed her water, a cell phone. She moved on and stopped only about a mile north of the disaster site in front of Firehouse Engine 9, Ladder 6, on Canal Street. The men were down at the towers. Replacements from Long Island were filling in as best they could. Jean Potter walked through the raised door into the garage.

"Hello," she said. "I'm Jean Potter, wife of a firefighter. Have you got work for me?"

The guys pointed to a phone that was ringing without interruption. "Great if you could take care of it."

For over an hour, Jean Potter answered phone calls, doing her best to console those on the other end of the line. Mothers, wives, sons, daughters looking for the men. Three hundred and forty-three firefighters lost their lives.

Peter Langone. Forty-one, he had promised his daughters a trip to Disney World.

Joseph Leavy. Forty-five, an aficionado of skyscrapers, one of the first firefighters to arrive at the World Trade Center.

Ronnie Gies. Forty-three, a firefighter for twenty-five years. His children'later saw him for the last time on an amateur videotape that showed him entering the towers.

James Amato. Forty-three, a captain who during the last big blaze had called his men back from a burning building seconds before the explosion. "Timing is everything," was all he would say later.

Vincent Giammona. He had planned to celebrate his fortieth birthday the night of September 11.

Terrence McShane. Thirty-seven, one of the few whose remains could be found.

Nearly all the men in leading positions in the New York City Fire Department were dead: Bill Feehan, first deputy commissioner; Peter Ganci, department chief; Terry Hatton, forty-one, chief of Rescue Squad 1.

Jean Potter had no inkling that her husband might well have been number 344.

On Board *Air Force One*, 10:37 A.M.

After President Bush learned that his wife, Laura, and his two daughters were safe, he asked jokingly how Barney the family dog was doing. "Nipping at the heels of Osama bin Laden now," Chief of Staff Andy Card kidded him in response.

At 10:41 A.M. *Air Force One* flew toward Jacksonville, Florida; from there fighter jets would escort it. Vice President Cheney, who had just followed the collapse of the second tower on TV, urged the president not to return to Washington too soon. He suggested flying instead to Offutt Air Force Base near Omaha, Nebraska, the headquarters of the Strategic Air Command. "We've got secure facilities there to update you," Cheney said.

Boston, 10:40 A.M.

The FBI agents' shock over what they were seeing on their TV screens could last only a few minutes. They had to get going. Who could have done it and where had they come from? Who knew whom in the planes? Who had sat in the strategically important seats near the cockpits?

The first detectives had been combing the passenger lists since 10 A.M. They saw Egyptian, Arabic, Lebanese names, names that didn't mean anything to them. Atta, Mohamed? Jarrah, Ziad? The officials sent the names through their computers and created rosters from the information they collected from the INS, the Immigration and Naturalization Service. By midday on September 11 it was clear that some of the hijackers came from Germany.

In the afternoon the agents received a phone call. A travel bag that was supposed to have been aboard American Airlines Flight 11 had been found. It belonged to Mohamed Atta. It got hung up somewhere on the conveyor belts at Logan Airport and never made it into the luggage hold of the Boeing 767. Very carefully the FBI agents opened the zipper: no bomb. The bomb had been the bag's owner himself.

Inside were clothes, a toiletries kit, and two written documents that Atta had intended to take with him into the inferno along with himself and thousands of others. These are the first items of proof: the typed confessions of a dead man. Documents of insanity. The papers contained the instructions for mass murder, promising "God's blessing" to the hijackers, as well as Atta's last will and testament.

Atta's bag gave FBI agents a look inside the man's head who had just staged the largest terror attack ever committed in human history. Since 8:45 A.M. Atta and his holy warriors had sent chills up the world's spine; now the detectives could see that world through the eyes of the hijackers.

Atta's papers portrayed a Western world eroded by greed, prostitution, drugs, loneliness. And they also portrayed the Islamic world the way these terrorists saw it: as the cradle of faith, the last oasis of culture, threatened by America, starved by the West, humiliated for centuries.

Atta knew both worlds, and toward the end he was consumed by the idea of smashing through the phony face of "the other." Living in the Western world had taught him how to launch an assault on this other life, had taught him what you had to do to turn billions of infidels into spectators of their own worst fears.

In the middle of the devil's chaos something like a heavenly counterattack took place. What else can you call it when 110 stories collapse within seconds into a mountain of steel and concrete—yet somehow create a cave of debris within which eleven people miraculously survive?

After the thunder of the destruction had died away, voices could be heard at about the level where the 4th floor of Stairwell B had once been. They belonged to men announcing themselves back into life. They belonged to firefighters Mike Meldrum, Matt Komorowski, Bill Butler, Tom Falco, Sal D'Agostino, and Captain Jay Jonas, all members of Ladder 6. They were from the Canal Street firehouse where Jean Potter was at that moment trying to calm their next of kin. Another voice belonged to David Lim, member of the New York Port Authority Police. The voices of Bacon and Cross, two firefighters, joined in the chorus. And then there were the slightly higher tones of a woman's voice. It belonged to Josephine Harris, an office worker with the Port Authority.

Josephine Harris had been sitting at her desk on the 73rd floor when the plane hit. She immediately started down. The problem was that the fifty-nine-year-old grandmother was not very steady on her feet. She had had to rest after nearly every step because of the pain in her legs.

She was on the 14th floor and at the end of her rope when she finally came upon help—Captain Jay Jonas and his men from Ladder 6. They had just dashed down the stairs from the 27th floor; the South Tower had collapsed and Jonas had given orders to evacuate.

"That's it, guys, let's get out of here. If one goes, the next won't be far behind."

They were running down the stairs when suddenly there in front of them stood Josephine Harris. In Jonas's head, the seconds were ticking away as loud as church bells. *Out of here, quick—but not without this lady.* Even if she weighs as much as a washing machine. David Lim, the policeman who had joined Jonas's unit along the way, and firefighter Bill Butler held Josephine Harris between them and carried her down until Jonas decided to make their work easier by looking inside offices and hallways for a chair to carry the "old lady."

That's when the North Tower crashed to the ground, as if someone had pushed the fast-forward button of a videotape.

Lim threw himself over Josephine to protect her but Butler was faster and so they both landed on top of her. The force of the tremor threw them down the stairwell like bales of hay. Captain Jonas, 240 pounds and a former football player, was able to save himself when the tower began to shake by taking a leap into the more stable stairwell.

It took some time before the survivors of the crash were able to see again. Dust and soot ate into their eyes like pepper spray. In the semidark the buried could hear the coughs and sighs of their companions. Nobody had been seriously hurt—a dislocated shoulder, a broken rib, a concussion maybe, nothing more.

When Jonas sat up on the 4th floor and brushed the garbage from his clothes, a voice was whispering from his radio. The voice belonged to Mike Warchola.

"Mayday," said Warchola. "We're trapped on the 12th floor of the North Tower. We're seriously injured. Help."

Warchola was a close friend of Jonas. Today was his last day of work before retiring. He belonged to Ladder 5 in Greenwich Village. Jonas got up and climbed over rubble and broken steps to go find Warchola. The 5th floor was a dead end. Steel and rubble had formed an impenetrable wall. Over the next five minutes Warchola twice radioed Mayday. Then nothing. He and four of his men were found two days later, lying peacefully, dead.

About three steps below the 5th floor was a hole in the stairwell about the size of a small window. Jonas looked through it. Here, too, nothing but steel and smoke. It appeared mere chance that these lowest floors in Stairwell B had remained intact. But what if they were totally enclosed in tons of steel? How long would it take the rescue team to dig their way through to them? Two days? Two weeks? Would anybody still be breathing?

Jonas is forty-four years old. After college, instead of a career with a six-figure salary, he opted for the New York Fire Department and had been putting out fires with passion for more than twenty-two years.

Picking his way through the remains of the stairwell he found a black firefighter's boot. And a bullhorn. It was the bullhorn of Rick Picciotto who, up in the 35th floor, had given orders to his firefighters to evacuate. The hurricane had reached him on the 5th floor and hurled him down two flights, where he was now. It was just after 10:30 when he heard the coughing and introduced himself.

Jonas and Picciotto assumed joint command of the group of survivors. Were they the luckiest guys in the world or members of a club of the damned? they wondered. Sure, they were alive, but for how much longer? The radio transmitters registered the last words of fellow firefighters: "Tell my wife that I love her." And the whispering voice of their battalion commander, Richard Prunty: "I'm not going to be able to make it out of here."

Marj, Lebanon, 5:30 P.M.

"Something's happened in New York," Samir Jarrah called out. He was sitting on the couch in his home in the Bekaa Valley near Beirut when he saw the towers collapse. The friends who were visiting joined him in front of the TV, drinking tea and staring. "That is terrible," said Samir Jarrah, who is sixty-one. "So horrible. So many innocent people."

They also saw the wreckage of the hijacked plane that had crashed in Pennsylvania—but they did not yet have any idea that Samir's son had been its pilot. They turned off the

TV, ate, and went to sleep. In February, Samir Jarrah had undergone open-heart surgery. Everything had gone well, but several bypasses had been put in, and on this Tuesday in September he still felt weak. He was able to cut himself some slack. Employees were running his two businesses.

He did not try to call Ziad when he saw the pictures from America; no one in his family tried. Ziad was in Florida, after all, far away from the burning towers. Ziad was safe, Ziad was learning how to fly, Ziad was going to be a pilot.

It wasn't until four days later, while the whole family was at their country house, that policemen would question them.

"Did I raise a terrorist?" Samir Jarrah asked himself. Terrorists came from the camps in Palestine. "They don't have any choice, they don't have any future, no life, they are dead already while they are still living. So they die and take along a few of those who made their lives so miserable." That's what terrorists were like until September 11.

But Ziad? His son?

Ziad was five years old when he built his first plane out of Legos and announced that when he grew up he would be a pilot. When he was twelve years old he went to the library to get books. "Always about flying. Nothing else existed for him," according to his father. Ziad was twenty-six years old when he flew his first Boeing: United Airlines Flight 93.

"Yet Ziad had everything," said the father. "He was a boy scout, he played basketball on a team, he made the family laugh, he went to the beach with his sisters, and of course, they wore bikinis all the time," his father said.

The Jarrah family is Muslim but not strict. Ziad had gone to the Hikmeh School, a Christian oasis behind tall concrete walls attended by both Muslims and Christians. "Ziad was tolerant, he never drew distinctions," says his teacher Mohamad Osman, forty-three. "He was good-looking, flattered the girls, and so he was always popular." He studied airplane engineering in Germany and, according to investigators, met Mohamed Atta and his fundamentalist friends. During the winter of 1999 he must have already had a notion about his eventual martyrdom: If only he could not just repair planes but also fly them, he told his father, he'd have better prospects for a career. His father accepted the idea, sent more money, and hoped that his son would soon come home to Lebanon.

Two days before the attack Ziad called home for the last time. He thanked them for the money he'd received. "He laughed and joked with everyone, as usual," his father said.

In his good-bye letter to his girlfriend, whom he planned to marry, Ziad wrote, "I did what I was supposed to do."

To this day his mourning father is certain: "I did not raise him to hate. On the contrary, I did all the right things."

Barksdale Air Force Base, Near Shreveport, Louisiana, 12:36 P.M.

In a second position statement recorded on video at Barksdale Air Force Base in Louisiana at 12:36 P.M., President Bush promised to hunt down and punish those responsible. "Freedom itself was attacked this morning by a faceless coward," said Bush, who appeared tense. The videotape was out of focus and grainy. "It was not our best moment," an administration official later admitted.

Before landing in Shreveport, the few journalists in the rear of the plane had been asked to turn off their cell phones so as not to send any signals that might betray the position of the plane. They were also instructed to report that the president was at "an unidentified location in the United States." Again the president expressed his wish to return to Washington, but Vice President Cheney advised against it. There were still a number of planes in the air and nobody knew whether any of them might be hijacked. His chief of staff was also against it. "Let's let the dust settle."

Bush argued with this assessment. He didn't want terrorists keeping the president of the United States out of Washington. "People want to see their president, and they want to see him now."

Bush phoned New York Senator Charles Schumer and

Secretary of Defense Donald Rumsfeld. Security officials were still concerned that the president's plane could be an easy target for a potential air attack, even on the ground.

At 1:37 P.M. Bush left Barksdale on *Air Force One,* headed for Offutt Air Force Base in Nebraska. The plane landed there at 2:50 P.M.

World Trade Center, Inside the Ruins of the North Tower

The people around Rick Picciotto and Captain Jonas steeled themselves for a long stay in their stairwell prison. No one grumbled when Jonas told them to turn off flashlights and radios in order to save power.

The men started to explore the stairwell. In addition to the filth that clogged their eyes and lungs was the smell of gasoline. A match lit in the dark or even a spark could mean the end.

During their search for an exit the men discovered a door on the 2nd floor. They opened it. Nothing but rubble and debris.

On the 3rd floor, another door. Again they opened it. Again nothing but rubble and debris.

On the 4th floor they discovered two sprinklers. At least now they had water. A little farther they found a toilet. And an elevator shaft that went down. It was black, no end. Picciotto decided it was too much of a risk. If no help arrived in a few days, they might try again.

The men were exhausted. David Lim, the policeman, went searching for his bomb-sniffing dog.

"Stop it," said Captain Jonas. "Your dog doesn't matter now. People are dying all around us."

At about noon, Jonas was again talking into his radio.

"Mayday. Mayday. This is Captain Jonas of Ladder Six. We are trapped in Stairwell B in the North Tower, floors two, three, four, and five. Come get us."

In response, Jonas heard a hoarse voice come out of the transmitter: "North Tower? The North Tower doesn't exist anymore!" Jonas's spirits sank. Until that moment they had hoped that only part of the building had collapsed. How many square feet of steel were on top of them? There was no one to answer the question. And no longer anyone in charge of the rescue mission, either. Many of the highest ranks were dead, their command centers demolished. Hayden was attempting to direct the chaos from West Street in the midst of the ruins; his office was the roof of a fire truck.

The only things they could do were wait, radio, and wait some more. Adrenaline dissipated, the pain of injuries grew. It was 1 P.M., 2 P.M.

Then Captain Jonas thought he was seeing things: It was starting to get light. It seemed to him as if the sun were shining directly into the stairwell. He followed the beams, step by step, and ended up back on the 5th floor. He looked through the window-sized hole. He saw steel and smoke, mountains of devastation, and a bit of blue sky. The remnants of Stairwell B were not buried in the rubble but rising out of it.

Picciotto joined him, Lim on his heels.

"Oh, my God," said Lim, softly. "How lucky can you get? How often you think this kind of thing happens?"

"Once in a billion."

A trench about ten feet deep and one hundred feet wide lay between them and freedom. It looked like a glacier from hell: sharp steel, endlessly deep crevices, blazing fires, no end in sight.

Minutes later, on top of the smoking pile of rubble, they could make out firefighters from Ladder 43.

Rick Picciotto was the first to be brought by rope across the treacherous abyss; then came the men from Ladder 6— Mike Meldrum, Matt Komorowski, Bill Butler, Tom Falco, Sal D'Agostino—then firefighters Bacon and Cross; policeman David Lim; and finally Josephine Harris. Only then did Captain Jay Jonas take his turn. It was 3 P.M. when his men lowered him down onto West Street. There he saw one of the most beautiful sights of his life: All his men had escaped death, along with Josephine Harris.

For twenty-two years, when people asked what kind of work he did, Jonas had always replied, "We go in, rescue people, put out the fire, and go home." This time the fire was stronger. But Jonas and his men did rescue a woman. And went home.

Jonas went over to Hayden's "office." They had last seen each other that morning at 9:03 when the second plane hit the South Tower and Hayden ordered him and his men into the World Trade Center. Hayden nearly wept.

"Jay, good to see you," he called out.

Jonas as well could barely hold back the tears. "Reporting in again, Chief. It's sure nice to be among the living."

Next the ambulance staff were fussing over Jonas's men. Only Jonas himself escaped treatment. He walked back to the firehouse on Canal Street.

Slowly it dawned on him that he owed his life to a tired lady. Everybody on the floors above and below was dead. "We all thought that Josephine was walking much too slow," Jonas would later say. "But really she was the one with the perfect timing. God gave us the courage to help her, and that's how we ourselves were saved."

Later the firefighters gave Josephine Harris, mother and grandmother and office worker from the 73rd floor, a Ladder 6 firefighter's jacket decorated with a green dragon—symbol of their station home in Chinatown. Below it was embroidered the following inscription: "Josephine—Our Guardian Angel."

Offutt Air Force Base, near Omaha, Nebraska, 4:00 P.M.

President Bush was sitting in an underground bunker and conducting the first consultation of the day with members of the National Security Council, via teleconference. Condoleezza Rice later reported that Bush opened the discussion by stating that what they were dealing with was an attack on freedom and "we're going to define it as such."

Not long after 4 P.M. the discussion ended. Bush repeated

his desire to return to Washington, and again the Secret Service advised against it. This time Bush overrode them. The American people expected him to give his televised address from the Oval Office, he told them, not from some bunker. At 4:36 P.M. the president's plane took off for the capital.

Washington, D.C., 7:00 P.M.

Bush returned to the White House. A squadron of six helicopters roared past the Washington Monument. Only at the last minute did *Marine One* break off from the group to land on the White House lawn; no one was supposed to know which helicopter the president was in. When he saw the column of smoke over the Pentagon, he said to his advisers, "The mightiest building in the world is on the floor. That's the twenty-first century war you just witnessed."

Bush assembled the most important members of his cabinet in the White House bunker: Dick Cheney, Secretary of State Colin Powell, Attorney General John Ashcroft, National Security Adviser Condoleezza Rice.

The White House, 8:30 P.M.

President Bush gave his third and last official statement of the day from the Oval Office. It lasted less than five minutes and was broadcast live on television.

Twelve hours after the attack, Bush was finally in the White House. "None of us will ever forget this day," he said. The American government would make no distinction between those who were terrorists and those who harbored them. "We go forward to defend freedom and all that is good and just in our world." An estimated eighty million Americans listened to these words sitting in front of their televisions, and could feel the weight bearing down on the president. He gave a discernible sigh.

Dan and Jean Potter looked for refuge at the home of Jean Potter's mother. Dust from the collapsed towers had made their own apartment uninhabitable, funereal. Jean's mother lived in Pennsylvania.

At around noon, after the collapse of the North Tower, Dan Potter had called his father, sobbing.

"Dad, Jean is dead."

"Nonsense," his father said. "She's on telephone assignment at the Canal Street firehouse."

Potter ran to his car and jumped in. He found her. Dust stuck to the two of them like cement, but when they lay sobbing in each other's arms the fear started to fall away. They wanted to get out of the city. When they stopped at a gas station on their way to Pennsylvania, people stared at them in silence. As if Jean and Dan Potter had not just survived but been resurrected.

PART II

In the "House of Followers"

FBI Headquarters, Washington, D.C., 9:20 A.M.

The Strategic Information and Operations Center of the Federal Bureau of Investigation is located on the fourth floor of FBI Headquarters. Seventeen minutes after the second crash into the World Trade Center, 250 agents rushed into the SIOC to begin an investigation. Monitors glimmered; people shouted past each other and worked the phones.

The FBI was in contact with the Pentagon, the State Department, the FAA, and Vice President Cheney—who had hunkered down in the Presidential Emergency Operations Center, the secure bunker underneath the White House. The lines there were secure.

First the FBI team feverishly gathered all the information they could. They had been left out of the loop on one critical fact, however. When the third plane crashed into the Pentagon, everyone here was completely shocked. Air traffic controllers had informed only the White House about the plane's suspicious flight pattern.

FBI Director Robert Mueller had been on the job a mere six days. He had been hired to overhaul the organization, whose record in recent times had been marred by scandals and mishaps. Now this.

Mueller determined that the most important thing was to prevent future attacks. He gave orders to arrest anyone who aroused suspicion, however petty the reason. The tactic is called "spitting on the sidewalk." The objective is to destroy any potential terrorist cells. He put seven thousand people to work. The largest operation in the history of the FBI had begun. Its formal name: Pentagon Twin Towers Bombing, or PENTTBOM for short.

Boston, Logan Airport, Around Noon

The detectives worked quickly. They already knew the names of the terrorists. And of course now they had Atta's suitcase.

They also had a car, a white Mitsubishi. An eyewitness had seen several Arab-looking men quarreling in front of it that very morning. Inside were the National Rent-a-Car rental agreement, flying manuals in Arabic, and a "ramp pass" that allowed access to restricted areas at Logan Airport. Some papers contained the same Arab names that appeared on the passenger lists. The names Charles and Drucilla Voss also appeared—the couple that had rented a room to Mohamed Atta in Venice, Florida; they were the first lead to Florida.

There were other leads, and they were continuing to point to a German connection.

Berlin, Office of the German Chancellor, 8:30 P.M. Local Time

Chancellor Gerhard Schröder appeared before the press.

At 3:03 P.M. that afternoon Schröder's press spokesman had called office director Sigrid Krampitz. "Turn on the television." Schröder conducted brief telephone conversations with his major advisers: Foreign Minister Joschka Fischer, Interior Minister Otto Schily, and Defense Minister Rudolf Scharping. After that, Schröder, Scharping, Schily, and Fischer met with the head of German intelligence, August Hanning. Then Schröder called the president of the German Republic, Johannes Rau, and after that French President

Jacques Chirac, British Prime Minister Tony Blair, and Russian President Vladimir Putin.

During the press conference Schröder called the attack an "assault upon our values" and pledged the "absolute solidarity" of the Federal Republic of Germany with the United States of America.

The chancellor looked tired.

Hamburg, Germany, September 12, 10:00 P.M. Local Time

Hamburg police officers cordoned off Marienstrasse in the Harburg section of the city. Plainclothesmen in black, unmarked cars with flashing lights sped toward the area.

Number 54 Marienstrasse is a plain-looking, pale-yellow, four-story postwar building located in a typical German lower-middle-class neighborhood. People don't know each other and aren't all that interested in doing so. Some who have lived here have been hiding from the world. Nameplates next to the doorbells are broken off; many of the houses don't have an intercom. Some who have lived here liked it that way. They didn't want to be found.

Here, on the first floor to the right of the stairs, Mohamed Atta lived with Said Bahaji and another man. The entire apartment consists of three square rooms whose total area is about five hundred square feet. It was more than just home. When Atta once sent his share of the rent to Bahaji, he scribbled the same notation on the money transfer slip: "for *Dar el-ansar*," which in Arabic means "House of Followers."

This "House of Followers" was modeled upon another house, also rented, located along Sayed Jalaluddin Street in the university district of Peshawar, Pakistan, a part of town where the affluent live. Called *Beit al-Ansar*, which also can be translated as "House of Followers," this was a white bungalow with a flat roof; it had squarely trimmed hedges and a closely cropped front lawn. Here, until he went into hiding, is where Osama bin Laden lived. And it was here that he welcomed those who came to learn how to wage "holy war."

At 10:18 A.M. on September 12 the FBI transmitted a list of nineteen suspects to the American Embassy in Berlin, which forwarded the six-page document to the Bundeskriminalamt, or BKA, the German equivalent of the FBI. Mohamed Atta, Marwan al-Shehhi, and Ziad Jarrah, as well as the names of many others suspected to have been involved in the attack, appear on this very first document, gleaned from reservation information, credit card accounts, postal addresses—all of which the FBI had collected in the course of one day. The document concluded by saying that the FBI would welcome any and all "trace information" regarding the suspects' activities in Germany, particularly those involving Atta and al-Shehhi. Officials in Berlin passed the list on to officials in Hamburg.

There was not much to discover at 54 Marienstrasse. Though the Hamburg police's best bomb-sniffing dog searched for twenty minutes, he didn't bark or stop once. Little was found aside from a few notes and some papers written in Arabic in the basement; once translated, they proved of scant interest.

Nonetheless, the raid was the beginning of the largest criminal investigation in history, involving practically every branch of government. In Germany alone, 17,000 pieces of information would be followed up on during the next weeks, 448 people and 19 businesses would be investigated, 39 locations would be searched, 452 banks and 43 credit card accounts would be checked, and mountains of files, computers, and videos would be confiscated.

The BKA established a six-hundred-member special task force called Soko USA, whose primary responsibilities were to coordinate the investigation with American authorities and then to figure out how the network was built, according to Germany's attorney general, Kay Nehm. Some of the most important early leads would come from cell-phone conversations.

Shortly before 1:30 P.M. the German police squad stormed a second house in the Harburg district of Hamburg. Two groups of policemen with machine guns swarmed into a first-floor apartment in a three-story corner building. A heavily armed squad in combat helmets formed a perimeter. However, Said Bahaji, the man they were looking for, was gone.

Instead the police found a frightened woman wearing a black chador, the shawl worn by religious Muslim women. Neşe Bahaji, Said's wife, and their six-month-old baby son, Omar, were taken into custody.

Hamburg-Harburg Technical University, September 13, 1:30 A.M.

University Chancellor Jörg Severin is a fairly easygoing administrator, but he is fiercely proud of his school's international profile: students at Hamburg-Harburg Technical University come from all over the world. Severin had been sound asleep but dreaming restlessly when the phone rang. It was the police commissioner, Justus Woydt.

"We need your database," Woydt said. Nothing more.

"At this hour of the night?" asked Severin. Then it dawned on him. "Oh, my God, New York?"

"Yes. Now," replied Woydt.

Fifteen minutes later Severin was standing at the school's main entrance. The police supplied the registrar with thirteen names. Seven of them appeared in the student directory. At this point it was still only a matter of "potential witnesses and suspects."

The next morning the school's president, Christian Nedess, was standing in the bathroom of his house when he heard the news. Two of the September 11 suicide pilots had studied at Hamburg-Harburg. "I nearly dropped my razor," said Nedess.

"Why here?" he wondered.

Berlin, Early October

That Hamburg should turn out to have been the nesting ground of the attack caught most German officials by surprise. For years the unstated policy regarding foreigners, however extreme their politics, was live and let live. In return it was expected that they would behave themselves while in Germany. What emerged from the investigation has been bitter medicine for German officials. Everyone knew that radicals were using Germany as a refuge, but there was an understanding that they wouldn't do anything to jeopardize the arrangement. "Don't spit on your own plate," an Arab proverb has it.

Before September 11 there were signs that the proverb had begun to lose some of its authority. On Christmas Eve 2000, almost nine months earlier, a SWAT team stormed two apartments in Frankfurt and took five Algerian men into custody. They were a bomb-assembly team, and it was alleged that they had been planning an attack on a Christmas Fair in the French city of Strasbourg. This tragedy was prevented "at the last minute," according to Interior Minister Otto Schily. The police confiscated an amateur video that showed tourists strolling along a street. An off-camera voice could be heard saying, "Here we see the enemies of God. You're on your way to hell, God willing."

Since then officials had been pushing for a reevaluation of the threat posed by Islamic terrorists. In the Office for the Protection of the Constitution—a special civilian agency established in postwar Germany to prevent subversive activities by extremists—a study group began devising ways agents might infiltrate radical circles. The danger had been recognized. Too late.

Ernst Uhrlau, director of secret services in the chancellor's office, was hit hard by this realization. Before Chancellor Schröder appointed him to his position, Uhrlau had been chief of the Hamburg Police; before that he had been head of the Hamburg branch for the Protection of the Constitution. He is quick on the uptake but slow to use words.

At the moment the first plane hit the first World Trade Center tower, officials in the chancellor's office were just winding up their weekly intelligence review. Nothing special had been on the agenda, and the ministers of the various departments—Secret Service, Interior, Defense, and Foreign—were heading back to their offices in a bantering, relaxed mood.

Uhrlau had just returned to his desk when a call came: "You may want to turn on the television."

Several hundred feet away, August Hanning, chief of intelligence, was sitting in his office talking to journalists in a general way about terrorists and terrorism when an aide handed him a slip of paper. Together with the journalists the intelligence chief watched CNN in disbelief for a few minutes. Then the telephones began to ring. Hanning ushered the journalists out of his office.

Within days these and other German officials knew that the hijackers from Hamburg were not their only problem. In their safes lay two BKA files, written several years earlier, in which officials in charge of national security urgently insisted that an exhaustive investigation be undertaken into the Al Qaeda organization. There had been unmistakable and repeated signs pointing to the conclusion that bin Laden's group had taken root in Germany. None of the pilots were mentioned by name in these papers, but others were—people who have since been identified as friends or even supporters of the Hamburg cell.

Attorney General Kay Nehm had always resisted launching an extensive investigation into Al Qaeda. The evidence was too flimsy and the legal difficulties insurmountable, he said. Nehm is a meticulous lawyer with a neat office; conversations with him can go on for a half hour before he makes eye contact. Pushing the limit is not his style.

Shortly after September 11, a conflict erupted between Nehm and the Schröder administration. American officials, who had started to arrest people as so-called key witnesses, couldn't understand why the same thing wasn't being done in Germany. The two different points of view clashed when American officials hurriedly informed German authorities that they had received a tip that a bin Laden representative was about to turn up at Frankfurt Airport. On what grounds should we hold him? German federal prosecutors asked. Just keep him locked up, replied their Washington counterparts. The potential problem resolved itself when the suspect failed to appear.

The situation escalated when the Bush administration put a German-Syrian businessman named Mamoun Darkazanli on the list of persons whose assets were to be frozen because of suspected links to terrorists. Nehm's office had explained to American officials that there simply wasn't enough information to bring charges. The fact that Darkazanli had been explicitly named as a suspect in the BKA files added to the Americans' irritation. There were increasingly sharp exchanges.

From this grew a suspicion within the Schröder administration that Nehm was being cautious only because he didn't want to admit that his earlier decisions had been mistakes. Nehm was ordered to attend the now daily security meetings in the chancellor's office. No sooner had he arrived at his first meeting than he was bombarded with criticism from the assembled ministers, as well as from Uhrlau. Further delay and inaction were out of the question. Nehm was outraged, but the scolding served its purpose. The case was broadened—and would now also include Darkazanli.

The investigation would be headed by two of the most experienced security officials in the country. The first was Walter Hemberger, who had already made something of a name for himself in the Bad Kleinen case, during which remnants of the German Red Army Faction had been run to ground. A passionate marathoner, Hemberger never did things halfway. Before long the walls of his office were covered with diagrams and charts tracing the interconnections of the Hamburg cell. The BKA's special commission—whose official title, Extraordinary Construction Commission, is a prime example of German policespeak—is headed by Manfred Klink, the second investigator. For many years, Klink was part of the leadership at the BKA in Wiesbaden, where he was responsible for security. Someone like Klink rarely makes the front pages anymore. That changes when you're trying to unravel the largest terrorist act of all time.

In the six weeks following September 11, investigators were constantly coming across new names and coming up with new suspects—small pieces in a growing mosaic. At times they came across some pretty bizarre people.

For example, in a correctional facility in the city of Hanover sat a certain Ali Z., a nineteen-year-old Iranian awaiting deportation. Long before September 11 he had been insisting that he be permitted to call the White House and the American Secret Service. He had something he needed to tell them. What that was he wouldn't say, other than that the current world order was ending.

Ali begged with such urgency that finally he was allowed to make the calls. The White House switchboard hung up as soon as they heard the caller was an Iranian sitting in a jail somewhere in Germany. The Secret Service dismissed him as suffering from serious delusions of grandeur. When on the Friday before September 11 Ali warned, once again, that "next week, something's going to happen," nobody listened. A doctor said that the young man was mentally unbalanced.

On September 13, two days after the attacks, people changed their minds. FBI special agents and BKA investigators sat down at the table with Ali Z. to listen to his story. The only problem was there was no story. Ali Z. rambled on about the threat to world peace, but otherwise it was obvious that he knew nothing. He was not acquainted with the hijackers and had no clue about possible motives for the attacks.

Lots of deranged people surfaced during these weeks; police listened to their stories with a mix of disgust, pity, and boredom. Then again, there were moments when the officers' tired ears perked up.

Around 6 P.M. one October evening, Zeljko E., a Kosovar Serb, entered a police station in the Altona neighborhood of

Hamburg, announcing that he wanted to turn himself in. The police checked their database for information about him, but their sluggish computer system was down again, and while waiting for it to come back up they put Zeljko in the lockup; a half hour later they knew that an arrest warrant had been issued for him in connection with a break-in.

The prisoner began demanding to be allowed to speak to someone involved with national security. When two BKA agents arrived, he told them that he had burgled a business and stolen printed material. Not money, not jewelry—paper, piles of papers and documents, all written in Arabic.

Zeljko said that he had wanted to find out if the stuff was worth anything. So, he told the BKA agents, he had dragged a suitcase full of these papers to a buddy of his who spoke Arabic. They soon realized that the documents might have something to do with the attacks in New York and Washington.

After making this astonishing claim, Zeljko called another friend from the police station and asked him to bring in the documents. The friend apparently replied he had turned them over to the police the week before. He told the police he was doing this on behalf of an organization to save world peace.

The papers—thousands and thousands of them—were found, hurriedly copied, and passed on to the BKA. They turned out to be a treasure trove. They revealed much about the business dealings of Mamoun Darkazanli, the businessman from Syria, whom the federal prosecutors were already investigating on suspicion of supporting a terrorist association—the same man American officials had put on their list.

Darkazanli continues to deny the charges that he was involved in the September 11 attacks, though it is clear that he was acquainted with many of the terrorists who took part in the attacks or with their preparation, as well as with Mamduh Mahmud Salim, Osama bin Laden's finance chief, now sitting in jail in the United States. Darkazanli had power of attorney over Salim's Hamburg bank account.

It makes for a great story. A petty thief pilfers files containing critical information about the largest terrorist attack in history and dutifully turns them over to the police. BKA agents do not buy this story for a minute; they suspect that some other secret service was trying to find a way of getting evidence into BKA hands. The question is, whose secret service?

Whatever the case, Manfred Klink's special task force had its work cut out for it. By the end of October, BKA agents were beginning to draw some conclusions. They had known for some time that the German connection to the attacks was not limited to simply harboring the three pilots. Traced phone calls and money transfers always led to the same place: the Harburg district of Hamburg—what someone who likes bad puns might now be tempted to call "Pearl Harburg."

In the six weeks following the attack, American and German investigators had established the money trail; and for the most part they had defined the network and its connections to Osama bin Laden's Al Qaeda organization.

Background: Osama bin Laden and Al Qaeda

While the ruins of the Pentagon were still smoking, former Supreme Allied Commander of NATO Wesley Clark officially pronounced Osama bin Laden responsible; the Saudi terrorist leader's organization was the only one in the world in a position to organize and finance such a complicated operation.

Abd al-Bari Atwan, editor in chief of *al-Kuds al-Arabi,* an Arab newspaper in London, gave credence to the lead. Bin Laden was said to have told him three weeks earlier that he was planning an attack on America of unheard-of dimensions. "We will stab America in its heart."

Osama bin Laden always enjoyed the legends spun around him. He contributed to them, and to his demonization as the West's Enemy Number One, through occasional television interviews. He loved to come across as mysterious—a master of disguises and user of multiple hideouts—but in truth there's nothing all that mysterious about the man's life.

He was born in 1955, the seventeenth of fifty-seven children of a Yemenite father in the Saudi Arabian city of Jiddah; his mother is a Syrian. His father was an extremely wealthy man who cultivated close ties to the royal family and was rewarded with lucrative contracts, including expansion of the holy sites in Mecca and Medina. Osama was taken care of by governesses and educated by private teachers; the few playmates he had were from aristocratic circles, which is how the shy, idiosyncratic boy came to be called "the Prince."

A successful family like the bin Ladens is part of a feudal Saudi system characterized by nepotism, extravagance, and an apparently never-ending rise in the price of oil engineered by OPEC. Weekend trips in his father's limousine brought Osama to a luxurious tent where he was supposed to learn about "nature." His mother also lived something of a double life. In Saudi Arabia she was not permitted to wear makeup, drive a car, or wear Western clothes, but as soon as she landed in a foreign country, she stripped off her *abaaya* and went about in Chanel outfits.

In 1968 Osama's father's helicopter, piloted by an American, crashed. The thirteen-year-old inherited $80 million. Two years later he treated himself to his first very own racing horse stable. When he was nineteen, he enrolled at King Abdul Aziz University in Jiddah; five years later he graduated with a diploma in engineering. Not much is known about Osama's time as a student. The magazine *Mideast Mirror* claims that "the Prince" led a loose life during his many trips to Beirut, that he "loved drink," and that more than once "got involved in a brawl over alluring nightclub dancers."

By his own account the year 1979 was a turning point for the not particularly religious bin Laden. This was the year Egypt and Israel signed a peace treaty, as well as the year the shah of Iran was toppled by the Islamic revolution;

but most important it was the year the Soviets invaded Afghanistan. "Filled with rage," bin Laden decided to give his life new meaning by organizing an Islamic resistance against the infidels. Nowhere did resistance seem more appropriate and just than in and around Kabul, Afghanistan.

At first Osama bin Laden did not himself take up arms. Whatever the heroic stories spread by those around him, it is highly doubtful that he ever took part in any significant fighting. One thing he did know how to do was bring in money. He often traveled to meet with the mujahideen, the warriors united to fight the Soviets. In 1984 he moved to Peshawar, the Pakistani city located only a few miles from the legendary Khyber Pass, the entry point to Afghanistan.

Bin Laden was described as tall and elegant, fond of wearing handmade Beal Brother boots and delicately woven fine Afghan tunics, and as the Good Samaritan, distributing sweets to the wounded and lifting the spirits of exhausted fighters with gifts.

There was, however, another side to bin Laden. He organized the building of strategic tunnels and weapons depots. And he wrote incendiary speeches, not simply against the godless Communists but also against the decadent West. Bin Laden was preparing for a future as a charismatic leader, a guardian of a fundamentalist Islam that would purge the world of sin and false religion.

Bin Laden's vehement anti-Americanism was probably no secret either to U.S. intelligence services or to the Reagan White House. Officials simply refused to let it affect policy. Washington was underwriting the Afghani underground resistance against the Soviets to the tune of $3 billion and promoting the recruitment of Islamic fighters—primarily in Arabic countries but also among Muslims in Asia, Europe, and even the United States. This was why some thirty-five thousand militants assembled for weapons training along the Pakistani border. The first multinational Muslim army, the first jihad, was financed with dollars.

One of the most enthusiastic of the CIA's accomplices was Sheik Abdallah Azzam, a Palestinian comrade of "the

Prince of Peshawar." His American headquarters were in the Alkifah Refugee Center on Atlantic Avenue in Brooklyn. Officially, the organization's mission was humanitarian, but on its letterhead, in Arabic, was printed "Office in the Service of Holy Warriors," leaving little doubt as to the organization's true purpose. Thousands of volunteers—or warriors—from around the world were recruited by Alkifah, and the Brooklyn branch was far from the only one. In the end, the organization had branches in thirty-eight American cities.

During a meeting in Oklahoma in 1988, Azzam made it clear that fighting the Soviets was but step one in the "holy war." "Brothers," he announced, "the superpowers are finished. The willpower that springs from our faith is what counts." A year later he held the first "Jihad World Conference" right under the nose of American security officials. If it hadn't earlier, it now became clear that the West would be targeted by God's warriors. "You have to be willing to risk Holy War wherever you can carry it out, even in America," Azzam preached.

Radical Muslims also gathered at a conference in Kansas City. Among those attending were high-ranking leaders of Palestine's Hamas group and FIS, the fundamentalist Islamic organization in Algeria. At this point the CIA still considered bin Laden, who in the meantime had developed into one of the leading organizers of the mujahideen, an ally worth supporting. Compared to the Russians, he was the lesser evil.

Once the Soviets, humiliated and beaten, withdrew from Afghanistan, bin Laden also went home—mission accomplished. By now, however, this financial wheeler-dealer had turned into a fanatic, the self-appointed leader of a global cause. He began caustically and openly to criticize the "corrupt" practices of the House of Saud, whose support of his efforts with the mujahideen had amounted to $100 million. Despite his scathing criticism of the ruling family, bin Laden was shielded by the protective hand of Prince Turki al-

Faisal, a longtime friend and head of Istakhbara, the Saudi Secret Service.

For a while bin Laden's life seemed to have quieted down. He spent the time growing his assets, starting more than sixty companies, many based in the West. He took care of private matters, becoming the father to ten children with three different wives, all from influential families.

There's ample evidence, however, that bin Laden didn't simply become a private citizen during these years. He regularly met with his confidant, the then-director of the Pakistani Secret Service and an éminence grise, General Hamid Gul. General Gul knew more than anyone about fundamentalist movements in the Islamic world and about impending developments in Afghanistan. Gul established a purportedly "humanitarian" organization for Arab fighters who stayed on in Afghanistan after the war against the Soviets had ended. Bin Laden brought some four thousand of these men to Saudi Arabia and organized and financed others in Pakistan and in the Sudan. They were awaiting their new tasks.

Another turning point in the life of Osama bin Laden came in 1990, when Iraq invaded Kuwait and he learned with horror that the Saudi royal family had requested that American troops be stationed in their country. When it became clear after the Gulf War that U.S. troops would remain permanently in Saudi Arabia, home to Mecca and Medina, Islam's most sacred sites, bin Laden called for open resistance against the Saudi regime. He attempted to drive the infidels out with the help of militant clerics such as Sheik Safar Hawali and Sheik Salman Auda and the pronouncement of fatwas or religious decrees.

In 1992 the Saudi royal family banished bin Laden, who settled in the Sudan, where he developed a close friendship with its de facto ruler, Hassan Turabi. Turabi was more than a guarantor of asylum; he was a fiery, highly intelligent Muslim, eager to take on the West and put it in its place. Turabi raised no objections when bin Laden brought more and more Arab Afghans into the Sudan for training in secret camps.

The government in Saudi Arabia realized the growing

danger in 1994, when it first warned bin Laden and then took away his citizenship. The year before, the first terrorist bomb had exploded in the World Trade Center. The organizer of the attack was revealed to be the blind Sheik Omar Abdel-Rahman, a frequent visitor to terrorist camps in the Middle East.

Bin Laden himself continued to stoke anti-Americanism, for example by boasting that his people had delivered a "humiliating defeat" to the United States in Somalia. American military personnel had lost their lives during an international humanitarian mission in Mogadishu; the corpse of an American soldier was dragged through the streets in triumph.

Saudi hit squads sent—with American knowledge—to kill bin Laden failed utterly. Political pressure from Washington finally forced the Sudanese government to part with its guest. This turned out not to be good news for the intelligence community. In the Sudan, bin Laden's activities could be monitored, but this was practically impossible in his new refuge, the far more chaotic Afghanistan.

In May 1996 bin Laden arrived by chartered jet at the airport of the eastern Afghani provincial capital of Jalalabad with an entourage that by now included four wives, thirteen children, and dozens of Arab Afghans. He was drawn to Kandahar, where the mysterious leader of the Taliban, Mullah Mohamed Omar, had established his headquarters. Bin Laden struck up a friendship with Omar, who was largely inexperienced in international politics. He gave Omar one of his daughters as a wife, built a magnificent house for his extended family, and threw several million dollars into road construction and sanitation facilities for the city.

After the Soviet defeat, the West forgot about Afghanistan. It watched with only vague interest while the various tribal factions and warlords maneuvered murderously for power. With the support of the ISI, Pakistani secret intelligence, students of Pashtun ethnic origin who had studied at Koranic schools in Pakistan established themselves as a power. These religious students, or "Taliban," quickly won over large parts of the country with the promise to unify it and eradicate corruption.

At points the Taliban and the United States were on good terms. Glyn Davis, one-time spokesperson for the State Department, said the United States had "no objections" to the enforcement of Islamic law in areas occupied by the Taliban. At a UN meeting, Robin L. Raphel, head of South Asian affairs in the State Department, praised the Taliban for exhibiting so much "staying power." A high-ranking government official enthusiastically gushed to old Afghan hand and author Richard Mackenzie, "Once you get to know the Taliban better you discover they've got a fabulous sense of humor."

Those were the days of Central Asian oil. White House wisdom held that crude oil and natural gas from in and around the Caspian Sea, pumped to the West via pipelines, might provide a valuable reserve in times of crisis. One of these pipelines was supposed to lead from natural gas–rich Turkmenistan straight across Afghanistan to the transoceanic ports of Pakistan, bypassing Russia and Iran. From there millions of barrels of fuel could be transported to consumers in the West. Such a project had no chance of success without stability in and around Kabul. Washington set so much store by this pipeline plan that it was willing to gamble—close its eyes and place all bets on the *Pax Talibana*.

It was clear from the very beginning, however, that the Taliban stood for the most rigid form of Islam: no jobs for women, no education for girls, no secular music. As yet they lacked a pan-Islamic ideology; the idea of "Talibanizing" other countries was still alien.

Osama bin Laden, on the other hand, did have such a vision. He brought together the Taliban and the Arab Afghans and founded a secret brigade called O55. On February 23, 1998, in Khost, Afghanistan, the World Islamic Front for Jihad against Jews and Crusaders, founded by bin Laden and blessed by Omar, made an appeal for worldwide terror: "It is the duty of every Muslim to kill Americans and their allies, military or civilian, wherever possible. This obligation remains in force until al-Aksa Mosque [in Jerusalem] and Haram Mosque [in Mecca] are liberated from their current death grip and American troops are defeated and withdraw from all Islamic countries, unable any longer to threaten a single Muslim."

Bin Laden later said that he considered each and every American a target; any citizen who paid taxes was guilty of abetting the system and thus was fair game. A Muslim who died during an attack on Americans was making a worthy sacrifice; bin Laden himself was ready to offer up his own son, he said.

Terrorist acts quickly followed this declaration of war: in August 1998, against American embassies in Nairobi, Kenya, and Dar es Salaam, Tanzania, that left 263 dead; in October 2000, against the U.S. destroyer *Cole* outside Aden, which killed 17. The FBI placed a $5 million bounty on the head of bin Laden, and in February of 2001 CIA Director George Tenet called his global terror network "the most immediate and most serious threat" to U.S. security.

Through a secret base in Afghanistan, bin Laden is supposed to have tried to buy components for an atomic bomb and biological weapons. Through a friend, an Egyptian flight instructor, he paid $200,000 to obtain ownership of a decommissioned T-39 jet sitting near Tucson, Arizona. His attempts to buy himself a state-of-the-art submarine in the United States using back channels didn't fall through until 2000.

Bin Laden himself rarely gets his own hands dirty. He gives the cells lots of leeway. *Newsweek* has described him as the "Chairman of the Board of Jihad, Inc. with subsidiary Jihad.com." He finances; others organize. The only prerequisite is an appropriate "Terror, Inc." orientation.

According to David Long, a specialist on terror and the Near East, bin Laden and his shadowy Al Qaeda organization have become practically invincible. "This is not an organization of terrorists in the traditional sense. It is more like a gathering place for diverse subgroups to obtain financing, support, and military training. It's a chameleon, an amoeba that constantly changes form and color but has only one leader: Osama bin Laden."

Bin Laden once boasted that he was active in fifteen countries, and that in addition to all the countries in the Middle East, Al Qaeda had cells in Russia, Great Britain, and the Netherlands. He was even the bearer of a Bosnian passport, issued at the new nation's embassy in Vienna, and said he had smuggled warriors into the crisis zone.

He created a special support base in Iraq, where on several occasions he met Kussai Hussein, the son of Saddam and possibly Iraq's next president. He also had connections with Islamic groups in the autonomous areas of Palestine, such as Hamas and Islamic Jihad.

Al Qaeda has at its disposal between three thousand and five thousand active members in some fifty countries, according to the British trade journal *Jane's Intelligence Review*. Terrorist subgroups that have become largely subsumed into the network or that are collaborating closely with them include the al Gama'a al-Islamiya in Egypt, the Algerian Armed Islamic Group, the Yemenite group Dscheisch Aden, the Abu Sayyaf group in the Philippines, and the Pakistani Kashmir Liberation Front. Connections to the Palestinian group Hamas and to Hezbollah, which are financed by Iran, are looser.

The terrorist as enraged slum dweller is a familiar concept. The terrorist as upstanding citizen is not unheard of. But the terrorist as middle-class role model is something new, and characteristic only of Al Qaeda.

Phone taps have captured conversations between terrorists and their support network in Europe, revealing how they think and talk. They speak cheerfully and chillingly of attacks and false passports. A man named "Farid" once had the following conversation with his buddy "Khalid" about an operation that has not yet been identified:

Farid: "Were you there too in Operation Ateta [code name for an as-yet-unidentified act of sabotage]?"

Khalid: "Yeah, I was in lots of places. There's nowhere I haven't been. It was fantastic when the order came from the emir. We'd studied the place beforehand and then with the explosives . . . bang, and a moment later it came down in a pile of dust, and a fire broke out that engulfed and burned God's enemies."

Farid: "And nothing was left."

Khalid: "Then came the order to destroy the farms and pharmacies."

Farid: "So you destroyed the whole village?"

Khalid: "Just about."

The capture of an Algerian named Ahmed Ressam, alias Benni Antoine Norris, gave investigators a picture of how "holy warriors" were trained in Afghanistan. Ressam was on a ferry between Victoria, Vancouver, and Port Angeles, Washington, when customs officials found bomb components and four fuses. The threat of 130 years in prison loosened his tongue. He confessed that he had intended to blow up Los Angeles International Airport. He also admitted to being a sleeper for Osama bin Laden and described the training camp routine in Afghanistan.

In 1998 Ressam had spent six months in a camp. Sometimes there were fifty people there, at other times one hundred; they came from Algeria, Jordan, Yemen, Germany, Turkey, and Chechnya. They exercised in small groups based on nationality, each on its own training grounds. During the first month they learned how to use "small weapons, pistols, a light machine gun and a heavy one." During the second month, said Ressam, explosives were the focus— how to use them and the proper selection of targets: "military installations, things like generating plants, gasworks, airports, railroads," or "hotels where conferences are held." During the third month they covered "urban warfare," tactics, and self-defense. "Wear tourist clothes." Advanced students moved up to another camp, where they learned how to make bombs. "We learned how to construct circuits," said Ressam. Why? "So we could blow things up."

On the last day of school—with an "excellent, congratulations, good-bye"—Ressam was given $12,000, a few chemicals, and a pamphlet. Then the graduates were sent out to wreak havoc in the world of the unfaithful.

Profiling the Terrorists

When they came to Hamburg in the 1990s, the September 11 perpetrators were ordinary young people—Muslims, of course, but also shining examples of Germany's vaunted capacity for integration. They turned into prototypes for a new type of terrorist: educated, well groomed, middle class. Somebody must have recognized that these young men from good homes were much too valuable for petty terrorist fare like car bombs. They deserved better than that. And they got it, though as is now clear the September 11 attack is one in which cost and results stand in bewildering relation: Nineteen young men killed more than three thousand people. These young men spent an estimated $100,000 for housing, training, transportation, and documentation, yet caused damage that may amount to hundreds of billions of dollars.

And the whole scheme could work only because Mohamed Atta, Marwan al-Shehhi, and the other pilots were capable of regarding their lives as a necessary expense.

Education preceded action. The path of the prospective pilots led from Hamburg to Afghanistan. American authorities are convinced that Atta and al-Shehhi (who supposedly called himself Abu Abdallah) stayed in a guesthouse of bin Laden's Al Qaeda network in Kandahar. Probably Ziad Jarrah did as well. At one point the young man told his great-uncle that there was only one path open to him: that of martyr.

When they left Germany for the United States in the summer of 2000, they left behind footprints. Investigators discovered no fewer than ninety-four copies of bin Laden's *Call to Fight the Infidels*. In one of Ziad Jarrah's former apartments they found a pronouncement that sounds like a prophecy: "The morning will arrive. The victors will come. We swear we will conquer you. The earth will tremble beneath your feet."

In addition to the three pilots, ten people are suspected to have taken an active part in preparing the attacks, according to the German attorney general's office; every case is under investigation. Two of these men were also supposed to have been sitting on the planes but failed to get visas. An arrest warrant has gone out for three of them, while another, the German-Syrian Mohamed Haydar Zammar, is thought to be in Morocco. The others, including Mamoun Darkazanli, remain in Germany.

The traces they all left in Germany were produced by red tape: entry documents, change of residence documents, university enrollment documents. Officials from the United States, which has no system of national identity cards and no compulsory residence registration, are amazed. Atta, for example, was registered as having at least three passports. Though duly recorded, this suspicious oddity was not noticed—and it would put Interior Minister Otto Schily into a rage weeks after the attacks.

One psychological profile of the terrorists of September 11 concludes that their preparation consisted of twelve steps. Step one involved the development of an extreme religious and political belief system. Step two was the hardening of their view of the West as the enemy. Step three was becoming convinced that a state of war existed. Step four was learning to see suicide, which is prohibited by the Koran, as an acceptable, even desirable, form of military strategy.

The fifth step, according to terrorist training theory, depicts the deed as an honorable one predetermined by Allah. From this follows step six: the idea that the murderers are chosen people, and that mass killing, step seven, represents the only effective action against an overpowering enemy.

In case of doubt there is the appeal to individual gain of step eight. The commando's spiritual leaders repeatedly and explicitly emphasized to future martyrs that they were certain to enter paradise. Communal gain is covered in the ninth step of these sermons: Here it is established that their heroic act would hit the enemy where it hurt; more effective symbolism could not be achieved.

The tenth step dehumanizes the victims, however many there would be, and however many were women, children, even fellow Muslims. None were worthy of compassion; they were mere appendages of the enemy. Osama bin Laden himself once characterized Muslims who fell victim to his attacks as "collateral damage."

The eleventh step calls for the formation of the cell, the subgroup. Group pressure grew, and with it group control, group solidarity.

Step number twelve involves repeating everything already learned. It was a step echoed in Atta's primer.

Remember your luggage, your clothes, the knife, and the things you need, your identification papers, your passport, and all your documents.

Mohamed Atta

The presumed mastermind of the nineteen killers—and, from all accounts, the coolest, calmest, and most collected of them all—arrived in Germany a conscientious student. He had already earned a bachelor of architectural engineering degree in Cairo and had come to Hamburg to get his master's and doctorate in Germany; at least that had been the plan of his father, Mohamed Atta senior, a lawyer in Cairo.

According to foreign residency files, Atta entered Germany for the first time on July 24, 1992. He did not have a visa and nobody asked him for one; he had come as the guest of a Hamburg couple, teachers who ran a German-Egyptian student exchange program.

Atta applied to the architecture program at the School of Applied Science in Hamburg, but was told there were no openings. He filed a complaint but withdrew it when he was granted admission to Hamburg-Harburg Tech.

In Germany, Atta (which in Arabic means "the gift") shortened his name from Mohamed al-Amir Awad al-Sajjid Atta to

Mohamed al-Amir. He seemed to have no trouble adjusting to his new academic surroundings. He was given credit for his Egyptian degree and so could begin coursework in his particular field of study, urban planning. His teachers thought highly of him. If he drew attention to himself, it was for all the right reasons—for his diligence and his abilities.

In this regard Atta's story was a rather different story from that of other "followers," several of whom changed their names and dates of birth to deceive the authorities about their identities. Ramzi Mohamed Abdullah Binalshibh arrived in Hamburg by boat on September 22, 1995. Born in Yemen in 1972, Binalshibh used the name Ramzi Mohamed Abdellah Omar (a fact that became known to the BKA only because someone happened to see a "Wanted" poster) and claimed to have been born in the Sudan in 1973. He applied for political asylum because, he said, he had been jailed by Sudanese police for two weeks after a student demonstration in Khartoum.

Officials did not find his story very credible. Four months later, Ramzi Omar's application was denied, and Binalshibh—alias Omar—filed a complaint. The complaint was denied in December of 1997. In May of 1998 a warrant was issued for Ramzi Omar, who had disappeared. That didn't matter to Ramzi Binalshibh, however, since the preceding December 3 he had reentered Germany on a "Schengen visa," a kind of European Union general visa named after the town in Luxembourg where it was first devised. On November 6, 1998, he moved to the House of Followers at 54 Marienstrasse.

Others arrived without bothering about formalities. Muhammad Bin Nasser B., born in 1946 in Indonesia, entered Germany in March 1972 with a tourist visa valid for two months; he stayed on illegally for thirteen years. He was arrested and scheduled for deportation in 1985 but managed get the German bureaucracy to grant him not only a delay, but then a residence permit and, in 1991, a work permit. He took a job in Hamburg's mail processing center and in November 2000 became a German citizen. At long last he was able to travel wherever he pleased.

Some of the suspects lived in Germany because they were German. Investigators were particularly vexed by the case of two terrorists who had seemed like such models of successful cultural integration. One was Said Bahaji, Atta's roommate, who disappeared after September 11. Bahaji had a German mother and a Moroccan father. The other was Mohamed Zammar, a Syrian who moved to Germany when he was ten to be with his father. Zammar became a citizen when he was twenty-one; his wife and his six children are living in Hamburg.

Yet Zammar was a role model for many radical Hamburg Muslims, having already experienced what the others longed for. In the way that in former times men told of their pilgrimage to Mecca, Zammar bragged about having fought in Bosnia and Afghanistan.

And there were others who had been granted asylum. One man came to Germany after having been sentenced in his home country to forced labor for life for murder and attempted murder. A member of Egyptian Islamic Jihad, and alleged to have connections with holy warriors in Italy and England, he was granted asylum precisely because his radical past protected him from deportation. Today he is an imam in Westphalia.

What is not clear is what role people like him played on September 11. Insubstantial but persistent connections to the Hamburg group surfaced repeatedly. One of this imam's followers, for example, engaged in numerous telephone conversations with Jarrah.

Investigators are absolutely convinced that somebody must have been leading Mohamed Atta along his deadly path. Yet Atta—whose passport photo has been reproduced hundreds of thousands of times in the weeks and months following the attacks—looks like the part he played. Eyes half shut, mouth set, expression defiant, his is the face of evil—or a reasonable facsimile of it. Atta's father has said this photograph had to have been doctored. It was someone else's scowling face that made his "dear son" look like a cold-blooded terrorist—"one of the most intelligent, determined, and dangerous of all hijackers," according to Secret Service experts later in charge of his case.

Who was this young man in gray trousers, sweater, and brown leather jacket? He was slim and slight, and had, according to a fellow student, "classical, almost Grecian features." Experts who have been working on the case have described him as rational, articulate, perfectionist, extremely intelligent, poised, and highly organized. To have withstood the psychological and physical stress of his actions he must also have been incredibly resilient. His fanaticism and anti-Americanism manifested themselves only rarely. Someone who hated so deeply and yet exhibited so little of the hatred clearly possessed an enormous capacity for self-control.

One former German friend describes him as reserved, even closed. "Atta gave the clear message he didn't want to talk about personal stuff." He was particularly uncomfortable around women, never shaking hands and responding only with a curt "yes" or "no" in conversations. The one time Atta felt an attraction for a young woman, he declined to act on it. The object of his affection was a city planner who wore jeans and shirts. He told friends he thought such dress was "undignified."

There must have been another side to Atta. "A cultural anxiety, the fear of being marginalized," is the friend's assessment. "His serious religious stance brought him to the edge. Consoling himself the way we Westerners do wasn't possible," says another fellow student.

When you try to talk to Atta's father, the old man ends up talking mostly about himself. He will tell you how he taught Mohamed "respect," "ambition in order to succeed," and, of course, "faith." He will also tell you that his son "had nothing to do with America. He was never there, not earlier and not just before the attack, either." Yes, he will admit, his son did feel hate—not for America but for Osama bin Laden, whom he hated as deeply "as one can possibly hate a person. You know why? Because my son is a real Egyptian with an upright character. Bin Laden bombed the Egyptian embassy in Pakistan. That was a blow to the honor of all Egyptians."

"Mohamed was different from others. He took life hard. He was always in a serious mood, always wanted to be the best," says Mohamed Atiya, a fellow student. "Mohamed was demanding, of himself and others," commented one of his former teachers in Cairo. Those who knew him as a boy in Egypt had only praise for him. He studied German and prepared for his trip. The German couple who brought him to Hamburg found him taciturn. "Not exactly sympathetic or open," is how the teacher, Mrs. M., now retired, remembers him. It was difficult to know whether he felt any gratitude to them for their efforts and hospitality.

What did become clear was that Atta was distressed to find that in Hamburg his faith was not the rule but the exception. His hosts and sponsors began to feel uncomfortable in their own home. Mohamed did not want to cook in pots that had ever cooked pork. Five times a day he took over the bathroom to wash himself, and afterward he ran to his room with arms upstretched in prayer—lest he come into contact with the unclean family dog. He closed his eyes when his hostess wore her nightgown, and he pretended her friends did not exist. At one point, he expressed something like doubt about his ability to remain pure. "Do you think that at my age it's still easy to abstain?" Any such self-doubts never surfaced again, at least publicly.

He never let down his guard. Once he had to have nose surgery because he was having terrible difficulty breathing at night. He insisted that his family not be informed about the operation. Nobody was supposed to worry. Not about him.

During the month of Ramadan, Atta would not eat anything before sundown. He started cooking at night. "That's when we asked him to leave," his hosts say.

It may well be that this expulsion started him on his new

and fatal course. Now he was forced to make new connections, and he found them among other Arab students in Harburg. He first moved into student housing. Bed, table, and wardrobe were provided by the Office for Student Affairs. The only thing he bought himself was a rocking chair, but it proved to be a problem because it took up too much space for him to pray.

Anger at the West started to flare up. He had grown up with a father who felt that Americans were trying to rule the world. "Sooner or later they'll occupy Egypt." The Cairo in which he had grown up was a city in transition—hotel chains and high-rises, symbols of degeneration, were springing up everywhere. Atta was consumed with hate. In Hamburg he found partners for his hatred.

In 1995 a fellow student at Harburg and a German expert in Islam went with Atta to Egypt on a study program. A small stipend enabled them to stay for three months. To save money, Atta lived with his parents.

Atta had applied for the scholarship the year before. "Given that I was born and raised in a developing country, I have had the chance to experience firsthand several aspects of the problems," he wrote on the application. "As the so-called new generation, we students have concerned ourselves with questions pertaining to the potentials and dangers of economic development, and we have discussed the topic critically but not without hope. In any case, we want to do something for our country even though we do not know exactly what that entails."

Atta seemed a different person in Cairo than he was in Germany. He took his friends all around the country, he went out with them at night, he even cracked jokes. "For a few weeks he finally loosened up," says one of his friends.

But the side that the other calls his "fundamentalist tendencies" was stronger. In their paper about the trip (part of the requirement of the scholarship), the three wrote about "poorly maintained" streets and "garbage in the streets and alleys." They described "the great riches" of Egypt and referred to the "Islamic monuments" whose importance has been "underestimated." For Atta, however, the central theme was that his country was turning into "McEgypt"; he bemoaned the "real estate speculation" in Egypt's "new cities" and the "decline of the old residential buildings." A supposedly historic city wall was being rebuilt in Cairo, and as a result old buildings would be torn down and residents relocated. The wall being "reconstructed" was nothing but a fake. Atta despised this kind of thing.

He despised lots of things.

Music, for example—little more than a godless distraction. He himself never went out dancing or to parties. Instead he listened to taped readings from the Koran. "You cannot interpret the Koran. The Koran is an absolute," he once explained. Atta was incapable of experiencing pleasure, say the psychologists who have worked on his profile.

He indulged in sweets and in nothing else.

Atta lived a double life. By 1995 he spoke perfect German and appeared to have adjusted to life in Germany, had a job with Plankontor, a business in Hamburg-Altona. He worked nineteen hours a week as a draftsman, earning about $850 a month. He had his own keys, answered the phones, and once brought some herbs for colleagues suffering from back pain. On the one hand he seemed to have found his way in the West. On the other he felt like a complete outsider.

His rigidity sometimes even drew the attention of his closest associates. The Hamburg group met regularly at Kuds Mosque on Steindamm Street. Younger members of the mosque were organizing a study group and wanted to publish a leaflet about it. Atta refused to go along with this. He would not contribute to it, or arrive on time for meetings, or follow the orders of the group leader.

Still, Kuds Mosque was a meeting place. Sooner or later everyone in the Hamburg cell turned up there. Every Friday, Atta and his friends took the subway from Harburg to Hamburg Central Station, then walked along Steindamm to the mosque. Here in a part of the city called St. Georg, Middle Eastern fast-food restaurants stand next to a pornographic movie house, an Arabic grocery store next to a house of prayer. More than ten mosques have settled around Stein-damm.

The entrance to Kuds Mosque is a glass door. Young men watch to make sure that only those who are welcome enter. The speaker of the Mosque Association, Aziz al-Alaoui, is a small man with a fierce look and full beard; he wears baggy cotton pants and wool sweaters—no kaftan.

An Asian grocery and an Olympic Fitness Club take up the ground floor of the building that houses the mosque. Whoever trains here has to be prepared to take on the world outside, a world of drug dealers, junkies, and beggars.

Prayer rooms—separate for men and women—are located on the second floor. Atta and his friends prayed on the right-hand side; a blue-green carpet with yellow stripes and a deep pile lends warmth to the room. On the floor above, the boys from Harburg could get a haircut; and next to the hair salon was a tea room–cum–grocery store that carried bags of grain and canned tomatoes.

At one point a German television crew used a hidden camera to film a preacher inciting hatred against the West. It's not surprising that the terrorists felt at home here. This is where Atta conceived and wrote his last will in 1996; two of his fellow students signed it.

Atta met not only brothers in faith at Kuds Mosque. He also met Germans who were sincerely interested in him and in Islamic culture. And at school there were students and professors who responded enthusiastically to his stories about Cairo. During a seminar on "Planning and Building in Developing Countries," Atta spoke eloquently about a number of issues facing countries like Egypt.

Atta was different from the other terrorists studying for professional degrees in Germany in the degree and intensity with which he felt the conflict between the Western world and developing countries. In his view skyscrapers were symbols of a Western civilization that had relegated his own culture to the sidelines.

Trips to the Arab world changed him. He returned from his pilgrimage to Mecca with a beard; he spent less time at school. His favorite professor at Harburg Tech, Dittmar Machule, reports that Atta did very little work during 1998. Machule was something like a substitute father for Atta. An intellectual man with wire-rim reading glasses, which he holds while he reads, Machule seems frail and moves deliberately. Since September 11 he has spent endless nights trying to understand how his unfailingly polite and sweet prize pupil could have changed into "a human robot who exploded at the push of a button."

The professor's office in Harburg is filled with bookcases sagging under the weight of books, picture albums, and notebooks; boxes containing student papers are piled up on the floor. On the walls and doors hang posters and photos of an excavation site in Syria to which he frequently devotes research. Machule is the ideal professor—always willing to lend a book and offer useful advice.

Machule was on fairly personal terms with Atta, but the young man repeatedly pulled back. He sometimes mentioned family problems at home in Cairo, then would disappear for a period of time—during which he could often be seen at Kuds Mosque. He would suddenly reappear at Machule's office, ready to discuss his thesis project with even greater seriousness than before.

In November 1998 Atta moved into the House of Followers on Marienstrasse. His roommates were Said Bahaji and Ramzi Binalshibh, the two suspected accomplices named in worldwide search warrants. Atta also founded the Islamic Club, a study group at Harburg Tech. "If I can't pray, I can't study," he explained to a Student Union representative who wanted to keep education and religion in separate compartments. Atta's reasoning prevailed.

Hidden by giant trees along the northern edge of the Harburg campus lies a narrow, dark brown wooden barrack with square, white window frames. This small building is home to most of the activities organized by students. To the door of Room 10, immediately next to the Protestant Student Society and the Short-Wave Amateur Radio Club, is a sign that reads "Islamic Club/Prayer Room" and a photo of Mecca.

Inside the small room is an old gray computer on a table near the door and some shelves with books. Arabic letters in gold embossing appear on the book covers. At the end of one shelf is the Koran. Otherwise nothing. As recently as the winter of 2001 you could read on page 62 of Harburg's activities catalog: "Islamic Club, Mohamed al-Amir, el-amir@tu-harburg.de."

In 1999, the year Atta became a full-blown terrorist, he passed his exams with grades equivalent to A– and A+. His final thesis was about the ancient city of Aleppo, located in modern Syria, and in particular about its older quarters: "Khareg Baben-Nasr: An Endangered Part of the Old City of Aleppo. Urban Development in a Section of an Islamic-Oriental City." He knew already that he would never work in city planning. At the top of his thesis he wrote, "My prayer and my sacrifice and my life and my death belong to Allah, Master of all Worlds."

After that, Atta traveled. He and al-Shehhi went to the Al Qaeda guesthouse in Kandahar. It was when they returned that they reported their passports were lost. New ones were issued—cleansed of suspicious stamps from Pakistan and Afghanistan.

Their minds, on the other hand, had been distorted.

Marwan al-Shehhi

He wore glasses and had peach fuzz. For a student he was pretty well-off. He had come from the United Arab Emirates to Germany in the spring of 1996 on a military scholarship to study English at the Goethe Institute in Bonn. Every month, roughly $2,000 was sent from the HBSC Middle East Bank in Dubai. Once a year he received a bonus payment of $5,000. Instead of parading his wealth, he moved into a modest room.

He wasn't ambitious, says a former teacher; he was somewhat immature and aimless. An average student, he liked to go to the movies and on Fridays came to class wearing a tie and jacket because afterward he went to prayers.

After the Goethe Institute, al-Shehhi did some more coursework in Bonn and then moved on to Hamburg, where he flunked out. In May 1998 he disappeared for six months. It is suspected that he went to a bin Laden training camp in Afghanistan. Part of a routine investigation shows that Marwan al-Shehhi returned to Bonn in January 1999. He had trouble with his exams and passed many of them only on a second try, if at all.

In many ways al-Shehhi was different from the rest. He was the only one who may have had an idea before he came to Germany of the war he would one day wage. It's also possible that many in the Emirates' military, where al-Shehhi underwent basic training, knew about his views. Like other hotspots, nothing much can be learned about the Emirates, a fact that pleases none of the investigators.

In Hamburg Atta and al-Shehhi became friends and comrades in terror. Perhaps it was because they were so different. Al-Shehhi was the joker and Atta the earnest strategist. First they became roommates. In 1999 al-Shehhi met the mysterious Ramzi Binalshibh, the Yemenite, and rather quickly exchanged his easygoing lifestyle for a far different one: preparation for mass murder. He stopped coming to class, and in December 2000 was officially dropped from the register.

A month earlier, on November 5, 2000, the Embassy of the United Arab Emirates reported al-Shehhi a missing person to the Hamburg police. His older brother came to Hamburg to look for him—without success. The same brother talked about their parents: about his Egyptian mother and his father, a Muslim preacher from the Emirates who took his son along with him to the mosques. If Papa was late, little Marwan was able to take over the call to prayer. Al-Shehhi's former friends were startled to learn that their buddy had a wife.

Ziad Jarrah

In the northern German City of Bochum, a young and a beautiful woman sits at home trying to comprehend it all. Aysel is a Turkish medical student. She was also the girl-friend of a terrorist, but of this she had no clue. Investigators ask her to explain to them the man she herself does not understand.

Ziad Jarrah had a long, narrow face and an easy laugh. He did not hate the West, at least not at the beginning. Arriving in Germany from Lebanon on April 3, 1996, he began coursework in German in Greifswald, a city on the Baltic Sea in what was the former East Germany. Jarrah loved to drink and he loved to party. "Once we drank so much beer we couldn't ride straight on a bike," says his cousin, who still lives in Greifswald. There he met the kind of man who can change a young Muslim's life.

In 1989 Abdulrahim al-M. traveled from Yemen to the eastern edge of Germany. A student of dentistry, he was thirty-six years old and still aspired to become a dentist, because in Yemen "as a doctor, you are the boss."

Twelve years later, in September 2001, Abdulrahim was still a student, now starting his twenty-third semester. He will most likely never become a dentist, though he has become a kind of boss. As the imam of a prayer room, he guides foreign students in prayer. They respectfully call him Abu Mohamed, or "father of Mohamed," and admire him for his wisdom and because he can read the Koran. Abu Mohamed is committed to his congregation, for which he is a spokesman.

"I have nothing to do with Germany," he says.

In September Abu Mohamed immediately became a target of investigators because of his contacts with the alleged terrorists. He refused to accept the idea that money transfers between his account and that of an alleged supporter of terrorism might also make him a suspect. Whatever his perspective on the matter, investigators still believe that he may have played a role.

Muslim students who end up in Greifswald automatically gravitate to Abu Mohamed. He knows how to get residency permits. He can find them places to live. He is willing to lend his car.

This is a bleak part of Germany. In winter, icy blasts of wind off the Baltic blow empty pizza boxes and dirty diapers from overflowing garbage cans across the open lots in front of the grim concrete boxes that make up student housing on Makarenkostrasse. A total of seven thousand six hundred students are registered in Greifswald. More than five hundred of them of them are foreign, and of these two hundred are Muslim. They shuttle continuously between dorm room and prayer room, prayer room and lecture hall—a half-mile stretch. They stay pretty much among themselves. Administrators had hoped the students would integrate into the community, but once when the dorms had to be vacated for renovation and students had to look for rooms in private homes, no one in Greifswald would take them in.

The prayer room is in a shabby bungalow located next to the barrackslike residence halls; it was once a day-care center. The windows are painted shut and the paint's peeling off the walls, on one of which someone scrawled, "Into the Ghetto."

Unhappy in Greifswald, Jarrah moved to Hamburg in 1997 and began to study aircraft engineering at the School of Applied Sciences. He was the only member of the cell not to live in Harburg or in any of the run-down sections of east Hamburg. A family in one of the nicer neighborhoods took him into their two-story home. Clean and well maintained, the house had lacquered brown shutters and a garden with rhododendrons. His former landlady did a portrait of him in oils. "He was such a bright young man," she says, "totally European." In her portrait of Jarrah he is smiling gently. But he was still a different person. During the winter term of 1997, he applied himself to his studies. "He was very religious but open at the same time. He put so much into it, working day and night with the most abstract formulas—he really wanted to become an engineer," says Heinz Krisch, dean of the school.

During the summer of 1998, Jarrah and a Moroccan student, Zakariya Essabar, were employed as work-study students in the paint and body shop of the huge VW factory in Wolfsburg, south of Hamburg.

He was also in love. Later he would phone Aysel nearly every day from America. He even called her from the cockpit of United Flight 93. Jarrah must have wavered until the last minute. He had been a pilot for some time already when he talked about wanting to have a wife and child. During the last summer he went to see Aysel—an unusual step for someone done with life and the world.

Experts who have studied the Jarrah case say it would be unsurprising for a man like him to find himself unable to follow through with the plan. He was far too emotional. Is it coincidence that Jarrah's plane was the only one that failed to reach its goal and instead crashed into a meadow? He had done the earlier steps—transformed himself from a disco dancer into a radical Muslim who prayed five times a day. According to an acquaintance, he wanted his girlfriend to wear a headcloth and even wanted her to cover her hands. But perhaps he had trouble with step number four, accepting suicide.

But Jarrah disappeared from school in the middle of winter term 1999. He told fellow students he planned to continue his studies in America, and went underground. Some family members suspect he was in Pakistan or Afghanistan; others vehemently disagree and won't even admit that he was ever out of touch.

Whether or not Ziad Jarrah considered jumping ship, by the summer of 2000 Mohamed Atta held tight to the net of terror; and it was strong enough to carry the weak and indecisive.

The Other Followers

In the months after the attack, investigators in the United States and Germany learned a great deal about the terrorists of September 11. In a vast scavenger hunt, a total of nearly seven thousand six hundred agents had collected every piece of evidence left behind by the terrorists. In Germany, as in the United States, the priority was to prevent future attacks. For that reason, the German BKA confiscated anything that might give them a clearer picture of the nineteen dead terrorists. They collected fingerprints and secured DNA samples; they confiscated cell phones, computers, and files, which piled up in police evidence rooms. "Have they been to your place yet?" worshipers inside mosques across Germany whispered to each other.

The German investigators know that discovery can be painful. For example, as soon as evidence started piling up against Mamoun Darkazanli, whom the CIA had long suspected of being bin Laden's Hamburg "commissioner," relations between the two countries turned icy. CIA officials started spreading the word that as long as a year before the attacks they had been urging German officials to take on Al Qaeda's Hamburg network—meaning, above all, Darkazanli. During a meeting with German Interior Minister Otto Schily, Attorney General John Ashcroft called Hamburg the terrorists' "central base of operations." Hamburg was "not the only place," Schily replied stoutly.

The truth is that mistakes were made on both sides. There were isolated leads in Hamburg pointing to those who would become members of the terrorist group. Said Bahaji's radical positions had drawn official attention more than once, and there were also hints about what was going on in Marienstrasse. But even the best bureaucracies can't cover every base, and when a single investigator from the Hamburg Office for the Protection of the Constitution is responsible for keeping tabs on every radical foreigner in the city, it's hardly surprising that the really dangerous ones disappear into the woodwork. Security officials call this phenomenon "seeing but not recognizing."

Four days after the attack German officials arrested Hassan R., a Moroccan suspected of being a contact person for some terrorists. Hassan R. worked for Ground Stars, a firm that loads and unloads planes at Hamburg Airport. There wasn't enough evidence to press charges, and he was set free the same day. During the investigators' search, however, they overlooked a pile of videos that contained proclamations of "Holy War." Hassan R.'s contacts probably were not all that innocent, though he insisted that he knew "these people from the mosque only superficially." Charges have now been brought against him for membership in a terrorist organization.

And officials in the United States overlooked the terrorists for the entire year they spent in America. The tricks Atta and his cohorts played with documents worked just as superbly in the United States as they had in Europe. As in Germany, signs went unheeded. Police in Minnesota had arrested Zacarias Moussaoui on August 16, twenty-six days before the attack. Moussaoui had come from London and had violated visa regulations for entering the country. His flight instructor had raised a red flag about him because he was interested only in practicing turns, not takeoffs or landings.

Some FBI agents had strongly urged that the computer and stack of papers confiscated when Moussaoui was arrested be examined quickly, but their superiors argued that more important things required their attention. Some, like FBI Director Robert Mueller, even said that Moussaoui had "little if anything" to do with the attacks. Today it seems likely to almost everyone that Moussaoui's arrest was the closest officials came to unraveling the terror plot. Evidence suggests that he would have been the twentieth man. Or perhaps even the leader of a fifth team. Moussaoui himself insists on his innocence. He wrote his mother from prison, "As far as the American story goes, don't worry. I didn't do a thing and in time I'll prove it, God willing."

In the meantime it's become clear just how close Moussaoui's connections to the Hamburg group were. One of the four German phone numbers he was carrying was to Ramzi Binalshibh's apartment. At least twice, a certain Ahad Abdallah Sabet wired money to Moussaoui in the United States from travelers' banks in the main train stations in Düsseldorf and Hamburg. On August 1, 2001, the amount was 23,571.59 marks (about $13,400), and two days later it was 9,487.80 marks (about $5,400). Earlier, this same Sabet received nearly identical sums from the Emirates. There is, however, no such person as "Ahad Abdallah Sabet," and his supposed address in Hamburg also does not exist. Fingerprints on the bank receipts show that the man behind this pseudonym was Ramzi Binalshibh.

In France Moussaoui's mother recounts that the last time she heard from her son was in 1996, when he left a message on her answering machine: "I love you and send you a kiss." Then he disappeared. Zacarias's brother Abd Samad says he assumed he was with his militant friends.

It took a considerable amount of time before the United States changed course in the Moussaoui case. As early as 1999 French officials announced that a warrant had been issued for Moussaoui's arrest due to his alleged connections to the Islamic Jihad that had claimed responsibility for the series of terror attacks in Paris in the mid-nineties. The French had warned the United States about this man before September 11.

Yet federal prosecutors did not indict Moussaoui until December 2001. Boeing flight simulation programs and information about crop dusters were found in his home. The case of the man suspected of being the twentieth hijacker is set for trial in Virginia, where he will face capital punishment.

As for the German investigators, they're relieved that their own picture of the Hamburg cell, with its three death pilots and supporters, has become mostly complete, however disturbing a picture it paints. What they find most astounding is how boldly and openly the terrorists behaved during the Hamburg period. Something sometime should have roused someone's suspicion. Yet, safe as they obviously felt, they also maintained their covers. Some worked on the assembly line at VW, others at the electric giant Siemens, still others at Hamburg Airport or at Premiere Cable Channel; and eight of them worked at a small company named Hay Computing. Holy warriors packed computers into boxes for $7.50 an hour, while money for their every need was arriving from the Emirates.

At some point they had all wanted to lead a Western lifestyle. Then that lifestyle was to be vanquished. In the meantime, it served as cover.

Manfred Klink's Special Task Force has not had an easy time getting below the surface. Few suspects have talked since September 11, and many in their circle of acquaintance have also been tight-lipped. Everyone in the Hamburg mosques attended by the hijackers says the same thing: Sure, we knew each other by sight, but who knew anything about what was going on inside their heads? Those guys were all good Muslims. When asked how they could have lived with people they maintain they knew only superficially, their answer is, "Generosity among brothers." What about that passport found in the drawer? "Someone we know who's here illegally put it there." And all those phone calls to Italy and Spain? "Oh, people we know. We can't remember their names." The weekend rental cars? Aren't they a little unusual for students who have to economize? "Oh, no, it's just more comfortable to go by car."

The few who have talked suggest that many more knew something than was first presumed. The group around Atta often sat apart in the mosques; whoever didn't share their views had no business sharing their circle. By 1999 the group had become so energized by their religion that Holy War against the unfaithful must have felt like an obligation. They showed their hatred in the Hamburg mosques, calling out, "Let the Jews burn. We'll dance on their graves."

These were the kind of slogans being taught in Al Qaeda training camps in Afghanistan.

Investigators are convinced that the pilots of the planes were not yet holy warriors when they first came to Germany.

They had a conversion experience; someone guided them through the years that followed. They believe it conceivable that one person pulled the strings that led the nineteen hijackers to their deaths and those of thousands of others—or a web of several people.

What role was played by people like Darkazanli, Binalshibh, and Zammar? Investigators believe that Darkazanli may have played the role of moneyman in the bin Laden network—he's a bright kind of guy who knows how to get along, a tradesman used to dealing with people from diverse cultural backgrounds.

In any case Darkazanli is the kind of man who turns up when he's needed—either with beard and kaftan or as a clean-shaven Western businessman. He himself says he became casually acquainted with Atta and friends only from going to the same mosques. His German is perfect and he handles himself well. He has come out of investigations with nothing sticking; Frankfurt's district attorney failed to convict him on money-laundering charges. At this point the court proceedings involve suspicion of supporting a terrorist organization. He still lives in Hamburg and, as stated earlier, continues to deny all charges.

Perhaps Binalshibh was to have been a hijacker, like Zakariya Essabar—another Hamburg follower—was to be at the beginning and Moussaoui at the end. He tried four times to get an entry visa for the United States and each time was refused. He became responsible for money transfers from Germany to the pilots in the United States.

While seeking asylum in Germany, Binalshibh lived first in temporary housing. Officials put him to work on a tree farm, but ten days later he was fired. "A weakling," according to his supervisor. He showed up for classes at Harburg only occasionally, and when he did he usually complained about women's "disgusting" low necklines. "He got F's in math, he was always reading the Koran under his desk," a former classmate reports.

The three-hundred-pound, six-foot-five Mohamed Zammar seemed like the ideal jihad warrior. He was the one who boasted about having fought in Bosnia and other places.

"Who are the biggest terrorists? The so-called civilized world!" Zammar thundered not long after the attacks, while sipping Turkish tea in a Hamburg mosque. "Who invented the atomic bomb? The Americans!" Many in the mosque keep their distance from him. But wherever in Europe mujahideen fighters have been arrested in recent years, the trail usually leads back to Zammar. The books about jihad found in Said Bahaji's home were inscribed by Zammar. The ninety-four confiscated copies of bin Laden's call to war against infidels were all photocopied by Zammar, a fact he happily concedes.

Zammar was a witness at the wedding of his helper, Said Bahaji, Atta's roommate and the man with whom the Hamburg investigation began. Investigators find Bahaji especially interesting. He wasn't on any of the planes on September 11; today he's presumed to be in Afghanistan. He would have something to say about the terrorist cell in Hamburg. He more than anyone mastered the double life. He grew up living it.

Bahaji grew up in Germany near the Dutch border. His family ran a restaurant that had both a discotheque and a bar. In 1984, when Said was nine, they moved to Morocco. "In the eyes of the Moroccans he was obviously a foreigner, just as he'd been in Germany," says his mother, who is German. She suspects that the roots of his fundamentalism began in a Moroccan school, where he had to start in the first grade. During Ramadan, students would check each other's tongue for redness, a sign of having eaten. Those caught were treated like outcasts. The family lived in the ancient city of Meknès, which combines elements of East and West. A McDonald's on one of the main boulevards fills up only after dark during Ramadan. Bahaji was a student at a school that, like the entire city, combined both modern and religious traditions. Some girls wore headcloths; others wore sunglasses.

Bahaji's parents' home is not far from the school. The mother has furnished the house as if she were back in Germany. She never really settled in Morocco and keeps going back to Germany. "Morocco is wonderful only for tourists," she says.

When Said arrived in Hamburg to study electronics, he was both strictly religious and boyish. He drove a dark VW Golf and loved Formula One racing. "Then, it is pure rave," he wrote on his home page. He knew everything about computers—"games, apps, the Internet. The only thing that counts for me is sitting in front of it." Bahaji felt lonely. "What a shame the Harburg students are so boring. They can't even open their mouths unless they're drunk," he wrote on his home page. Drinking, of course, was taboo for him.

As a German citizen, Bahaji had to do military service. He joined the seventy-second Tank & Rifle Battalion in Hamburg's Fishbeck district. He was discharged after five months because of asthma and allergies. The photo on the warrant that circulated around the world after September 11 was cropped; on the original, Bahaji can be seen wearing the uniform of the German Army.

He met Atta and Binalshibh, and the three of them moved to Marienstrasse. Bahaji took care of day-to-day business. He signed the lease, and the rent was paid out of his account. At last there was a task, a place for the young man who had never felt wanted anywhere else. He had lost contact with his home in Morocco. His father hasn't seen the boy for years. When Said married a Turkish woman named Neşe, his father was unable to come to the wedding. "I didn't have enough money," he said. Said paid the bride money—3,000 marks ($1,700)—in two installments. However, his father knew about his six-year-old grandson.

He also knew that Said had said his good-byes on September 3. He announced he was leaving for an "internship" in Pakistan. The last sentence on Said's home page reads, "O.K., I'm done!" It was the end of August. According to confidential evidence the White House showed NATO countries to convince them of Al Qaeda's complicity, Osama bin

Laden was calling his loyalists and supporters home to Afghanistan.

The vital element in this chain of evidence was this command from headquarters to flee in advance of the great attack. It must have reached Hamburg sometime in late August or early September. At any rate, on September 3 Bahaji boarded Turkish Airlines Flight 1056 from Hamburg to Istanbul, and from there continued on to Pakistan. He and two others spent the night in Room 318 of the Embassy Hotel in Karachi. The last trace of him was found in Quetta, a city less than forty miles from the Afghani border.

A final message reached his wife six days after the attacks. "Thanks to Allah I am well. I have arrived safely," he wrote. "Unfortunately, I won't be able to call often because calling's very expensive. Please say hello from me to everyone in your family and mine. All the best."

Like so many other bin Laden loyalists, Bahaji would have to fight for his life in Afghanistan. He has not been heard from again.

Six days before the attack, Binalshibh, using his old name, Ramzi Omar, booked a flight on Lufthansa from Düsseldorf to Madrid. He never used the return ticket booked for two weeks later. Binalshibh's whereabouts are still unknown.

Zakariya Essabar, the twenty-four-year-old Moroccan who tried and failed to get an entry visa for the United States, and who might have been a possible twentieth hijacker, is at the top of the German BKA's most-wanted list. He was last seen in Hamburg at the end of August.

The last one to disappear was Mohamed Zammar. He's assumed to be in Morocco—not on the run but on vacation. He has told people he plans to return to Germany, where he is under suspicion but has never been charged.

The European Network

Manfred Klink's Special Task Force investigators have learned that Europe acted as a way station for terrorist groups like Osama bin Laden's—a kind of base for acquiring money and useful items like transmitters and electronics components. Today, they note, Europe is a target area. When the investigators first undertook their work, they assumed that the Hamburg terrorists were a small, isolated cell, able to function because of local support and influence. Today investigators believe that a loose network spans all Europe. It no longer matters who belongs to which Islamic group. What holds them together is neither Islam nor ideology but religious delusion coupled with a hatred for the United States.

In Italy the investigators have come across the Varese Group, planners of a poison gas attack who are intertwined closely with that bomb assembly group in Frankfurt, who, officials say, were planning an attack on Strasbourg.

Investigators have discovered an Al Qaeda cell in Spain and arrested eight people. During a wiretapped phone call, one of them said, "In our classes we're already into flight instruction, and we've even slit the throat of the bird." There were the usual interlocking connections. The phone number of Abu Dahdah, nom de guerre of the man arrested in Spain and presumed to be the leader of the cell, was found in Hamburg. Investigators are convinced that Dahdah was also in contact with Darkazanli, Said Bahaji, and Ramzi Binalshibh.

Four men were arrested in Rotterdam for planning attacks on American institutions in Paris.

The police in Great Britain are only now starting to make life difficult for fundamentalist groups like Abu Qutada, who have issued calls to battle against the unfaithful.

The CIA estimates that worldwide there are six to seven million radical Muslims who sympathize with Osama bin Laden's ideas and that some 120,000 of them are willing to fight.

Even American officials doubt that bin Laden gave direct orders for the attack on the World Trade Center; such orders were not really needed. In that crude, out-of-focus thirty-nine-minute video—nearly ruined by the cameraman's constant coughing—the Pentagon presented to the world, bin Laden is shown wearing sneakers, a turban, and a camouflage jacket. He seems to be sitting down for a meal with his followers. They discuss September 11. Bin Laden says he was notified "the previous Thursday that the event would take place that day." Presumably that means that the head of Al Qaeda set the ball rolling but had nothing more to do with the actual planning; by that Thursday the flights had all been long since booked.

Bin Laden, it seems, was September 11's premeditator, not its executioner.

"The brothers, who conducted the operation, all they knew was that they have a martyrdom operation and we asked each of them to go to America but they didn't know anything about the operation. . . . They were trained, and we did not reveal the operation to them until they are there and just before they boarded the planes. . . . Not everybody knew: Mohamed from the Egyptian family was in charge of the group."

"Mohamed"—that is, Mohamed Atta.

The sky smiles, my young son, for you march towards heaven.

PART III

Aftermath

Bloomfield, New Jersey

She doesn't look like someone who suffered third-degree facial burns only nine weeks before. Her nose used to be black, she says. Now it's a little bit red, like the rest of her face. That too will settle down, thanks to the doctors' skill.

Thirty percent of Virginia DiChiara's body was burned when she walked out of the elevator, through a veil of burning jet fuel, and onto the 78th floor of the North Tower. Face, hands, arms, shoulders, back. The hands are the worst, she says. She wears black gloves.

She lives in Bloomfield, New Jersey, in a comfortably furnished, pretty house with a yard, with the two golden retrievers who saved her life on September 11. The weather was so gorgeous that day that Remy and Sydney wanted to run around the yard a little longer. DiChiara decided to let them while she drank a second cup of coffee. So she arrived later than usual at the World Trade Center and was still in the elevator when the plane hit, rather than where she worked in the Cantor Fitzgerald offices on the 101st floor. Nobody on the 101st floor survived.

"I lost a lot of friends," she says, the only time during a two-hour interview when her eyes fill with tears.

DiChiara sees a psychologist twice a week. "I have to come to terms with a lot of things," she says. Her brother died in a fire when she was six years old. Immediately she changes the subject.

Still she seems strong. She talks articulately about her terrible experiences and always laughs at the hard parts. She scratches often, hard and deep. Burn wounds itch like hell. Now and again one of the golden retrievers trots up and puts his snout on the table. A little petting, please. She extends a hand with a black glove.

It's hard for Virginia DiChiara not to feel up to par. She's not yet really able to move her hands, and she still can't grip properly. She will, but it will take time. "I'm the kind of person who likes results," she says. Now she has to think in terms of weeks, months. In a year she'll be back to normal again, say the doctors.

She exercises daily. She starts earlier and does more than before. Bending and stretching her fingers, over and over again. Bending and stretching. For days on end there's no sign of progress. Then at last the fingers stretch and bend a fraction of an inch farther.

It takes a long time. Everything takes a long time—showering, getting dressed. "I'm like an old lady," DiChiara says and laughs. She's forty-four. She can't use makeup, her skin can't tolerate it yet.

She goes for massage therapy Monday to Friday, to revitalize the burned parts of her body. "They kill me," she says, again with a laugh. "They beat me up like hell." But she loves to go. It all helps.

Many were touched by what happened to her. She gets mail every day, and she tries to write back. She's already pretty good at holding a pen, but she tires easily.

The telephone rings, not the first time during the conversation. The first days at home she received hundreds of calls. So many pep talks can be exhausting. She gets help from her mother and friends. Someone's always with her.

She misses work terribly. "I'm a workaholic," she says. She's an auditor at Cantor Fitzgerald, and her job is to see that all deals follow the law. It's not the kind of job that promotes friendships. She's got a strong character, though, and plenty of heart—just the right mix for her job. She can go back to work in three months.

She takes off her gloves to give her hands some air. It's a shock to see them—two clumps of raw red flesh. For a while they just sit on the table. Then DiChiara has to scratch again.

She doesn't hate anyone on account of her hands. She has no personal wish for revenge. She's in favor of the war against the Taliban and Al Qaeda, lest there be another September 11.

Port Authority Office, Jersey City, New Jersey

Jan Demczur has brought along his pail and squeegee in case they are of interest. They figure at the center of his story, after all. He wears a yellow tie under his windbreaker.

He doesn't know his way around the place anymore. The Port Authority has moved temporarily into a flat office building between two gas stations located at the Jersey City exit of the Holland Tunnel. The Port Authority once owned the World Trade Center, and most of its eight thousand employees worked there. The new building looks like a hastily converted garage. There are no windows. It's like a beehive—too many people in too little space, a desk crammed into every empty corner. Employees even work in the cafeteria, their desks and computers wedged between the tables. Police officers, draftsmen, construction workers—they have all been given a desk here until new office space is found. It feels like an emergency shelter, which, in truth, is what it is.

Demczur blinks. Then he spots George Phoenix and Al Smith, two of the men who were trapped in the elevator with him. He laughs, and they do too. That morning of September 11, after going their separate ways through the streets of downtown Manhattan, Demczur and Phoenix ran into each other by chance. They all said they'd get together again—the way you do. Demczur had scribbled their names on a notecard.

Three of the six men can't make it today: Iver and Paczkowski have appointments, and Colin Richardson's still not able to talk about September 11.

We walk to the cafeteria. Demczur puts his bucket down next to the table, still wearing his windbreaker, as if he were on a short break and about to go back to work. The "break" stretches on for five hours. For Demczur it never ends; since the collapse there are no more windows to be cleaned. The window-washing operation he worked for was located on the 35th floor of the South Tower. The company still exists but is rethinking its business, at least that's what they tell Demczur. He says that's okay with him. He doesn't feel ready yet. He wakes up at night soaked in sweat. During the day he's tired and lacks energy. On trains he feels shut in. He went to see a psychologist who said the anxiety would probably disappear, and that if it didn't it should be looked into further. Right now Demczur's getting a third of his paycheck. He's not giving up. When he arrived in the States he had nothing to his name. Now he has a family and a home. There are still plenty of windows in New York.

Phoenix, Iver, and Richardson are Port Authority engineers and still have their jobs. At the moment, Acting Director Paczkowski is busier than ever. Only the window cleaners and postal workers lost their jobs.

That's how it goes.

After the towers collapsed, Al Smith partied, to celebrate being alive. After that he called up to find out whether he had a job. Well, they said, there's no longer a post office in the World Trade Center. So no need for postal workers, right? For two months he got a couple hundred dollars' transition money, then nothing. He knows he shouldn't say anything, but sometimes he wishes those who lost jobs would get some of the money provided for families of the deceased.

"After all, we're victims too," says Smith.

He wasn't mentioned in the first stories about the elevator ride that ran in one of the papers. Nobody knew his name.

During the huge memorial service held in Yankee Stadium he started a conversation with a reporter from *The New York Times* and told him his story. At first the reporter didn't want to believe it, but later when the others mentioned there'd also been a black guy in the elevator with them, the reporter called back, and Al Smith was granted his place in the story. But that doesn't pay the bills.

At some point, Phoenix has to go back to work. Demczur and Smith hang out in the warehouse as long as possible. They keep running into old buddies. Smith talks with the cafeteria ladies, telling his story over and over. They listen with mouths agape. He looks good.

Demczur and Smith talk on, but sooner or later it's time to leave. They hand in their visitor passes. Demczur has jotted everything down on notecards: more phone numbers, which papers have published stories about their elevator adventure.

We're in the parking lot and cars are thundering past. Demczur asks if we could give him a lift. His home's not far away. Sitting in the car, he carries the bucket on his lap. About two miles away we pull into the small street he lives on. His house is small and white, with a skinny tree out front.

"Where the tree is," Demczur instructs us.

He looks radiant. Shivam Iver said that Jan was his guardian angel.

Demczur takes the pail with him into his house. No use for it today either.

Nadi-Sid Gun Club, Cairo

Mohamed Atta senior weeps. He squirms. He shouts. But he does not answer questions.

He says that Mossad, the Israeli Secret Service, carried out the attacks.

"We're talking about an insane plot with an insane concept but at the same time a meticulous and exact execution.

Only Mossad is capable of this. It shows how the Zionists have operated ever since Moses led them out of the Red Sea." His son could never have committed such an act.

"My son in front of two hundred and forty levers and lights? Steering a huge plane from high altitude down to the desired level? Hitting the steel girdle of a building dead center, like hitting a pencil with a bullet? Something like that requires an enormous amount of talent and know-how! That's an enormous undertaking!"

"Your son, Mr. Atta, trained for a long time."

"No, no, no."

Nadi-Sid Gun Club is a place where wealthy Egyptians shoot rifles, or sit on the terrace killing time, drinking espresso while others shoot. Atta senior is wearing an unbuttoned shirt. His glasses are smudged by hands that have been handling newspapers. He smokes Cleopatras, an "American blend."

Atta, a lawyer by profession, is a loud and moody kind of person. Early in their marriage, he moved his wife and their three children to the Cairo area from a small town in the Nile Delta. At first they lived in the middle-class suburb of Giza. Leaving downtown Cairo, you keep going toward the pyramids, and a few miles before the sphinx, turn left; the five-member Atta family lived modestly in a house at an intersection, two flights up on the left. Later, when Atta's law firm became well established, they moved to a more elegant neighborhood. There's a theater across the street and on the front of the building is a Pepsi sign. The building's lobby has potted plants and a mirror. Atta lives on the eleventh floor, a lonely old man—his wife left him years ago and his two daughters rarely come to visit.

Lonely and angry.

"Liars, all liars!" he screams. He will sue every last one of the journalists, at least those who wrote that his son was gay.

He doesn't want to talk up here: the neighbors, you know. So the door closes again and it's off to the gun club.

Interviews with Atta's father are somewhat strange. For

one thing, you're never alone with him. People at neighboring tables hide behind their newspapers, pretending to read; waiters who were there just a minute earlier stop by again. Secret Service, of course. The second reason interviews with Atta are somewhat strange is that they aren't really interviews.

America, he insists, "invented terrorism."

"The first terror organization was the Ku Klux Klan, which was native to Mr. Bush's home state. There are five thousand groups like that in the USA and we see the products of American education: little boys bring machine guns to school and kill their teachers and classmates. Then the movie industry brings the terror home to people all over the world."

He believes it was American or Israeli agents who killed his son—"with acid, the way they always do it."

He takes a deep breath and it's suddenly quiet on the terrace, except for the sounds of gunfire.

"Why would they do that? What purpose could possibly be served by such a conspiracy?"

"The Zionists want to drag a young Egyptian through the dirt because Egypt's a thorn in the side of the Zionist racists," says Atta.

"Don't you feel any grief, aren't you at all worried that your son, of all people, might possibly have flown into the World Trade Center on September 11?"

"No, why should I? He was still alive after the attack. He called me twenty-four hours and forty-eight hours after the attack."

That was the last time. Because after that, says the father, "they indeed killed him."

Upper East Side, Manhattan

Jill Gartenberg stands like a soldier at the entrance of her apartment on the Upper East Side. She is thirty-four and stands very straight. Her handshake is firm but her eyes look tired; a faint smile plays around her mouth.

How are you?

"Okay," she answers.

You can see immediately that she's pregnant. It's November now, and she's in her fifth month. She's expecting another girl.

Gartenberg walks to the couch in small steps, feet splayed, the way pregnant women walk. Another woman—blond and pale—is sitting in the living room. She's a friend who's there to listen in and to make sure that Jill isn't asked any unfair questions. When the phone rings, Gartenberg asks her friend to find out who's calling. Everyone who calls for the next one and a half hours has to wait. Jill doesn't want to lose her composure. The doorman downstairs is informed in advance about every visitor. The living room's been picked up and Nicole's toys are neatly put away. Jill's two-year-old daughter is asleep. The living room's a simple rectangle. A photograph of her husband, Jim, stands on the coffee table. He's got a friendly face.

We talk a little about the past. How she and her husband met at the University of Michigan. They'd been married for seven years and known each other for ten. On September 11, Gartenberg left home at 7:15 A.M. He wanted to be done early; it was supposed to be a short day. Normally he worked long hours, well into the night. But she doesn't want to complain about him anymore. He came home early twice a week so he could put Nicole to bed, and he was there for the family on weekends. Everything was fine. She has a video of him playing with their daughter. A happy father wearing shorts.

"I talk with Nicole about it, but I've got no idea how much she understands. I show her pictures of the World Trade Center. I tell her Daddy was inside and that he's not coming back ever again. I tell her he loves her and would love to be home with her. Maybe it's a blessing she's still so little. There's no way she can understand the way a five- or six-year-old understands—it's all so inconceivable."

When the plane hit, Jill Gartenberg was on her way to work. She's a speech therapist and has a small private practice. Jim's first call didn't reach her. He left a message on the machine in her office.

"I can play the tape for you," she says and leaves the room for a minute.

When she returns, she's carrying an answering machine.

"Jill, there's a fire on our floor. I love you, Jill. Tell everyone that I love you. I don't know whether I can get out. Jill, I love you so much," he calls out.

"The message was recorded at 8:46 A.M.," says Jill. "Do you want to hear it again?"

She holds the little silver machine in her hand. The tape makes a whirring sound as it rewinds.

The man calls out. Jill holds the machine firmly, her gaze far off. At some point, she places the answering machine next to the photograph. The voice and the picture.

"I can show you letters." She gets up and opens a small writing desk. Most of the letters are about the short telephone conversation between James Gartenberg and Channel 7, WABC, on the morning of September 11. While he was inside the burning tower, his voice was live on TV. Jill Gartenberg has never seen the tape on which her husband can be heard talking to the TV station announcers. It's probably just as well. A woman from Illinois had praised James Gartenberg's courage and composure while he was talking to the announcers—brave, courageous, thoughtful. An elderly couple visiting New York wrote: "He's a shining example of all that's right about America."

Jill Gartenberg also hopes that her husband didn't die for nothing, that he's a hero.

The small apartment's located on the fifth floor of a new building. Outside, the evening rush-hour traffic rumbles up First Avenue. The Upper East Side is where James Gartenberg grew up. He went to school just around the corner, and that's where his mother lives as well.

She wonders what else she might have said to him on the phone. What was there to say?

"Sometimes I don't get it, that this is supposed to be my life," she says at one point. "My two children will grow up without a father. It's not fair."

For a moment it looks as if she's about to cry. But she doesn't.

MTA Council, Long Island City

Jan Khan clears his throat. He clears it after every sentence, sometimes after every word. It may be a nervous tic that predates September 11. Or perhaps it's his way of coping with the terrible memories: leaving a small pause before delivering the next word about hell.

He was in hell—on the Lower Level of the World Trade Center—when the South Tower collapsed. He talks about it distantly, in a calm, expressionless monotone. The only indication that remembering is hard is that he clears his throat so often.

His life chugs along normally. He commutes daily to work, no longer to Manhattan but to Long Island City, where the Council has found new office space. Hawking loudly, he recalls what happened, here in a room without windows. The offices are only temporary; plans are to return to Manhattan. Khan will go under one condition: that never again will he have to work above the twelfth floor.

Khan was born a Muslim and his wife goes to a mosque regularly, but he doesn't practice. Both are in favor of the campaign in Afghanistan and see it as a war against criminals rather than a war against Islam.

The problem is, he and his family *look* like the criminals. Some Americans think so, at least. Khan is from Guyana, of Indian descent. In the eyes of some people he looks like an Arab or Afghan, and these days some people suspect them all of being terrorists.

His son has had one such experience. Khan clears his voice. He doesn't want to go into it and changes the subject. America has been his country for ten years. He came here most of all because of his children. He wants them to have a future.

Blue Ribbon Bar, Brooklyn

Smiller's still at Fuji Bank, which is now a subsidiary of Mizuho Holding. He wants to leave, though; he's wanted to for a long time. Since September 11 he's been taking concrete steps in advance of giving notice. Next year he plans to start studying library science. At the beginning of December he passed an aptitude test with flying colors.

Meanwhile he's involved in the installation of the new computers for Fuji. They're now on the twenty-fifth floor of a high-rise on Broadway. Smiller's happy because now he can leave the building to have lunch. When he was in the World Trade Center his office was too high up to make going out worth it.

The atmosphere at the bank is just fine. Only the top four directors lost their lives; everyone else returned to work in the course of several weeks. The employees feel Fuji was very generous. Whoever didn't feel up to it was encouraged to stay home.

Because of limited space in Manhattan, the bank had to find a place in New Jersey for its traders. Smiller's happy he doesn't have to hear the hoots and squawks of greed anymore. On the other hand, he misses the capitalist war whoops.

"The way they'd clamor over million-dollar amounts," he admits, "was also pretty sexy."

The fear of more attacks that plagued Smiller in the early weeks has eased some. He and his wife have looked at some houses near Woodstock, in the Catskills, but he doesn't plan to flee New York in a hurry. Even the news that men close to bin Laden may have bought the plutonium they needed to build atomic weapons doesn't rob him of sleep. *The Washington Post* reported that during an Al Qaeda meeting, a terrorist wagged a gas container and proclaimed that it contained the bomb.

"If there had really been any plutonium inside, the guy would be dead by now," says Smiller.

Smiller may not feel immediately threatened, but he feels threatened enough to be interested in Islam. So he ordered a book about it on-line—Bernard Lewis's *The Muslim Discovery of Europe*. His conclusions? The Islamic world is not particularly curious about the West, and that's how it's been for the last thousand years. Ignorance seems to be a core reason for hatred.

Smiller does not accept arguments about Americans making up only 5 percent of the world's population but burning 25 percent of the world's energy and having to support governments like Saudi Arabia's to keep things that way. America can't make the world fair, he says. America is accused of either being isolationist or of acting like the world's policeman.

September 11 turned Smiller—an ultraliberal who thought the Bush administration was a joke—into a patriot. He thinks the way the war's been conducted is ideal and that those who object that in the long run it will only increase hatred and create more terrorism are wrong.

"The fact that we kicked the shit out of them made an impression. People who use violence don't understand any other language. And that's exactly why our attacks were successful. Our bombs made the future that much harder for Al Qaeda."

Yaffa's Tea Room, TriBeCa

Anthony DeBlase has a gruff voice. He really is a spiritual person, he says. He often talks to God. When it's a lousy day, he says, "God, this day is really no masterpiece, but so what, I know you're busy."

There are more and more days like that now. Even before September, things weren't so great, he says. To be honest, things haven't been great since the day his wife left with the kids. "I still don't get it. She had everything. Good money, new kitchen, new tits. Why did she have to leave?" DeBlase's proud he doesn't talk like one of those blow-dried Wall Street boys.

By 7 in the evening Yaffa's is probably the noisiest place on the block. Other than Ground Zero, of course, where the bulldozers roar. The bar is DeBlase's choice. Noise can help. He's not doing so well, not even when he's sitting broad-shouldered in front of his computer, struggling with the bond markets. Inside him it still looks like it does two blocks down the road at Ground Zero, he says.

He's still got his apartment on Greenwich Street. Mornings and evenings he gets that smell in his nose from the disaster scene and tries not to think about what he's really smelling.

"It's good that you came, from so far away," he says. "It's also good the Europeans are willing to send soldiers to Afghanistan."

For Anthony DeBlase, the World Trade Center was the essence of New York City. Stuffed to the last square foot with people from all over the world busy making money. DeBlase loved it. Whenever he and his brothers returned from a trip, they always knew where home was—over there, where the Towers were.

No longer. Towers gone, wife gone, brother Jimmy gone. Crushed? Burned up? Vaporized? No one will ever know. Two days after the attack, the paychecks stopped coming. Now Anthony collects money for his nephews.

"Once, as boys, we swore we'd kill whoever killed one of us. You do that kind of thing as boys. I better not tell you what I'd do to the ones behind this. Each and every bomb has my personal blessing."

Their mother, Anita DeBlase, went to Ground Zero on September 12 with a sign she made herself. "Missing" was written in big letters above a photo of Jimmy. Underneath the photo it read, "Six feet, 295 lbs." When a policeman stopped her, she told him that Mayor Giuliani was waiting for her. When Giuliani showed up, she pushed through the crowds until she reached him.

"Please, my son's in that rubble," she said.

The photo of Mayor Giuliani holding Anita's hands circulated worldwide.

A thousand people came to Jimmy DeBlase's funeral in Manalapan, New Jersey. Anita read a prayer she'd written herself for her son, and her husband wore a suit for the first time since they got married. "It's unbelievable that we will never feel your dynamic personality, never hear your melodious laughter, or see your handsome face." Then she had to sit down.

"How good of you to come," said Anthony DeBlase. He made signs of a hug, then disappeared among the crowd at the bar.

Offices of Lava Trading, Broad Street, Manhattan

Chuck Allen is once sitting again on the high floor of a skyscraper overlooking water—but now it's the East River rather than the Hudson. Allen is the amateur pilot and computer specialist at Lava Trading. It's a spectacularly clear day but there's not a single jet trail in the sky. Airspace over the city has been closed for half an hour.

It's a Monday morning, the very day an American Airlines flight has crashed in Rockaway, Queens, on the other side of the East River.

"Okay, it's strange. They say on the radio it's an accident, not a terrorist attack."

Allen has a spare quality about him, and the tremendous composure of someone who believes that nearly any situation can be dealt with. Not a hint that only recently he barely escaped death. It took his computer team six weeks to get Lava Trading's data flow back up to speed. Now it clicks along just like before. That was his biggest worry.

"For someone who's spent twenty years of his life in the Middle East, you know, where there's always a danger of some kind of explosion, getting thrown off course is something one gets used to."

He can't help thinking about why he didn't check the other offices to see whether people were waiting there.

"I wish otherwise, but it simply didn't occur to me."

His wife, Sabah Allen-Hassounah, is a journalist and a native Palestinian. On the morning of September 12 she received an urgent phone call from Washington. They were looking desperately for Middle East experts.

Duane Street Firehouse

When Peter Hayden arrives at his office, the blue pants of his uniform are splashed with mud. He's just come from the memorial service with Mayor Giuliani amid the rubble of the World Trade Center. The attack happened three months ago to the day.

On one of the walls of Hayden's office hangs a traffic sign with the word "whining" crossed out. Haydn's blue eyes appear tired and sad, as if he hasn't been able to sleep.

"No," he says, "nights are okay again." It's the pile of wrecked steel that eats him up. "There's nothing but death down there."

On September 11 Hayden was commander of all the fire districts below Forty-third Street. He set up his command post in the lobby of the North Tower and held his position until the South Tower collapsed. By evening it was clear that the fifty-five-year-old Hayden was one of the few veteran leaders of FDNY to have survived the day. Hayden stood on top of a fire truck on West Street amid the devastation and with the other FDNY survivors tried to dig out those buried beneath the debris. Or at least locate them. His blue eyes fill with water.

"There were almost none. Most of them were ground to dust."

Even now, three months after the disaster, he's still searching. Almost every day, twelve hours a day. The results are devastating. On his desk lies a sheet of paper dated December 10 with the list of those found.

Bodies recovered by the FDNY/NYPD: 131
Of these . . . FDNY: 117
Total of whole bodies: 232
Total of identified dead: 503
Body parts: 10,416

Naturally, Hayden suffers feelings of guilt. From the very beginning he knew it was going to be impossible to extinguish a fire that covers twenty floors or more. What should he have done? Should he not have sent his crew into the burning towers to help those lost or cut off on higher floors? Hayden had spoken to many of them from his lobby phone.

"We had to try," he says, adding in a bitter voice, "there's no way you can prepare for attacks of this enormity." Where there's that much destructive will, tens of thousands of training hours don't help.

It doesn't really make things better that all of America feels proud of his men. What are New York City firefighters supposed to do next time the terrorists come—with chemical or nuclear weapons? They'll have to go to the disaster scene, of course, since it's their job to help. He feels certain New York will be targeted again. Nowhere else is there such a collection of symbolic targets.

Late on September 11, when Hayden went home to his wife in Rockaway Beach, he asked her what she would think if he put in for early retirement.

"I used up my nine lives in a single day."

His wife prays for him but doesn't believe for a moment that he'll retire early.

The attack on the World Trade Center was more than a mere fire, which is why it pushed FDNY to its limits. It is hard to maintain a firefighter's passion in the face of suicidal terror.

On the one day Hayden took off in early October, he was walking his dog in his Rockaway neighborhood when he heard an explosion. He looked up and saw an airplane ripping apart. A part of the plane circled slowly down toward him like a corkscrew. *Here we go again,* he thought, before barely escaping the falling wreckage. He tied up his dog and pitched in with the rescue efforts.

"Of course it was terrorism," says Hayden. The FBI and every other official can tell him a hundred times it wasn't, but he saw how the plane broke apart, they didn't.

There's one thing that all the terror, all the disappointments and mistrust among officials, hasn't destroyed: Hayden's loyalty to his job. Apparently he does have a few more lives left in him.

Meknès, Morocco

What mother would not stand up for her son? Would not protect him, trust him, worry about him? What mother would say, "Yes, my son is a terrorist"?

Anneliese Bahaji sits at home in Meknès, Morocco—"not my native country"—watching German TV day after day. She says that any morning there could be news about her son, Said, who's suspected of involvement in the Hamburg cell and now presumed to be a fugitive.

She wears a knit sweater and pants, her hair tied back with a scarf. Her face looks rigid and worn, and she often stares into space. She can talk quickly and easily about some things, but when you ask her what she's feeling, the room goes quiet for a long time.

For the past weeks Anneliese Bahaji has not been able to talk with anybody, not even with her husband. The two of them live alongside but not with one another. In the past their cultural differences lent excitement to their marriage, but now they keep them apart. She travels back and forth between Germany and Morocco, and every time she's in Germany she declares once again, "Morocco's only beautiful to tourists."

Whom to talk to? The girlfriends she had when she worked for a designer outfit have long since gone back home, and she's never made friends with Moroccan women.

So she sits in front of the TV screen and thinks about her Said.

She clings to any hope that her son isn't guilty. Didn't he once talk about going to live in the United Arab Emirates? About building a future for himself and his wife in some Islamic country?

"He just had a baby. You don't plan a terror attack when you've just had a baby," she says. "It's probably all a stupid coincidence, and when he was in Pakistan he fell in with extremists who pressured him. People always used him, maybe people had him do things he knew nothing about."

Besides, why would he use his real passport if he were trying to go underground? Why, she asks, does he try to call her?

On October 1 investigators recorded a call made to Mrs. Bahaji in Germany. Said had been missing for four weeks. While the prerecorded message was still running, a forlorn voice kept calling out, "Hello? Hello?" The caller hung up just as Anneliese Bahaji reached the phone.

"They could have blackmailed him, threatened to hurt his wife and child. Who can really say?"

When the Bahajis moved to the father's native land in 1984, they were closing the book on their life in Germany. He had mismanaged two discotheques. The family was in debt.

It felt as if Germany had robbed Abdallah Bahaji of everything he'd had—now, even his son. Today he's a farmer, a bent figure who walks slowly across his fields. He wears a heavy wool sweater and an even heavier green quilted jacket. His face is tanned and deeply furrowed. Abdallah Bahaji is a doer, not a talker. Here on the fields near Meknès, September 11 and the New World Order seem far away.

Abdallah would have loved it had Said settled in Morocco rather than in Germany. He could have been one of those landowners who have others work their fields for them. He could have been part of the upper class.

"Said always thought Morocco was too corrupt," says Anneliese Bahaji.

The father hardly knew that Said had become a strict Muslim.

"Islam's something you carry in your heart, not in your clothes." He can't comprehend why his son's wife has to hide her face behind a veil.

The father lost his son years ago. Yes, they talked on the phone every so often, but what can you really say in a phone call? As a boy Said was more of a thinker, too delicate in his father's eyes.

"Once, when we went hunting, we shot a pheasant and he didn't want to go fetch him. Since then Said never eats pheasant." The father smiles; stories like this are always a little embarrassing to a man like him.

In those days whenever Said didn't like something he simply shut himself up in his room. "He just wouldn't answer," says Abdallah.

He believes that his son wasn't really prepared for all the troubles that awaited him in the cold German climate.

"Don't let them trick you, I told him before he left."

Elmont, Long Island

The house in which the Praimnaths live seems something like a shrine to propriety. Your feet sink into carpet the color of swimming pool blue. A full-color wedding photo radiates from the wall. The rococo-style armchairs have heavy plastic covers. The air is slightly scented. Stanley Praimnath is happy and sees no reason to hide it. Why should he, especially after September 11?

"It was a very evil deed. Why didn't they crash into the towers at night, when no one was working there?" Two girls are giggling in the kids' room.

Praimnath prayed and the right wing of the United Boeing tilted slightly upward and he survived. He tells the story of his rescue to everyone, most of all on Sundays at the Bethel Assembly of God.

"Listen to me. I'm a living example that prayer helps in

times of want. I called out to the Lord and he immediately answered. Immediately! God's finger can push aside an airplane."

Praimnath has come a long way from his life in Guyana. He contributes a tenth of his Fuji Bank income to his church. He says this is a no-brainer. If God hadn't given him a job, he wouldn't have any money at all.

His company has moved to New Jersey. The commute to his new office is now longer. But the road to God has grown shorter.

Dania, Florida

On the second floor of his fitness center Bert Rodriguez leans against the ropes of the boxing ring and seems pleased with himself. Self-doubt is rare for Rodriguez.

Two men are training at the other end of the hall. One is a dwarf with a paunch. He's kick boxing a sandbag suspended from the ceiling by a chain. A few feet away, an enormous man is hitting a punching bag.

"It's hard to believe," says Rodriguez, "but in the ring, the little guy could be dangerous to the huge guy. First impressions are often deceptive."

Rodriguez bounces against the ring ropes. The ring is constructed of iron springs, plywood, foam rubber, and a thick cloth covering stained by water, sweat, and blood.

Rodriguez was Ziad Jarrah's kick-boxing trainer. Jarrah first came in for instruction four months before the attack. During the weeks that followed Rodriguez spent approximately eighteen hours in the ring with him. For eighteen hours teacher and student hit at each other and talked about God and the world. When it was over Rodriguez felt respect for his student. That didn't change, even after the attack.

"You can say a lot about the terrorists, but the accusation that they were cowards is nonsense."

Someone who sits in the cockpit of a jet and sees the front of a skyscraper racing toward him and still pushes on the lever is worthy of respect. It doesn't matter how crazy Jarrah's and the others' ideals were. Questionable ideals are better than none, according to Rodriguez.

Rodriguez has been an Asian martial arts practitioner for forty-six years. He started as a six-year-old in New York. Today he's a master with a slew of titles and a good reputation in southern Florida. He instructs agents from the Drug Enforcement Agency. He taught Miami police officers and several army units how to disable an opponent.

Rodriguez always fights—it doesn't matter whether he's talking about buying or selling real estate, food, women and relationships—and he never gives in. He has to have the final word. The ring has become home. It is the vantage point from which he judges people and the world. He was the ideal teacher for Ziad Jarrah.

Some people have asked Rodriguez whether he regrets having taught a terrorist. Rodriguez doesn't understand this kind of question.

A few years ago, the walls of Rodriguez's gym were decorated with weapons. On the way to the ring everyone passed by a collection of knives, daggers, lances, maces, and clubs. Somewhere in the middle a snake was slithering around in a crate—a cobra or sometimes a rattlesnake. Rodriguez would encourage his students to put their hand into the crate and try to grab the snake behind its head. The weapons and snakes scared away too many customers, so now they're gone. Today, Rodriguez's gym is divided into two worlds. On the ground floor fitness seekers pedal their bikes. On the upper floor fighters train.

Rodriguez believes that reaching into the snake crate is a smart exercise if you want to win in the ring.

"You don't lose against an opponent," he says. "You lose against your own fear." Come eye to eye with your own fear and conquer it and you'll probably conquer your enemy too. Nobody reached for the snake more often than Rodriguez.

Some people consider Rodriguez a mental case. Rodriguez doesn't mind. If you ask him, most of his critics never do more than pay off their mortgage and add a few pounds on their hips every year. They wouldn't last more than a minute in the ring.

It's early afternoon and Rodriguez is sitting calmly at the edge of the ring wiping the sweat off his shaved head. He's just completed three hours of training and he's still breathing easily. He runs seven miles three times a week and almost daily goes a few rounds in the ring. He has one meal a day, in the evening. "The way predators do."

That's how Rodriguez sees himself: as a predator who won't shy away from poisonous snakes. He believes himself to be part of an elite, a small circle of men and women who can master their fear of fear and do extraordinary deeds. Most people wind up on treadmills, fighting their own bellies, not the world. Since the attack, Jarrah, too, belongs to this elite.

"Now this is a reasonable gut," says Rodriguez and lifts up his shirt. Six well-contoured stomach muscles, the ribs arching above. On the left you see a few scars.

"Knives," he says with pride.

In the beginning Jarrah seemed to be another of the ones who belong downstairs on the treadmills. He jogged obediently and lifted weights. The best thing he had going for him was he didn't have a big mouth. He wasn't one of those who train five minutes and then stand there talking macho crap. He came into the gym, changed, worked his way through the program, showered, said good-bye, and left.

Karen, the receptionist, liked how he behaved. Jarrah ended up booking twenty hours. Rodriguez canceled the last two lessons because he was out of town at a kick-boxing tournament.

Rodriguez is a popular trainer because he knows a lot of ways to hurt, cripple, or kill people, and because he doesn't bore his students with Far Eastern philosophy. There's no complicated choreography to what he teaches. You don't even have to be particularly athletic. You just have to be willing to hurt other people and to tolerate your own pain. That's it. If you ask Rodriguez, "Do you hurt or harm people during your lessons?" he answers, "Of course." By the tenth lesson students better know how to fight off a baseball bat. If not, they're in trouble.

When Rodriguez thinks back to his work with Jarrah, he remembers his punctuality, politeness, and self-control.

"He wasn't a fantastic fighter," says Rodriguez, "but he knew his own weakness and was ready to learn."

In Rodriguez's world, there's no shame in getting knocked to the ground, then getting up and getting knocked down again. On the contrary, it's a virtue.

Rodriguez stands up to fetch boxing gloves from the side room. Before putting them on, he bandages his knuckles. He does it without looking. He's done it a thousand times.

"It's good to trust in your abilities," says Rodriguez while he forces his hands into the gloves. He thinks it makes sense to find something worth fighting for. America became great because of people who dared to risk their lives, not because of those who believed in collective power.

Rodriguez grew up in Cuba. When he got to New York, he fought prejudice. He also fought with the police. He has a scar near his heart—made from a bullet from a pistol fired by a police officer. As a young man he made money by visiting people who were behind in their payments. His job was to help them catch up. He says that he always went alone, that he never needed a partner.

Rodriguez goes into the ring to fight a guy wearing a U.S. Coast Guard T-shirt. He could be Rodriguez's son; the only thing that separates him from his ideal weight is a few pounds of muscle in the right places. He doesn't stand a chance against Rodriguez. Rodriguez's punches cut through his defenses like a chain saw through butter.

Rodriguez sits down again.

"The problem was the guy couldn't land a blow 'cause he was constantly wondering what I'd do next. He wasn't active, but reactive. Like our society."

Rodriguez complains that more and more Americans don't rely on themselves but on someone else to take responsibility for their possible defeat. They hire a lawyer. Or count on the group, the team.

Believing in the team can have fatal consequences. That became apparent, Rodriguez preaches, on board Flight 93. The passengers rebelled against the terrorists and failed. This is a topic he cares about. He stops leaning into the ropes with his upper body and sits upright.

"First they planned to scald Jarrah and his gang with boiling water. Then they had to call their families. Then they had to confer with each other. Then they had to summon their courage and, finally, half an hour later, they moved on the hijackers. No wonder they failed. The hijackers had time enough to get organized."

Rodriguez truly believes that the passengers on Flight 93 made fatal mistakes. He would have done it better. He would have marched into the cockpit and tried to finish off the terrorists. Maybe he would have succeeded. Maybe he wouldn't.

Rodriguez has said what he has to say. He steps out of the ring to go change. He smiles. He feels good. He's got an answer for everything.

Before he leaves, he puts on his baseball cap and turns the visor around. The cap was made especially for him and his kick boxers. When he wears it backward, like he usually does, it reads "Killer Instinct."

Westfield, New Jersey

How did a blind man escape from the 78th floor of the World Trade Center? Thanks to the self-sacrifice of his fellowmen? Through God's grace? Because of unbelievable good luck?

That's what Mike Hingson hears constantly—how grateful he must feel to his fellowmen, to God, to his lucky stars. That he may have contributed something to his own rescue usually doesn't really occur to them.

This by itself gives Mike Hingson a reason to talk. He

wants the world to understand that even a blind man didn't have to live through this day of disaster as a victim, but as someone who could control his own fate. He opens the door to his white, single-family home in the suburban village of Westfield, New Jersey. He's an average-sized man with light, unfocusing eyes who moves graciously and self-assuredly to greet people.

Roselle, his Seeing Eye dog, yelps and pulls on the fringes of the living room rug. Right at the moment she's free to act like a normal dog. Mrs. Hingson is sitting at the dining room table in a wheelchair; she and three woman friends are bent over bits of fabric and a color wheel. Today's quilting day. They're sewing blankets in patriotic colors, to be sold at a bazaar for a September 11 benefit. Three quilts have already been completed.

Hingson prefers that we have lunch at a Chinese restaurant, where we can sit and talk undisturbed. He takes a walking stick and leaves Roselle behind in the living room. In the taxi he asks the driver, "What do you see now on the left? A school? Take the next right, it's a sharp one." He knows the roads by heart. "See a mailbox over there? It's right there." He gets out of the parked car, walks toward the curb, listens, takes out his stick, and begins to walk.

Hingson is very good at concentrating, listening, focusing his brain on the central issue: This is where I've got to go. Now it's just to the Chinese restuarant, to the counter to order imperial chicken, then to find a table.

On September 11 the goal was survival. There was this horrible moment when he thought, *If I don't pull myself together, I'll be dead.* They were outside on the corner of Broadway and Fulton Street, thinking they were safe, that Roselle could relax. Hingson was holding on to David Frank's arm. David had stopped to take a picture as a keepsake and let go of his friend. At exactly that moment the South Tower collapsed. David ran.

"He just left me standing there," Hingson says. The way he says it makes it sound as if all emotional coloration had been removed in advance. It does not sound like a reproach. At most there is an air of disbelief about it.

He says he tried to think about what to do in case he stumbled on the debris and fell.

"I think I would have been crushed if that had happened." Instead—and here he sounds proud—he took Roselle's leash and asked her to go on. They managed on their own until he heard David's voice saying, "I'm sorry, Mike. May I take your arm?"

In the middle of that dust cloud Hingson suddenly had an advantage, because he knew how to be guided by sounds and Roselle. He helped a woman who couldn't see because her eyes were caked over with dust.

"I can't see anything," she cried.

"I don't see anything either, but I have a dog," he replied.

David, too, had to be calmed again and again, or so it seemed to Hingson. It wasn't a situation in which David was responsible for him but in which the three of them—David, himself, and Roselle—were a team. Adrenaline surged through their bodies and saw to it that they survived.

Now their heads have to cope with what happened. At times you almost envy Roselle, who apparently didn't experience that day as a shock.

"A dog isn't prone to analyze," says Hingson. "She lives in the moment, so she's fine. We humans don't know anymore what's normal. We're looking over our shoulders all the time now, thinking, What's next? Something threatening? First thing we've got to figure out is what 'normal' means nowadays."

On the way home he says his priorities have changed. His job at Quantum Software is still centered around figures and sales, but to him other things count more now. The fact that there are people you can count on, and dogs too. And that there are killers, people "who've forgone the right to be called human." They'll be called to justice, he says, swinging his body out of the taxi.

"If not in the courts, then by God. Thanks for coming. Good-bye."

He walks toward the house, by himself, tapping his cane.

At the end of November, Chief Jay Jonas went to Vienna, Austria, for the first time in his life. His grandparents had emigrated from there. He and his wife were flown there so that he could receive a "Man of the Year" award on behalf of the New York Fire Department. On stage with him were Paul McCartney, Hans-Dietrich Genscher, Mikhail Gorbachev, and the British billionaire Richard Branson.

"A lovely evening," says Jonas, then adds that he was glad when he got back home.

Home is a wood-frame house in a village at the foot of the Catskills, seventy miles north of New York City. His three children romp around in the yard. His wife works as a physical therapist, and in the afternoons, after Jonas comes home from the night shift, he has responsibility for the kids. He doesn't mind. He loves his kids. In a few days, he says proudly, his fifteen-year-old will be dancing in the *Nutcracker*. It's oddly wonderful to see a 240-pound former football player gaze dreamily at his daughter as she leaves for a ballet recital.

The award Jonas received in Austria is a statue of *The Thinker* by Rodin. It sits unobtrusively on the kitchen counter, not far from the coffeemaker. You can almost imagine Jonas asking his wife, "Dammit, honey, where'd I put *The Thinker*? I can't seem to find it."

The story of Chief Jonas and Ladder Company 6 is one of the few September 11 stories with a happy ending. The firefighters were helping an old lady down the stairs when the North Tower collapsed above them. Five hours later, they were able to break free of the ruins. They pulled the lady safely out of the smoky inferno by carrying her on a makeshift metal stretcher. Later on, they presented her with that jacket on which was embroidered, "Josephine—Our Guardian Angel."

Chief Jonas is the classic strong, silent type. He is a professional whose eyes light up as soon as he talks about his city and his job. His city is New York. Every day he drives to New York, and as soon as he crosses the George Washington Bridge he gets goose bumps.

Before joining Ladder Company 6 in Chinatown, Jonas worked in a Puerto Rican neighborhood, and then in a Dominican one. He loves New York's melting pot aspect. Any given day on the job is a little like taking a trip around the world.

Jonas likes to banter with Billy Butler, one of the guys from Ladder Company 6. Butler's a former prison guard. He has a mustache and, like Jonas, lives near the Catskills. He loves to hunt. Jonas calls Butler "Grizzly Man." When Butler asks why Jonas doesn't shoot animals, he replies, "The only place I go hunting is the meat department at the supermarket. Hey, Butler, I'm a city boy."

Jonas is enraged that they attacked this city, this center of tolerance, this melting pot of races and cultures, this high point of human coexistence. He will be outraged for the rest of his life.

Jonas was promoted a few months ago. He's now one of the fire chiefs for all of Lower Manhattan. It's a grim time to take on this kind of responsibility. He's gone to so many funerals of fellow firefighters, including close friends, that he's stopped counting. Recently his assistant said to him, "Chief, it's starting to taper off. Only thirty-some funerals left." The remark hit Jonas like a ton of bricks. Only thirty funerals, he thought to himself. In the entire history of the FDNY more than eleven hundred firefighters have lost their lives. Nearly a third of these died on September 11—343 in all.

It's tough to get an award for fighting this kind of disaster. Maybe near the coffeemaker is the right place for it.

Midtown Manhattan

Once again Rafael Kava's sitting across from the entrance door, only now he's on the twenty-ninth floor. But it's still

Manhattan. Mutual Forwarding's found an office in Midtown. The view's not as good, but Kava's got a new electric typewriter. He sits quietly at his desk, where he doubles as receptionist and secretary. He still has his briefcase and his hat. His glasses are too big for his face.

It's afternoon and he's not alone like he was that morning. The whole family's buzzing around the small office—Kava's nephew, his nephew's wife, the great-niece, the great-nephew, and his great-nephew's wife. It's a family business. They're very busy just before Christmas and they all look agitated but not stressed out. Albert Cohen, Kava's nephew, the head of the small shipping company, shows up for a moment with an orange. That's what you get for refreshment at Mutual International Forwarding—oranges, bananas, clementines.

Kava has a friendly smile; he hardly speaks any English. He acts out the way the plane crashed and he fell off his chair. How he took his hat and briefcase. All in pantomime: the windows—plop, they fall out. Next, thick, black smoke. Poooh. Away! Out of here! Down! Saved! Kava smiles like a child. Then we sit in silence. You can understand why all the other occupants of the 89th floor assumed the old man hadn't made it. He looks frail, so helpless. Outside, darkness settles in, the city starts to glisten. Kava briefly types something on his large electric typewriter. At some point, after 5 P.M. when it gets quieter, his nephew Albert Cohen shows up and translates.

Now Rafael Kava recounts in French how he left the burning office. He appears very calm while he describes the inferno. It's no different from his pantomime. All the others from the 89th floor emerge out of the darkness. The MetLife people, Diane from the law firm, Walter from Cosmos Services and, of course, Theresa, his "angel."

"There's the true hero," says Albert Cohen and stops translating. Now he himself has to tell the story. How he was standing outside while the tower burned. He'd emerged from the Brooklyn-Battery Tunnel some minutes after the tower was hit. Everything had already been cordoned off.

Cohen wanted to run in, but they wouldn't let him. He said he saw the second plane; he heard the sudden thrust. He knew immediately what kind of plane it was, and the airline. Being in shipping, he's spent a lot of time at airports. He says he can identify almost instantly nearly every airline in the world. His uncle watches him. Albert Cohen says that he's furious with the terrorists.

"We lived in Cairo as Jews without harming anyone. We're tradespeople, not warriors. We arrived in New York without a penny to our name. We built up an existence here, and this is our home now. All we want is to live in peace."

His uncle stares through his huge glasses. It looks as if he'd rather be typing again on his large typewriter.

Rafael Kava also trusted others on September 11. He walked down eighty-nine flights, while Theresa Moya held his hand. They had arrived at the foot of the Brooklyn Bridge when the tower they'd been in collapsed. He did not let go of her hand. They kept on walking, all the way across the bridge to downtown Brooklyn. They waited for a few hours in front of the courthouse and in the evening they went to the Marriott Hotel. His nephew had him picked up from there. He was home in Staten Island just before 7 P.M.

Mutual International Forwarding resumed work the following day. A shipping company can't afford to take a break. They had been working in the North Tower two years before the World Trade Center officially opened, and they were working again a day after it collapsed. They moved into Cohen's daughter's apartment. Rafael Kava rested for two days after his long descent. Then they sent him to the small office they have at Kennedy Airport. For two weeks, they ran the business out of a customer's conference room, until they found space here on Fortieth Street at the corner of Fifth Avenue. It's amazing how much empty office space is available in Manhattan. The other refugees from the 89th floor also found new quarters quickly. The MetLife people are working out of their main office in Manhattan. Strategic Communications, the ad agency, rented a whole floor on Park Avenue South, and Drinker, Biddle & Reath has moved temporarily to their New Jersey offices.

It takes Rafael Kava a bit longer to get to work, but otherwise not much has really changed for him. It was some fifty years ago that he had to leave Egypt. He lives with his sister on Staten Island.

He simply goes on.

Hollywood, Florida

When the World Trade Center collapsed, Susan Khalil's understanding of the world collapsed with it. Until then she had always believed in people's innate goodness. For example, when Hani, as she still calls him, moved into her home, she offered him her complete hospitality. Susan Khalil, born Samek, tried as hard as she could to be a good hostess, to encourage him and to help him.

"Five years later you get these pictures on TV," she said. "The shock, the shame."

And then the fear. Fear of neighbors, reporters, attacks by Muslim extremists. Susan Khalil was deathly afraid of the FBI investigators, even though the special examiners were friendly and she told them everything she knew through her tears, everything that happened way back when.

When the young visitor entered Susan Khalil's life, her first thought was, poor guy. A skinny kid was standing in front of her, chest caved in, pimply skin, wisps of a beard on his chin. His eyes flickered here and there, and he was constantly pulling up his shoulders as if he wanted to crawl inside himself. He stuttered so much he was hardly able to get out a "hello." *He has bad breath,* thought Susan Khalil, *and his shirt needs washing badly. Poor guy, he's probably completely intimidated, overwhelmed by America. He's also probably homesick.* And so she beamed at him and gave him a double dose of kindness.

The name of the young visitor was Hani Saleh Hassan Hanjour. Born August 3, 1972, in Taif, Saudi Arabia, Hani was twenty-three when he moved in with the Khalils in

March 1996. He looked eighteen and acted like a fourteen-year-old struggling to get through puberty. They had told Hanjour's older brother that he could live with them in Hollywood, Florida, for a month, maybe even a few weeks longer.

He wanted to live in Hollywood so he could look around for the right flight training school. It was a dream of his, he confessed while blushing, to become a commercial airline pilot. Susan thought it was a great idea. She admires pilots, her own brother is a pilot.

The bungalow on Canal Road is modest, and there's no separate guest room. Susan decided that her three-year-old son Adam's room, the one decorated with Mickey Mouse posters, could be turned into a guest room. Susan put the toys in a box, wiped off the shelves in the closet, put new sheets on the bed and a small bunch of flowers on the night table. Everything was ready; her son would be allowed to sleep in his parents' bed for the time being.

Susan Khalil could never have suspected that five years later the young man's name would enter history as a mass murderer. Or that he would turn into her very own personal nightmare.

"Oh, my God, all at once you're pulled into the middle of it," she says. "You just can't grasp it. We're a totally average family, that's what I mean."

This "average" family consists of Susan and her husband, Adnan. He comes from Saudi Arabia and works in Hollywood as an English teacher. Physically, they're complete opposites. He's tall and dark, she's short and pale. He has an oriental presence, loud, funny, is an enthusiastic cook. She seems maternal, quiet, and maybe carries a few extra pounds on her hips. Their marriage couldn't be happier.

They have two children. The older daughter's already left home, and Adam is now eight. Between taking her son to school, housekeeping, and going to the mall, Susan experiments with being an artist. She paints colorful cactus plants against empty desert landscapes. The colors are luminous, the mountains glow as if glazed.

"I need harmony around me," she explains, "in my paintings and my life. Maybe I've always been too trusting."

She doesn't want to repeat the mistake. It requires a heroic effort of diplomacy to meet her in the weeks following September 11. At first she's willing to grant an interview, then not, then maybe she will after all, then probably not, then yes it's okay but under no circumstance at home. She suggests Friday's as a meeting place but at the last minute changes her mind, the Red Lobster's a safer place. And under no circumstances is a photographer to be in the vicinity, understood?

Susan Khalil is not a difficult person. She is simply afraid.

She's waiting in a booth at the Red Lobster, her handbag placed visibly on the table as a means of identification. She has chosen a seat as far away from the other diners as possible. She picks at her crabmeat salad and talks about her sinister houseguest. Although Hani Hanjour, the man who probably steered the Boeing 757 into the southwest section of the Pentagon, lived in her house, he remained as intangible as a phantom the entire time. Hanjour: the ghostly guest, the man without qualities.

It must have been a strange time. Susan Khalil put herself out. Every morning a radiant smile. What did Hani want for breakfast? Coffee, tea, cornflakes? Or toast with eggs?

Oh, anything, he didn't care.

Her guest chewed listlessly on whatever she put in front of him and rarely ever said thank you. When she asked him something just to make conversation, he blushed, lowered his head, and mumbled something she could hardly understand.

"Back then I thought maybe it was because his English was so poor. Or that because I was a woman and as a Muslim he wasn't used to having contact with women. Today, however, I ask myself whether already back then he wasn't in contact with these—how should I put it—these conspirators. Perhaps this horrendous plan already existed, and he was simply ashamed to face me."

Susan Khalil looks around and scans the restaurant to see whether anybody's watching her, pushes her half-eaten crab salad to the side, and fights back her tears.

"The thing I ask myself, although of course it's absurd, is was there anything I could have done to prevent it? Should I have noticed something?"

It was tough being together in the same house. The cheerful American became more and more tense. The inhibited Arab tried to flee from her kindness. Her joyful morning salutation was rarely returned. She prepared meals three times a day for him but he was hardly ever hungry. He hid in his room, not even watching TV like Adnan urged him to do to improve his English, not reading newspapers or books either but always and only reading the Koran, the Koran, the Koran. Susan Khalil's a faithful Christian, but this monkish devotion spooked her.

When she knocked at his door for lunch or dinner, Hanjour would sneak past her absently, almost guiltily, only to slip back into his room as soon as the meal was over. Susan Khalil felt helpless in the face of such rejection.

"I mean, what was I supposed to do with him? Shake him? Force him to talk to me? He was still a guest, after all. So I said to myself, All right, Susan, respect him and give him time."

She did give him time. Nothing changed. So Susan Khalil finally gave in to the bizarre situation. She made an effort to look at the positive side—her houseguest, for example, would play engagingly and lovingly with her son Adam, sometimes for hours on end. He taught him Arabic words and was happy when the little guy repeated them after him; he let him ride on his back and piled up building blocks with him.

"For a mother, it was touching to see how he opened up in that setting."

Other habits weren't quite as touching. Hygiene, for example. He took showers rarely, and the odor could be almost overpowering. He didn't brush his teeth, either.

238

"After two or three weeks, there was a brown film over his teeth. I couldn't bear to look at him."

Susan Khalil had a talk with her husband, who tactfully took his guest aside and learned that he didn't even own a toothbrush. Susan Khalil found it hard to comprehend.

"It's absurd. Back in Saudi Arabia his family was really well off. We always had tons of toothbrushes in the house, I always bought them in large bags. All he needed to do was ask, but he didn't dare."

She shakes her head. "I wanted to be kind of a friend to him, but I never was."

One day Hani Hanjour moved to Oakland, California. He'd found a school where he could first take a language course, then enroll for pilot training. Susan Khalil tried hard not to show her sense of relief.

On his last evening with the Khalils, the young Arab nearly engaged in a real conversation with Susan. They were standing in the kitchen. With an embarrassed gesture, he pulled $100 out of his pocket and tried to place it in Susan Khalil's hand. She was offended and fended it off. He was there as a guest, not as a boarder.

No, no, the $100 was for Adam, "the very, very good boy," explained Hanjour with a twisted smile. Susan should give him the money when Adam was older, with greetings from Hani. In case he still remembered.

Adam would certainly remember, said Susan Khalil, and accepted the money. And Adnan and she wouldn't forget him, either, she added. Way back then she could hardly know how right she was.

Le Café Crème, Manhattan

Mark Oettinger wears a flannel shirt. He's blond, and his hair's parted neatly and combed close. He's got broad shoulders and carries a gray tool bag through the streets of Midtown. He's a very polite, caring New Yorker: Watch out for the car, lady! The road's clear now, lady.

Oettinger's a carpenter, a woodworker. On September 11 he had a job on the 10th floor of the North Tower. He was setting up furniture for the Bank of America. From 7 am to 8:45 A.M. he joined furniture, and after that he saved lives. At least that's what you read about him in New York. That and that he was about to go join the war to get his revenge.

Oh, well, you may say. Afterward everyone wants to be the one who said to the others, "We've got to get out. I know the way." That's normal. And maybe there's even a need to exaggerate a little in order to make looking back more bearable, maybe a need to be a hero, or to promise to become an even greater hero in the army.

Oettinger carries his bag into the restaurant on Madison Avenue. He puts it down carefully next to the delicate little bistro table. All day long, he carries that bag with him, starting in the morning when he leaves his home in Brooklyn. Here in Upper Manhattan he doesn't seem to feel at home. And then again he does. Just now, he's been in Times Square in the Condé Nast Building. He was doing a job for *Vanity Fair*.

He talks again about how he led people—women in particular—out of the North Tower. He says he had no choice. He had to keep going back to look for more, even if it was not his job.

Why did he do it?

"Because I'm soft," he says. "I didn't want to be alone."

He smiles somewhat absentmindedly and then recalls the moment when the South Tower came down and a cloud as dark as the night sky in winter descended. He ran in the direction of air he could feel on his face. All of a sudden, like a door opening, the grass looked green; a fountain was burbling. He was standing in front of City Hall Park. It was unbelievably still. Only then, he says, was he able to cry.

He cried for the others and for himself. He cried for the people who worked with him who'd had a job farther up in the towers—Chris, Pat, Brian. Everyone was mourning the firefighters and policemen. But there were normal people, too, he thinks, people who were also just doing their job, people who worked backstage, behind the scenes, making sure that Manhattan kept working.

They weren't the kind of people who usually sit in Le Café Crème to the sounds of piano music, among well-dressed people discussing the advantages of Napa over French Chardonnay.

Brian, Chris, and Mark were people you weren't supposed to see in the lobby of the World Trade Center. They had their own stairwells, their own elevators, their own basement storage rooms. It was a good place to work, says Oettinger. He liked being in the basement, among the small, pleasant passageways, the hidden storage rooms. People used to tell newcomers that in some of the wall closets you could still find beer bottles left by the original construction workers.

They saw themselves as society's underpinnings, as the ones who'd never wind up on top but who derived pride from the idea that even up on top they couldn't do without us.

Mark had worked his way up. He grew up in New Jersey. His family was of limited means and his father died when he was ten. His mother managed to raise eight children with the help of the Bible and rigid notions of justice and morality. Mark was the youngest, a shy, muscular boy. During school vacations, he earned good money in construction. He learned from his mother about right and wrong and about how to be polite to women.

He went into the army, he explains, because college never worked out and you've got to do something. It was a bit of an adventure, but only maneuvers, not war with real dead people. Different from September 11. Maybe, he wonders, that was a preparation for this?

He never anticipated a huge disaster happening in his lifetime, or that he'd be there and turn into a big rescuer. But it was fitting. Treat the ladies well. You know, young man, what's good and what's bad.

Mother's youngest has turned into a gentle giant who drinks from a china cup with care and speaks almost like a minister, in a ceremonious, melodic voice. He talks about his clients and furniture building. He says he has a good reputation in Manhattan. His clients like him and many are repeat customers. He will do anything, literally anything, to make his clients happy. That's his ambition, his reward, and his bread and butter.

He's the kind of guy, he says while critically examining the furniture in Café Crème, who goes into old houses to look over the wood, the way others go to art shows. Sometimes he lies awake at night and worries about where to put a particular column a client is insisting on. Will it look any better if I move the ceiling panels to the left?

His tools are now lying somewhere in Ground Zero, smashed to bits. His boss told him he could go ahead and buy whatever he needed, wasn't that kind of him? He did exactly that. After two days he already wanted to go back to work. He couldn't bear sitting still in his tiny Brooklyn apartment. He asked his company to assign him the next client on the list. It was on the thirty-first floor in Upper Manhattan. It wasn't that easy to get back into an elevator, but it was okay.

This new life? It's different now when he turns on the TV and sees dead people. Images of the real dead move across his mind. A man like Mark gets enraged then. He learned from his mother—God bless her—what was right. He takes the death penalty for granted and is surprised anyone questions it. Why not the death penalty? Isn't the American system of justice already too lenient? At least that's what he usually hears.

He thinks it's good for America to avenge itself. He was in the National Guard. He's a reserve corporal of the Twenty-eighth Infantry Division. His family had planned a celebration at the Jersey home of his oldest brother for the weekend after the disaster, but Mark couldn't go; he had to go on maneuvers. He says he's ready to serve when he's called up. Maybe to guard airports, maybe even a tour of duty.

"Nothing's certain anymore, these days," says Corporal Oettinger. But his bags are packed.

He sounds more like a person who wants the world back the way it was, or, better still, a more peaceful world altogether. These days he dreams about a farm. He's bought forty-one acres of land in Pennsylvania, among rolling hills where the grass is almost always green. Build a house. Raise animals. Perhaps forget.

But forgetting Ground Zero probably isn't possible. He spent the whole day looking for people. He couldn't leave. He also looked to see if he could recognize any furniture, but there was nothing to recognize, nothing but dust.

He's been back to Ground Zero. He listened while some of his rescue worker friends told him their stories. About turning over the body of a young women and finding her child underneath. About an arm they found, a woman's, and when they pried open her fingers they found inside the fist of a baby.

No, really, he does not want to forget. He even kept some mementos. He rummages through his gray bag and pulls out something. A present, "for a nice lady like you." It's the brass key from a safety lock, engraved with these words: "World Trade Center. Do not duplicate."

Greenwich Village Firehouse, Houston Street and Sixth Avenue

An inflatable snowman and a strobe-lit Christmas tree are all that's left from the Greenwich Village Firehouse Christmas party. There were magicians, carolers from the neighborhood, even a clown who was supposed to help the kids laugh again—the fifteen whose fathers went to work the morning of September 11 and never came home.

The station lost eleven firefighters. One would have been too many, but eleven? They were all experienced men, like Mike Warchola, who planned to retire on September 12, having worked twenty-four years in FDNY. Like Louie Arena, who brought in his broken lawn mower in case they had any spare time to repair things. All at once eleven of the best, funniest, ablest buddies gone—how does your team recover from that? John Ottrando, driver of Engine 24 and the first to arrive at the World Trade Center, shakes his head. "At first, you don't. You have to mourn, it feels like you're paralyzed. But you have to go on." When the siren goes off, he and his crew have thirty seconds, then off they go. Flashing lights respect no man's troubles.

But when things are calm, it's a help to surviving wives, children, and firemen that in times of mourning FDNY functions like one big family. For those who put their lives on the line on September 11, it's also good to see how a reputedly harsh and fast-paced city like New York has taken the time—for months now—to shower both its dead and living firefighters with love, respect, and money.

Ottrando has set up a big yellow notebook to record the donations. Some people gave $2, some gave $1,000 or $2,000. Others brought loads of iced tea and baked goods. Back in the garage are boxes full of shirts and stuffed animals. Ottrando is forty-four years old and the father of two sons. What was he supposed to do with a fluffy blue bunny? "No idea," he says, "but it's touching. Maybe it's from children who hoped it would make me feel better."

Nobody asked for these donations. Stuffed animals, cartons of Coke, buckets of candy, all arrived spontaneously. A woman from across the street sewed ten dresses, one for each of the firefighters' daughters. Another woman asked whether they could make use of cemetery space; she didn't want to seem morbid, but she had two cemetery plots to donate. In one firehouse in Brooklyn, the men gathered money donations, put them in black garbage bags, and stored them in the shower. Since then the collecting has become better organized. Each of the widows is expected to receive about $880,000.

With all this tender attention, the fire stations have come to resemble places of pilgrimages. Nevertheless, Ottrando is not able to regain the unequivocally good feeling he once had for his brotherhood, the New York City Fire Department.

The men had bad fires to deal with before September 11. But since September 11, many firefighters feel the WCT disaster is just prelude to a new kind of war. "I never planned to be a soldier," says Ottrando. As a child, he was once sick in bed for days after shooting a sparrow with a BB gun. He looks out the window, past the glowing little red helmets and plastic hydrants that someone had hung in the window for Christmas decoration. "It helps to be liked," he says, even if sometimes his arm gets tired from waving back.

The other day on Carmine Street he could hardly drive through. It was one of those warmer days, and all the people sitting in the sidewalk cafés and restaurants started to applaud. More and more people came out of buildings, and the whole thing turned into a kind of procession. Ottrando realized at that moment that he had chosen the right profession after all.

Marj, Bekaa Valley, Lebanon

The father wipes away his tears with little towels. He has bags under his eyes, his head slumps between his shoulders, his arms hang limply. He looks strangely crooked in his green turtleneck. Father Jarrah receives us in his family's sitting room. Here in the village of Marj in the Bekaa Valley, about twenty-two miles east of Beirut, is the family seat of the Jarrahs. It's a weekend area for people who live in Beirut. There are four sofas, a crystal chandelier, and heavy green-and-red brocaded drapes; nine upholstered armchairs are lined up along the walls. Ziad Jarrah was the rich son of wealthy parents.

Outside in front of a green wrought-iron gate, peddlers open the trunks of their beat-up little cars and put out potatoes for sale. Worn-out Mercedes-Benzes and limos struggle along the potholed road. An enormous, splendid mosque stands just a few houses farther along.

Ziad Jarrah spent weekends and summers in his parents' vacation home. Otherwise his childhood coincided with the civil war in Beirut where the fronts of buildings were strewn with bullet holes. The Jarrah family has a six-room apartment there in Hamad Street, seventh floor in a nine-story high-rise. The ground-floor lobby boasts an abundance of marble. That's where his mother, Nafisa, is now hiding; according to her husband, "She's no longer capable of talking." Jarrah's two sisters, Dania, twenty-seven, and Nisri, twenty-three, both business students, are keeping her company. No one is allowed to see them.

How does a family accept the death of a son or brother? It's heartbreaking but possible.

How then does a family accept the death of a son or brother who was one of the terrorists in the largest terrorist attack ever?

Father Jarrah simply does not believe it. Ziad, he says, was a modern young man and led a modern young man's life. He had whatever he wanted.

His father had sent him to only the best Christian schools, from elementary through high school, "the most expensive schools in all Beirut. They were about education, not religion." He gave his only son nothing but the best. "I spoiled him. He could get whatever he wanted. More."

"Some days we skipped school and played soccer," says Mazen Mamiche, a friend from school. "Ziad wasn't ambitious, he cracked jokes about his teachers." His dad would give him the keys to his Mercedes for weekend outings. Neighbors remember days when the Mercedes would zip out of the lower-level garage with Ziad at the wheel and three girls in the backseat.

He was not a good student. He hid his poor grades from his parents as much as possible, and when he couldn't hide them any longer and he confessed, Ziad's father arranged to have him tutored in math, physics, and chemistry. Even then

Ziad flunked his high school finals. Two years later he was able to graduate from a public high school.

In his teens he dreamed of becoming a pilot, but that seemed out of question; his family decided that he should first go overseas to get a solid education. He took up aircraft engineering. Every month, father Jarrah sent 1,200 marks to Hamburg. Then it was 1,500 marks, then $2,000 after Jarrah went to study in the States. Ziad often asked for money. His father is a manager in the government's social security agency. He's a high-level public servant, and he paid without asking questions. On the phone with his son he was interested in only one thing: "Are you at the top of your class?"

Ziad sent home an official paper, something his parents believed was an important document. "He needed only one more year before finishing his studies," his father believed. In truth Ziad had yet to get through the preliminaries. What he'd sent to Beirut was nothing but a certificate of university registration.

In this room there is nothing that reminds them of the son they once knew.

Ziad's Uncle Jamal is a forty-six-year-old bank director who dresses in a gray pin-striped suit and is something like the family spokesperson. Jamal Jarrah collects documents and newspaper clippings in red, yellow, and blue plastic folders. He serves his guest tea and always acts professional, as if explaining a business report.

"Ziad was not a hijacker," he says. "To this day they have no proof Ziad was the pilot."

What about the cockpit voice recorder?

"That's not Ziad's voice."

What about the good-bye letter to Aysel, the kick-boxing lessons in Florida, the message on Atta's cell phone? What about all the documents about death in martyrdom?

"Fabricated. False. Inventions."

But why?

"The Americans shot down the plane, so they've got to make it look hijacked." This way Uncle Jamal can still talk about an "accident" and explain that his nephew is "missing."

Jamal Jarrah has an explanation for everything. So to him it seems normal that Ziad, who never missed a party in Beirut, would pray five times a day in Hamburg. Thus unfolds a picture of the perfect nephew, utterly smooth, with nary a weakness or inconsistency.

Ziad a mass murderer?

"Makes no sense," says Jamal Jarrah. "He had a family, he planned to marry his girlfriend Aysel and find a good job."

Of course it doesn't make sense. How could it?

All the concern and all the money, all the parties and the many girls—somehow it wasn't enough. Maybe a young man like Ziad, so used to feeling corroborated, was especially vulnerable to outside influences while in a foreign country. Probably a spoiled young man like Ziad stumbled into the terrorist milieu the same way a Western teenager might fall in with a religious sect on a vacation trip to Asia. A mother's and father's pet like Ziad would be too weak to resist. The professionals who drafted psychological profiles of the hijackers consider him to have been indecisive and impulsive as well as immature, unstable, and unprofessional. Many times before September 11 he must have had doubts; nevertheless, he went along with it.

"He was lonely in Hamburg," says Ziad's cousin who had gone to Greifswald at the same time.

In Beirut he complained that girls always wanted to marry him after the first kiss. But in Germany he was instantly committed to Aysel. Then he found a group of friends who were regulars at the mosque.

All of a sudden there were two worlds and Ziad in the middle, going back and forth and wanting somehow to bring them together. He tried until the very end.

Friends noticed the changes, but apparently not his family. Ziad never had a beard, says his father, who "was strongly opposed to it." Yet photographs show his son with a short, well-kept, full beard. Some relatives suspect he was in Afghanistan or Pakistan. Impossible, says his father. "He always told me everything."

As if to prove it, the father takes visitors into the inner courtyard of their country home. There on the pale stone stands the black Model 300 Mercedes, automatic transmission, leather seats. It was bought September 9, two days before "the accident," as they say around here. The car was registered September 11, 2001, license number Z 140810. On the rear left a sticker: "D" for "Deutschland."

On that September 11 they were looking forward to Ziad's wedding, to his return to Beirut. The Mercedes was a symbol for it all.

Samir Jarrah drives along a side street, a narrow path along the edge of the village. He stops and leaves the car in front of an unplowed field. "For Ziad and Aysel," Ziad's father shouts into the drizzling rain, and laughs. He bought this land for the mansion he planned to build for his son and daughter-in-law.

No, the whole thing makes no sense, not even after talking about it for hours.

Fifth Avenue, Manhattan

The Potters are shy people. It was by chance that their picture appeared in the tabloids on September 12. After that the phone didn't stop ringing for months. Everyone wanted to interview the Potters. The Potters, however, didn't want to speak. Many of their best friends were dead. The last thing they wanted was to profit from the disaster.

They turned down everyone. Until Sabine Schenk called from *Der Spiegel*'s office in New York.

"She sounded like such a warm person, so human, so kind," says Dan Potter. He convinced his wife. The way back to September 11 was an afternoon strewn with tears, but some laughter too.

In the beginning of December the Potters bought a one-bedroom apartment in the Westchester suburb of Bronxville.

They couldn't take it any longer. Manhattan is expensive. Besides, it's filled with bad memories. Out the bedroom window of their apartment in Battery Park City, where the World Trade Center towers once stood, was a gigantic construction site—and cemetery. At night the largest ruin in the world is lit as bright as daylight. The other day Dan Potter said to his wife, "There lie the ashes of people we had dinner with a couple months ago."

The Potters' nights are still short. They go to bed at ten. Jean wakes up around midnight with disaster nightmares—cars colliding, planes crashing, bombs exploding. Dan holds her. Sometimes it takes hours before they get back to sleep. On some days, Jean has to be out the door very early. She's still working for the Bank of America, whose offices have now moved uptown on Fifth Avenue.

Dan Potter can't jump a fire rig anymore. Two of his vertebrae were dislocated on September 11 and often his left leg turns numb. He's supposed to have an operation. Half his buddies are for it, the other half emphatically against. He's afraid. He would rather retire than go into a hospital.

This decision's not an easy one. FDNY has been the family he's lived with longest, twenty-three years. The firehouses he worked in were the magical gathering places of their neighborhoods. He likes standing at the entranceways and greeting people—children, grandmas, pretty girls, would wave to him. Inside, the other guys would be sleeping, watching TV, showering, cooking. Firefighters are famous for their cooking skills. You often see them hanging out in the city's supermarkets, shopping for osso buco or Irish stew. New York firefighters are cosmopolitan when it comes to food.

Besides the sharing among friends, he'll miss the action. Action is in his blood; it lifts his spirits, and sets his adrenaline off. Action has an obvious, simple, unquestionable goal: to save people's lives, no matter what age, color, or class. Maybe American courtrooms don't treat people as equals. But when it comes to a fire, everybody's equal.

Potter will miss not belonging to this brotherhood. It incarnates the principles of America like no other—bravery, freedom, community, equality.

Not that Dan Potter says he thinks about all this. But he knows.

"I'm just a firefighter," he says, and laughs his generous laugh. Then he reveals his secret plan: to still work as a firefighter—as an instructor somewhere out in the country.

APPENDIX

The Hijackers and Their Helpers in Germany

THE PILOTS

Mohamed Atta, alias Amir, Egyptian, born in 1968, steered American Airlines Flight 11 into the North Tower of the World Trade Center. Presumed leader of the terror pilots, he studied city planning for seven years at Hamburg-Harburg Technical University, and founded an Islamic Club there in 1999. He is thought to have been in a training camp in Afghanistan in 1999.

Marwan al-Shehhi, born in 1978, from the United Arab Emirates, steered United Airlines Flight 175 into the South Tower of the World Trade Center. A trusted companion of Atta, he had been in Germany on a military scholarship since 1996. He is thought to have been in a training camp in 1999.

Ziad Jarrah, born in 1975, Lebanese, crashed with United Airlines Flight 93 into a field near Shanksville, Pennsylvania. He had been in Germany since 1996 studying airplane engineering at Hamburg Polytechnic. In 2000 and 2001 he underwent pilot training in Florida. He reported his passport missing at about the same time as al-Shehhi and Atta.

Hani Hanjour, born in 1972, a Saudi, struck the Pentagon with American Airlines Flight 77. He had been in the USA since 1996, and had a hard time getting his pilot's license.

THE MUSCLEMEN

Abdulaziz Alomari, born 1979, from Saudi Arabia
Wail Alshehri, born 1973, from Saudi Arabia
Waleed Alshehri, born 1978, from Saudi Arabia
Satam al-Süqami, born 1976, from the United Arab Emirates
Fayez Ahmed, born 1977, from Saudi Arabia
Ahmed Alghamdi, born 1979, from Saudi Arabia
Hamza Alghamdi, born 1980, from Saudi Arabia
Mohald Alshehri, born 1979, from Saudi Arabia
Salim Alhamzi, born 1981, from Saudi Arabia
Majed Moqed, born 1977, from Saudi Arabia
Ahmed al-Haznawi, born 1980, from Saudi Arabia
Ahmed Alnami, born 1977, from Saudi Arabia
Saeed Alghamdi, born 1979, from Saudi Arabia

THE LOGISTICS MEN

Khalid al-Mihdhar, born 1975, from Saudi Arabia
Nawaf Alhamzi, born 1976, from Saudi Arabia

THE HELPERS

Said Bahaji, German-Moroccan. Electronics student at Hamburg-Harburg Technical University and one of Atta's closest accomplices. Fled to Pakistan before the attack.
Ramzi Binalshibh alias Omar, Yemeni, arrived in Germany in 1995, at first under a false identity and requesting political asylum. He planned to undergo flight training in Florida, but American authorities refused him an entry visa.
Zakariya Essabar, Moroccan. 1997 in Germany, studied applied medicine. He is supposed to have become Binalshibh's replacement as pilot and applied twice for a visa but was turned down.
Habib Zacarias Moussaoui, resident of London, took flight training courses in Oklahoma, was arrested before the attacks in Minnesota on account of violations of his entry visa conditions. He is supposed to have possibly been a member of another hijacking squad. He received wire transfers of

some $15,000 from Hamburg and Düsseldorf, and was carrying the telephone number of one of the German "supporters."

Lutfi Raissi, Algerian with a French passport, was arrested in Great Britain on September 21, 2001. Raissi is supposed to have been the flight instructor who trained Hani Hanjour, the pilot who steered American Airlines Flight 77 into the Pentagon.

Chronology of the Attacks

1992

July 24: The Egyptian Mohamed Atta arrives in Germany and lives first with a teacher couple in Hamburg who have invited him to stay.

November 23: Atta begins a course of study in city planning at Hamburg-Harburg Technical University.

December 1: Atta starts a part-time job for Plankontor, a company in Hamburg (until July 1997).

December 31: Atta registers himself as residing in Hamburg.

1993

February 26: A car bomb explodes in the underground garage of the World Trade Center in New York, killing five.

July 28: Atta moves into "Am Centrumshaus," a student housing complex in Hamburg.

1994

Atta takes a trip to Istanbul, and continues on the journey to Syria.

1995

Atta takes a pilgrimage to Mecca.

August 1 to October 31: Atta in Cairo on a study program.

September 22: The Yemeni Ramzi Binalshibh arrives by

ship in Hamburg and applies for asylum in Pinneberg under the name of Ramzi Mohamed Abdellah Omar.

1996

The German-Moroccan Said Bahaji begins studies at Hamburg-Harburg Technical University.

January 17: Binalshibh's application for asylum is rejected, a decision he appeals.

April: Hani Hanjour lives with the Khalil family, in Hollywood, Florida.

April 3: The Lebanese Ziad Jarrah arrives in Germany and begins a three-month language course in Greifswald. There he comes to know his girlfriend Aysel and comes into contact with a radical Islamicist.

April 11: Atta writes his last will.

April 28: Marwan al-Shehhi arrives in Germany. Military authorities of the United Arab Emirates grant him a scholarship. He lives first in Bonn, where he spends a year learning German at the Goethe Institute.

1997

Al-Shehhi attends a course of studies in Bonn.

February 5: The Moroccan Zakariya Essabar arrives in Germany, and attends a course of studies at Anhalt/Köthen Polytechnic.

June 11: In Greifswald, Jarrah qualifies for the study of medicine.

September 30: Jarrah begins to study airplane engineering at Hamburg Polytechnic.

1998

January: Al-Shehhi switches to a course of studies in Hamburg.

February: Osama bin Laden founds the World Islamic Front for Jihad against Jews and Crusaders.

May 25: After a final rejection of his asylum claim, Binalshibh alias Omar goes underground and a warrant is issued against him.

July 16: Jarrah and Essabar take part in a work/study program at the VW plant in Wolfsburg, south of Hamburg.

July 29: Atta extends the Tunisian Béchir B. a power-of-attorney to settle all his affairs.

August 7: Bombs planted in the American embassies in Nairobi and Dar es Salaam by Osama bin Laden's Al Qaeda network cause the deaths of 263 persons and injure more than 4,500.

September 16: In Grüneck, near Munich, Mamduh Mahmud Salim, the alleged financial manager of Al Qaeda, is arrested. Investigations begin into the affairs of Hamburg businessman Mamoun Darkazanli on account of possible membership in Al Qaeda.

October 1: Essabar moves to Hamburg, where he studies applied medicine at Hamburg Polytechnic.

October 2: Found during the search of an apartment in Turin belonging to three alleged terrorists suspected of having planned attacks on American installations in Europe—weapons, munitions, and the Hamburg address of Mohamed Haydar Zammar, one of the presumed conspirators.

November 1: Atta, Bahaji and Binalshibh move into 54 Marienstrasse in the Harburg district of Hamburg.

1999

According to CIA findings, Atta visits an Al Qaeda guesthouse in Kandahar, and al-Shehhi stays in an Al Qaeda Kandahar guesthouse under the name Abu Abdallah.

January 1: Bahaji begins his German military service, but is given an early discharge on May 15 for health reasons. In mid-year he marries. Wedding guests: the suspected terrorists and their supporters; Zammar is witness.

January 27: Atta founds the Islamic Club at Hamburg-Harburg TU.

August 26: Atta turns in his thesis.

September 1: Essabar moves into 54 Marienstrasse. Al-Shehhi moves to Wilhelmstrasse, Hamburg. He registers for the winter semester at Hamburg-Harburg TU.

November to January: Jarrah disappears from Hamburg;

possibly he is on a visit to Pakistan or Afghanistan. At the end of the year Atta and al-Shehhi report their passports missing. Jarrah is not seen at Hamburg Polytechnic.

2000

January 15: Logistics men Khalid al-Mihdhar und Nawaf Alhamzi arrive in Los Angeles on a flight from Hong Kong.

February 9: At the Hamburg resident registry office, Jarrah reports his Lebanese passport, No. 1151479, missing.

February 12: Seventeen soldiers die during a suicide attack upon the destroyer USS *Cole* in Aden, Yemen.

May to August: Some $22,500 are deposited in al-Shehhi's Dresdner Bank account from the United Arab Emirates. Binalshibh repeatedly wires money from al-Shehhi's account to the hijackers, who are now in the USA.

May 29: Marwan al-Shehhi arrives in Newark, New Jersey.

May 31: Atta attempts to fly to Chechnya, but is not allowed to enter without a visa.

June 2: Atta arrives by bus—this time with a visa—in Chechnya, where he meets with an Iraqi agent.

June 3: Mohamed Atta arrives in Newark.

June 29: Ziad Jarrah arrives in Newark.

July 19 to September 18: Atta und al-Shehhi receive nearly $110,000 from the United Arab Emirates, in four installments.

July 26: Binalshibh sends 3,853 marks to al-Shehhi, in the USA.

August: Atta and al-Shehhi begin flight training at Huffmann Aviation in Venice, Florida.

September 25: Binalshibh sends 9,629 marks to al-Shehhi, in the USA.

October 24: Essabar has himself issued a new passport, though the old one is still valid.

December 12: Essabar applies for a US visa, and is rejected.

December 18: al-Shehhi is dropped from the student registry.

December 21: Atta and al-Shehhi receive their pilot licenses.

December 26: Arrest of members of the Meliani Group in Frankfurt: they had planned to attack the Christmas Fair in Strasbourg.

December 29: In Opa Locka, Florida, Atta and al-Shehhi rent six hours on a Boeing Flight Simulator and practice making turns.

2001

January 4: Atta flies from Miami to Madrid.

January 10: Atta flies from Berlin to Miami.

January 23: Zacarias Moussaoui arrives from London in the USA and without any flying background trains on a Boeing 757/400 flight simulator.

January 28: Essabar once again applies for an American visa and at the same time receives a cash deposit of 11,300 marks in his account. The visa application is denied.

March to June: The musclemen arrive: Salim Alhamzi, Majed Moqed, Hamza Alghamdi, Mohald Alshehri, Ahmed Alghamdi, Fayez Ahmed, Satam al-Süqami, Wail and Waleed M. Alshehri, Abdulaziz Alomari, Saeed Alghamdi, Ahmed al-Haznawi, Ahmed Alnami. They come in on flights to Miami, Orlando, and Washington, D.C.

April to July: Atta and al-Shehhi rent Apartment 122 in the Tara Gardens Condominium, 10001 West Atlantic Boulevard, Coral Springs, Florida.

May to September: Jarrah takes kick-boxing lessons at the US-1 Fitness Center in Dania, Florida.

April 26: Atta is stopped by a road control officer in Fort Lauderdale, Florida.

April 28: Jarrah rents himself a room at the Bimini Motel on North Ocean Drive in Hollywood, Florida, for one month.

May 2: Atta receives Florida driver's license No. A 300540-68-321-0.

June 21: In an interview with an Arab journalist Osama bin Laden warns of a major, heavy attack on American targets.

June 29: Atta travels to Las Vegas, where he meets Salim

Alhamzi and Hani Hanjour. Atta stays in the EconoLodge on Las Vegas Boulevard South.

July 5: Atta is again stopped by a traffic officer, this time in Delray Beach, Florida.

July 7: Atta flies from Miami via Zurich to Madrid, rents a car that he later returns in Barajas with 2,000 additional kilometers on the odometer. Investigators suspect that he met there with suspected Al Qaeda followers around Abu Dahdah.

July 19: Atta flies from Madrid via Berlin to Atlanta.

August 1: Moussaoui receives 23,571.59 marks from the travel bank at the Düsseldorf Central Train Station, sent by Ramzi Binalshibh. In Falls Church, Virginia, Hanjour und Khalid al-Mihdhar procure new identification papers.

August 3: Moussaoui recieves another 9,487.80 marks from Hamburg, again sent by Binalshibh.

August 13: Atta travels to Las Vegas for a second time. Again he stays in the EconoLodge.

August 16: Moussaoui is arrested in the USA for violations of entry visa conditions.

September 4: Bahaji puts up at the Hotel Embassy in Karachi.

September 5: Bahaji sends his wife an E-mail from Karachi and flies on to the Pakistani city of Quetta, near the border with Afghanistan. Binalshibh flies to Madrid via Düsseldorf.

September 6: Al-Shehhi transfers 5,000 marks to Binalshibh's account.

September 7: Atta and al-Shehhi get into a fight with a waitress at Shuckum's Bar in Hollywood, Florida.

September 8: Atta transfers $7,860 to Mustafa Ahmed Alhawsawi in the United Arab Emirates.

September 9: Al-Shehhi, Wail Alshehri, and the other hijackers check out of the Panther Motel in Deerfield Beach, Florida.

September 10: Al-Shehhi transfers $5,400 to a helper. The hijackers split up among various hotels in Boston. Atta and Alomari drive a rented car to Portland, Maine.

September 11: Atta and Alomari board a commuter flight

from Portland to Boston, where they check in with the other members of their group for American Airlines Flight 11. Jarrah and his group check in at Newark for United Flight 93. Al-Shehhi and his group check in at Boston for United Airlines Flight 175. Hanjour and his team check in at Dulles Airport for American Airlines Flight 77.

Timetables of the Hijacked Flights

AMERICAN AIRLINES FLIGHT 11 (MOHAMED ATTA & HIS GROUP)
7:59 Takeoff from Logan International Airport, Boston.
8:15 Suspected moment of hijacking.
8:28 Airplane veers sharply to the south.
8:38 Last radio contact with the cockpit.
8:45 Impact with the North Tower of the World Trade Center.

UNITED AIRLINES FLIGHT 175 (MARWAN AL-SHEHHI & HIS GROUP)
8:14 Takeoff from Logan International Airport, Boston.
8:37 Flight 175 requested by air traffic controllers to keep a lookout for American Flight 11.
8:42 The hijackers take over the airplane.
8:43 The Federal Aviation Administration declares Flight 175 hijacked.
8:50 Flight 175 changes its route in the direction of New York City.
9:03 Impact with the South Tower, WTC.

AMERICAN AIRLINES FLIGHT 77 (HANI HANJOUR & HIS GROUP)
8:20 Takeoff from Dulles International Airport, Washington.
9:00 Airplane makes a 180-degree turn and assumes course toward Washington.
9:24 The FAA announces that Flight 77 has possibly been hijacked and is heading in the direction of Washington.

9:37 Airplane disappears from radar screens.
9:38 Impact into the southwest side of the Pentagon.

UNITED AIRLINES FLIGHT 93 (ZIAD JARRAH AND HIS GROUP)

8:42 Takeoff from Newark International Airport, New Jersey.
9:00 United Airlines warns all of its aircraft of possible hijackings. Flight 93 answers: "Understood."
9:16 The FAA announces that Flight 93 has possibly been hijacked.
9:28 Passenger Jeremy Glick calls his wife and learns of the attacks on the WTC.
9:35 Airplane changes direction and assumes course toward Washington.
9:59 Todd Beamer gives the signal for the passengers to attack the hijackers: "Ready, guys? Let's roll."
10:01 Screams and curses from the cockpit, the plane zigzags in midair.
10:06 Crash near Shanksville, Pennsylvania.

Excerpts from the Terrorists' Manual

The attached manual was located by the Manchester (England) Metropolitan Police during a search of an Al Qaeda member's home. The manual was found in a computer file described as "the military series" related to the "Declaration of Jihad." The manual was translated into English and was introduced earlier this year at the embassy bombing trial in New York.

DECLARATION OF JIHAD [HOLY WAR] AGAINST THE COUNTRY'S TYRANTS MILITARY SERIES

[Emblem]: A drawing of the globe emphasizing the Middle East and Africa with a sword through the globe

[On the emblem:] Military Studies in the Jihad [Holy War] Against the Tyrants

In the name of Allah, the merciful and compassionate

PRESENTATION

To those champions who avowed the truth day and night ...... And wrote with their blood and sufferings these phrases ...

... The confrontation that we are calling for with the apostate regimes does not know Socratic debates ..., Platonic ideals ..., nor Aristotelian diplomacy. But it knows the dialogue of bullets, the ideals of assassination, bombing, and destruction, and the diplomacy of the cannon and machinegun.

... Islamic governments have never and will never be established through peaceful solutions and cooperative councils. They are established as they [always] have been by pen and gun, by word and bullet, by tongue and teeth.

In the name of Allah, the merciful and compassionate

Belongs to the guest house

Please do not remove it from the house except with permission.

[Emblem and signature, illegible]

INTRODUCTION
Martyrs were killed, women were widowed, children were orphaned, men were handcuffed, chaste women's heads were shaved, harlots' heads were crowned, atrocities were inflicted on the innocent, gifts were given to the wicked, virgins were raped on the prostitution altar ...

After the fall of our orthodox caliphates on March 3, 1924 and after expelling the colonialists, our Islamic nation was afflicted with apostate rulers who took over in the Moslem nation. These rulers turned out to be more infidel and criminal than the colonialists themselves. Moslems have endured all kinds of harm, oppression, and torture at their hands.

Those apostate rulers threw thousands of the Haraka Al-Islamyia (Islamic Movement) youth in gloomy jails and detention centers that were equipped with the most modern torture devices and [manned with] experts in oppression and torture. Those youth had refused to move in the rulers' orbit, obscure matters to the youth, and oppose the idea of rebelling against the rulers. But they [the rulers] did not stop there; they started to fragment the essence of the Islamic nation by trying to eradicate its Moslem identity. Thus, they started spreading godless and atheistic views among the youth. We found some that claimed that socialism was from Islam, democracy was the [religious] council, and the prophet—God bless and keep him—propagandized communism.

Colonialism and its followers, the apostate rulers, then started to openly erect crusader centers, societies, and organizations like Masonic Lodges, Lions and Rotary clubs, and foreign schools. They aimed at producing a wasted generation that pursued everything that is western and produced rulers, ministers, leaders, physicians, engineers, businessmen, politicians, journalists, and information specialists. [Koranic verse:] "And Allah's enemies plotted and planned, and Allah too planned, and the best of planners is Allah."

They [the rulers] tried, using every means and [kind of] seduction, to produce a generation of young men that did not know [anything] except what they [the rulers] want, did not say except what they [the rulers] think about, did not live except according to their [the rulers'] way, and did not dress except in their [the rulers'] clothes. However, majestic Allah turned their deception back on them, as a large group of those young men who were raised by them [the rulers] woke up from their sleep and returned to Allah, regretting and repenting.

The young men returning to Allah realized that Islam is not just performing rituals but a complete system: Religion and government, worship and Jihad [holy war], ethics and dealing with people, and the Koran and sword. The bitter situation that the nation has reached is a result of its divergence from Allah's course and his righteous law for all places and times. That [bitter situation] came about as a result of its children's love for the world, their loathing of death, and their abandonment of Jihad [Holy War].

Unbelief is still the same. It pushed Abou Jahl—may Allah curse him—and Kureish's valiant infidels to battle the prophet—God bless and keep him—and to torture his companions—may Allah's grace be on them. It is the same unbelief that drove Sadat, Hosni Mubarak, Gadhafi, Hafez Assad, Saleh, Fahed—Allah's curse be upon the nonbelieving leaders—and all the apostate Arab rulers to torture, kill, imprison, and torment Moslems.

These young men realized that an Islamic government would never be established except by the bomb and rifle. Islam does not coincide or make a truce with unbelief, but rather confronts it.

The confrontation that Islam calls for with these godless and apostate regimes, does not know Socratic debates, Platonic ideals nor Aristotelian diplomacy. But it knows the dialogue of bullets, the ideals of assassination, bombing, and destruction, and the diplomacy of the cannon and machinegun.

The young came to prepare themselves for Jihad [holy war], commanded by the majestic Allah's order in the holy Koran. [Koranic verse:] "Against them make ready your strength to the utmost of your power, including steeds of war, to strike terror into [the hearts of] the enemies of Allah and your enemies, and others besides whom ye may not know, but whom Allah doth know."

I present this humble effort to these young Moslem men who are pure, believing, and fighting for the cause of Allah.

It is my contribution toward paving the road that leads to majestic Allah and establishes a caliphate according to the prophecy.

According to Imam Ahmad's account, the prophet—God bless and keep him—said. . . . [a few lines of Hadith verses, not translated].

FIRST LESSON
GENERAL INTRODUCTION
Principles of Military Organization:
Military Organization has three main principles without which it cannot be established.

1. Military Organization commander and advisory council
2. The soldiers (individual members)
3. A clearly defined strategy

Military Organization Requirements:
The Military Organization dictates a number of requirements to assist it in confrontation and endurance. These are:

1. Forged documents and counterfeit currency
2. Apartments and hiding places
3. Communication means
4. Transportation means
5. Information
6. Arms and ammunition
7. Transport

Missions Required of the Military Organization:
The main mission for which the Military Organization is responsible is: The overthrow of the godless regimes and their replacement with an Islamic regime. Other missions consist of the following:

1. Gathering information about the enemy, the land, the installations, and the neighbors.
2. Kidnaping enemy personnel, documents, secrets, and arms.

3. Assassinating enemy personnel as well as foreign tourists.
4. Freeing the brothers who are captured by the enemy.
5. Spreading rumors and writing statements that instigate people against the enemy.
6. Blasting and destroying the places of amusement, immorality, and sin; not a vital target.
7. Blasting and destroying the embassies and attacking vital economic centers.
8. Blasting and destroying bridges leading into and out of the cities.

Importance of the Military Organization:
1. Removal of those personalities that block the call's path. [A different handwriting:] All types of military and civilian intellectuals and thinkers for the state.
2. Proper utilization of the individuals' unused capabilities.
3. Precision in performing tasks, and using collective views on completing a job from all aspects, not just one.
4. Controlling the work and not fragmenting it or deviating from it.
5. Achieving long-term goals such as the establishment of an Islamic state and short-term goals such as operations against enemy individuals and sectors.
6. Establishing the conditions for possible confrontation with the regressive regimes and their persistence.
7. Achieving discipline in secrecy and through tasks.

SECOND LESSON
NECESSARY QUALIFICATIONS AND
CHARACTERISTICS
FOR THE ORGANIZATION'S MEMBERS
   1. Islam: The member of the Organization must be Moslem. How can an unbeliever, someone from a revealed

religion [Christian, Jew], a secular person, a communist, etc. protect Islam and Moslems and defend their goals and secrets when he does not believe in that religion [Islam]? The Israeli Army requires that a fighter be of the Jewish religion. Likewise, the command leadership in the Afghan and Russian armies requires any one with an officer's position to be a member of the communist party.

2. Commitment to the Organization's Ideology: This commitment frees the Organization's members from conceptional problems.

3. Maturity: The requirements of military work are numerous, and a minor cannot perform them. The nature of hard and continuous work in dangerous conditions requires a great deal of psychological, mental, and intellectual fitness, which are not usually found in a minor. It is reported that Ibn Omar—may Allah be pleased with him—said, "During Ahad [battle] when I was fourteen years of age, I was submitted [as a volunteer] to the prophet—God bless and keep him. He refused me and did not throw me in the battle. During Khandak [trench] Day [battle] when I was fifteen years of age, I was also submitted to him, and he permitted me [to fight].

4. Sacrifice: He [the member] has to be willing to do the work and undergo martyrdom for the purpose of achieving the goal and establishing the religion of majestic Allah on earth.

5. Listening and Obedience: In the military, this is known today as discipline. It is expressed by how the member obeys the orders given to him. That is what our religion urges. The Glorious says, "O, ye who believe! Obey Allah and obey the messenger and those charged with authority among you." In the story of Hazifa Ben Al-Yaman—may Allah have mercy on him—who was exemplary in his obedience to Allah's messenger—Allah bless and keep him. When he [Mohammed]—Allah bless and keep him—sent him to spy on the Kureish and their allies during their siege of Madina, Hazifa said, "As he [Mohammed] called me by name to stand, he said, 'Go get me information about those people and do not alarm them about me.' As I departed, I saw Abou Soufian and I placed an arrow in the bow. I [then] remembered the words of the messenger—Allah bless and keep him—do not alarm them about me. If I had shot I would have hit him."

6. Keeping Secrets and Concealing Information: [This secrecy should be used] even with the closest people, for deceiving the enemies is not easy. Allah says, "Even though their plots were such that as to shake the hills! [Koranic verse]." Allah's messenger—God bless and keep him—says, "Seek Allah's help in doing your affairs in secrecy."

It was said in the proverbs, "The hearts of freemen are the tombs of secrets" and "Moslems' secrecy is faithfulness, and talking about it is faithlessness." [Mohammed]—God bless and keep him—used to keep work secrets from the closest people, even from his wife A'isha—may Allah's grace be on her.

7. Free of Illness: The Military Organization's member must fulfill this important requirement. Allah says, "There is no blame for those who are infirm, or ill, or who have no resources to spend."

8. Patience: [The member] should have plenty of patience for [enduring] afflictions if he is overcome by the enemies. He should not abandon this great path and sell himself and his religion to the enemies for his freedom. He should be patient in performing the work, even if it lasts a long time.

9. Tranquility and "Unflappability": [The member] should have a calm personality that allows him to endure psychological traumas such as those involving bloodshed, murder, arrest, imprisonment, and reverse psychological traumas such as killing one or all of his Organization's comrades. [He should be able] to carry out the work.

10. Intelligence and Insight: When the prophet—Allah bless and keep him—sent Hazifa Ben Al-Yaman to spy on the polytheist and [Hafiza] sat among them, Abou Soufian said, "Let each one of you look at his companion." Hazifa said to his companion, "Who are you?" The companion replied, "So-and-so son of so-and-so." In World War II, the German spy, Julius Seelber [PH] managed to enter Britain and work as a mail examiner due to the many languages he had mastered. From the letters, he succeeded in obtaining important information and sent it to the Germans. One of the letters that he checked was from a lady who had written to her brother's friend in the fleet. She mentioned that her brother used to live with her until he was transferred to a secret project that involved commercial ships. When Seelber read that letter, he went to meet that young woman and blamed her for her loose tongue in talking about military secrets. He, skillfully, managed to draw out of her that her brother worked in a secret project for arming old commercial ships. These ships were to be used as decoys in the submarine war in such a way that they could come close to the submarines, as they appeared innocent. Suddenly, cannonballs would be fired from the ships' hidden cannons on top of the ships, which would destroy the submarines. 48 hours later that secret was handed to the Germans.

11. Caution and Prudence: In his battle against the king of Tomedia [PH], the Roman general Speer [PH] sent an emissary to discuss with that king the matter of truce between the two armies. In reality, he had sent him to learn about the Tomedians' ability to fight. The general picked Lilius [PH], one of his top commanders, for that task and sent with him some of his officers, disguised as slaves. During that mission, one of the king's officers, Sifax [PH] pointed to one of the [disguised] slaves and yelled. "That slave is a Roman officer I had met in a neighboring city. He was wearing a Roman uniform." At that point, Lilius used a clever trick and managed to divert the attention of the Tomedians from that by turning to the disguised officer and quickly slapping him on the face a number of times. He reprimanded him for wearing a Roman officer's uniform when he was a slave and for claiming a status that he did not deserve.

The officer accepted the slaps quietly. He bowed his head in humility and shame, as slaves do. Thus, Sifax's men thought that officer was really a slave because they could not imagine that a Roman officer would accept these hits without defending himself.

King Sifax prepared a big feast for Lilius and his entourage and placed them in a house far away from his camp so they could not learn about his fortifications. They [the Romans] made another clever trick on top of the first one. They freed one of their horses and started chasing him in and around the camp. After they learned about the extent of the fortifications they caught the horse and, as planned, managed to abort their mission about the truce agreement. Shortly after their return, the Roman general attacked King Sifax's camp and burned the fortifications. Sifax was forced to seek reconciliation.

B. There was a secret agent who disguised himself as an American fur merchant. As the agent was playing cards aboard a boat with some passengers, one of the players asked him about his profession. He replied that he was a "fur merchant." The women showed interest [in him] and began asking the agent—the disguised fur merchant—many questions about the types and prices of fur. He mentioned fur price figures that amazed the women. They started avoiding and regarding him with suspicion, as though he were a thief, or crazy.

12. Truthfulness and Counsel: The Commander of the faithful, Omar Ibn Al-Khattab—may Allah be pleased with him—asserted that this characteristic was vital in those who gather information and work as spies against the Moslems' enemies. He [Omar] sent a letter to Saad Ibn Abou Wakkas—may Allah be pleased with him—saying, "If you step foot on your enemies' land, get spies on them. Choose those whom you count on for their truthfulness and advice, whether Arabs or inhabitants of that land. Liars' accounts would not benefit you, even if some of them were true; the deceiver is a spy against you and not for you.

13. Ability to Observe and Analyze: The Israeli Mossad received news that some Palestinians were going to attack an Israeli El Al airplane. That plane was going to Rome with Golda Meir—Allah's curse upon her—the Prime Minister at the time, on board. The Palestinians had managed to use a clever trick that allowed them to wait for the arrival of the plane without being questioned by anyone. They had beaten a man who sold potatoes, kidnaped him, and hidden him. They made two holes in the top of that peddler's cart and placed two tubes next to the chimney through which two Russian-made "Strella" [PH] missiles could be launched. The Mossad officers traveled the airport back and forth looking for that lead to the Palestinians. One officer passed the potato cart twice without noticing anything. On his third time, he noticed three chimneys, but only one of them was working with smoke coming out of it. He quickly steered toward the cart and hit it hard. The cart overturned, and the Palestinians were captured.[1]

14. Ability to Act, Change Positions and Conceal Oneself:

a. [An example] is what Noaim Ibn Masoud had done in his mission to cause agitation among the tribes of Koraish, those of Ghatfan, and the Jews of Koreitha. He would control his reactions and managed to skillfully play his role. Without showing signs of inconsistency, he would show his interest and zeal towards the Jews one time and show his concern about the Koraish at another.

b. In 1960, a car driven by an American colonel collided with a truck. The colonel lost consciousness, and while unconscious at the hospital, he started speaking Russian fluently. It was later discovered that the colonel was a Soviet spy who was planted in the United States. He had fought in Korea in order to conceal his true identity and to gather information and critical secrets. If not for the collision, no one would have suspected or confronted him.

[1]This story is found in the book *A'n Tarik Al-Khida' (By Way of Deception Methods)* by Victor Ostrovsky [PH]. The author claims that the Mossad wants to kill him for writing that book. However, I believe that the book was authorized by the Israeli Mossad.

THIRD LESSON
COUNTERFEIT CURRENCY AND FORGED DOCUMENTS

Financial Security Precautions:

1. Dividing operational funds into two parts: One part is to be invested in projects that offer financial return, and the other is to be saved and not spent except during operations.
2. Not placing operational funds [all] in one place.
3. Not telling the Organization members about the location of the funds.
4. Having proper protection while carrying large amounts of money.
5. Leaving the money with non-members and spending it as needed.

Forged Documents (Identity Cards, Record Books, Passports)

The following security precautions should be taken:

1. Keeping the passport in a safe place so it would not be seized by the security apparatus, and the brother it belongs to would have to negotiate its return (I'll give you your passport if you give me information).
2. All documents of the undercover brother, such as identity cards and passport, should be falsified.
3. When the undercover brother is traveling with a certain identity card or passport, he should know all pertinent [information] such as the name, profession, and place of residence.
4. The brother who has special work status (commander, communication link, ...) should have more than one identity card and passport. He should learn the contents of each, the nature of the [indicated] profession, and the dialect of the residence area listed in the document.
5. The photograph of the brother in these documents

should be without a beard. It is preferable that the brother's public photograph [on these documents] be also without a beard. If he already has one [document] showing a photograph with a beard, he should replace it.

6. When using an identity document in different names, no more than one such document should be carried at one time.

7. The validity of the falsified travel documents should always be confirmed.

8. All falsification matters should be carried out through the command and not haphazardly (procedure control).

9. Married brothers should not add their wives to their passports.

10. When a brother is carrying the forged passport of a certain country, he should not travel to that country. It is easy to detect forgery at the airport, and the dialect of the brother is different from that of the people from that country.

Security Precautions Related to the Organizations' Given Names:

1. The name given by the Organization [to the brother] should not be odd in comparison with other names used around him.

2. A brother should not have more than one name in the area where he lives (the undercover work place).

FOURTH LESSON
ORGANIZATION MILITARY BASES
"APARTMENTS — HIDING PLACES"
Definition of Bases:
*These are apartments, hiding places, command centers, etc. in which secret operations are executed against the enemy.

These bases may be in cities, and are [then] called homes or apartments. They may be in mountainous, harsh terrain far from the enemy, and are [then] called hiding places or bases.

During the initial stages, the Military Organization usually uses apartments in cities as places for launching assigned missions, such as collecting information, observing members of the ruling regime, etc.

Hiding places and bases in mountains and harsh terrain are used at later stages, from which Jihad [holy war] groups are dispatched to execute assassination operations of enemy individuals, bomb their centers, and capture their weapons. In some Arab countries such as Egypt, where there are no mountains or harsh terrain, all stages of Jihad work would take place in cities. The opposite was true in Afghanistan, where initially Jihad work was in the cities, then the warriors shifted to mountains and harsh terrain. There, they started battling the Communists.

Security Precautions Related to Apartments:

1. Choosing the apartment carefully as far as the location, the size for the work necessary (meetings, storage, arms, fugitives, work preparation).
2. It is preferable to rent apartments on the ground floor to facilitate escape and digging of trenches.
3. Preparing secret locations in the apartment for securing documents, records, arms, and other important items.
4. Preparing ways of vacating the apartment in case of a surprise attack (stands, wooden ladders).
5. Under no circumstances should any one know about the apartment except those who use it.
6. Providing the necessary cover for the people who frequent the apartment (students, workers, employees, etc.)
7. Avoiding seclusion and isolation from the population and refraining from going to the apartment at suspicious times.
8. It is preferable to rent these apartments using false

names, appropriate cover, and non-Moslem appearance.

9. A single brother should not rent more than one apartment in the same area, from the same agent, or using the same rental office.

10. Care should be exercised not to rent apartments that are known to the security apparatus [such as] those used for immoral or prior Jihad activities.

11. Avoiding police stations and government buildings. Apartments should not be rented near those places.

12. When renting these apartments, one should avoid isolated or deserted locations so the enemy would not be able to catch those living there easily.

13. It is preferable to rent apartments in newly developed areas where people do not know one another. Usually, in older quarters people know one another and strangers are easily identified, especially since these quarters have many informers.

14. Ensuring that there has been no surveillance prior to the members entering the apartment.

15. Agreement among those living in the apartment on special ways of knocking on the door and special signs prior to entry into the building's main gate to indicate to those who wish to enter that the place is safe and not being monitored. Such signs include hanging out a towel, opening a curtain, placing a cushion in a special way, etc.

16. If there is a telephone in the apartment, calls should be answered in an agreed-upon manner among those who use the apartment. That would prevent mistakes that would, otherwise, lead to revealing the names and nature of the occupants.

17. For apartments, replacing the locks and keys with new ones. As for the other entities (camps, shops, mosques), appropriate security precautions should be taken depending on the entity's importance and role in the work.

18. Apartments used for undercover work should not be visible from higher apartments in order not to expose the nature of the work.

19. In a newer apartment, avoid talking loud because prefabricated ceilings and walls [used in the apartments] do not have the same thickness as those in old ones.

20. It is necessary to have at hand documents supporting the undercover [member]. In the case of a physician, there should be an actual medical diploma, membership in the [medical] union, the government permit, and the rest of the routine procedures known in that country.

21. The cover should blend well [with the environment]. For example, selecting a doctor's clinic in an area where there are clinics, or in a location suitable for it.

22. The cover of those who frequent the location should match the cover of that location. For example, a common laborer should not enter a fancy hotel because that would be suspicious and draw attention.

FIFTH LESSON
MEANS OF COMMUNICATION AND TRANSPORTATION

In the name of Allah, the merciful and compassionate

Means of Transportation

Introduction:
It is well known that in undercover operations, communication is the mainstay of the movement for rapid accomplishment. However, it is a double-edged sword: It can be to our advantage if we use it well and it can be a knife dug into our back if we do not consider and take the necessary security measures.

Communication Means:

The Military Organization in any Islamic group can, with its modest capabilities, use the following means: 1. The telephone, 2. Meeting in-person, 3. Messenger, 4. Letters, 5. Some modern devices, such as the facsimile and wireless [communication].

Communication may be within the county, state, or even the country, in which case it is called local communication. When it extends expanded between countries, it is then called international communication.

Secret Communication Is Limited to the Following Types: Common, standby, alarm.

1. *Common Communication:* It is a communication between two members of the Organization without being monitored by the security apparatus opposing the Organization. The common communication should be done under a certain cover and after inspecting the surveillance situation [by the enemy].

2. *Standby Communication:* This replaces common communication when one of the two parties is unable to communicate with the other for some reason.

3. *Alarm Communication:* This is used when the opposing security apparatus discovers an undercover activity or some undercover members. Based on this communication, the activity is stopped for a while, all matters related to the activity are abandoned, and the Organization's members are hidden from the security personnel.

Method of Communication Among Members of the Organization:

1. Communication about undercover activity should be

[2]Cell or cluster methods should be adopted by the Organization. It should be composed of many cells whose members do not know one another, so that if a cell member is caught the other cells would not be affected, and work would proceed normally.

done using a good cover; it should also be quick, explicit, and pertinent. That is, just for talking only.

2. Prior to contacting his members, the commander of the cell[2] should agree with each of them separately (the cell members should never meet all in one place and should not know one another) on a manner and means of communication with each other. Likewise, the chief of the Organization should [use a similar technique] with the branch commanders.

3. A higher-ranking commander determines the type and method of communication with lower-ranking leaders.

First Means: The Telephone: Because of significant technological advances, security measures for monitoring the telephone and broadcasting equipment have increased. Monitoring may be done by installing a secondary line or wireless broadcasting device on a telephone that relays the calls to a remote location . . . That is why the Organization takes security measures among its members who use this means of communication (the telephone).

1. Communication should be carried out from public places. One should select telephones that are less suspicious to the security apparatus and are more difficult to monitor. It is preferable to use telephones in booths and on main streets.

Second Means: Meeting in-person: This is direct communication between the commander and a member of the Organization. During the meeting the following are accomplished: 1. Information exchange, 2. Giving orders and instructions, 3. Financing, 4. Member follow-up.

Stages of the In-Person Meeting: A. Before the meeting, B. The meeting [itself], C. After the meeting

A. *Before the Meeting:*
   The following measures should be taken:
   1. Designating the meeting location, 2. Finding a proper cover for the meeting, 3. Specifying the meeting date and time, 4. Defining special signals between those who meet.

1. Identifying the meeting location: If the meeting location is stationary, the following matters should be observed:
   i. The location should be far from police stations and security centers.
   ii. Ease of transportation to the location.
   iii. Selecting the location prior to the meeting and learning all its details.
   iv. If the meeting location is an apartment, it should not be the first one, but one somewhere in the middle.
   v. The availability of many roads leading to the meeting location. That would provide easy escape in case the location were raided by security personnel.
   vi. The location should not be under suspicion (by the security [apparatus]).
   vii. The apartment where the meeting takes place should be on the ground floor, to facilitate escape.
   viii. The ability to detect any surveillance from that location.
   ix. When public transportation is used, one should alight at some distance from the meeting location and continue on foot. In the case of a private vehicle, one should park it far away or in a secure place so as to be able to maneuver it quickly at any time.

   If the meeting location is not stationary, the following matters should be observed:
   i. The meeting location should be at the intersection of a large number of main and side streets to facilitate entry, exit, and escape.
   ii. The meeting location (such as a coffee shop) should not have members that might be dealing with the security apparatus.
   iii. The meeting should not be held in a crowded place because that would allow the security personnel to hide and monitor those who meet.

iv. It is imperative to agree on an alternative location for the meeting in case meeting in the first is unfeasible. That holds whether the meeting place is stationary or not.

Those who meet in-person should do the following:

i. Verifying the security situation of the location before the meeting.

ii. Ensuring that there are no security personnel behind them or at the meeting place.

iii. Not heading to the location directly.

iv. Clothing and appearance should be appropriate for the meeting location.

v. Verifying that private documents carried by the brother have appropriate cover.

vi. Prior to the meeting, designing a security plan that specifies what the security personnel would be told in case the location were raided by them, and what [the brothers] would resort to in dealing with the security personnel (fleeing, driving back, . . .)

2. *Finding a proper cover for the meeting:* [The cover]

i. should blend well with the nature of the location.

ii. In case they raid the place, the security personnel should believe the cover.

iii. should not arouse the curiosity of those present.

iv. should match the person's appearance and his financial and educational background.

v. should have documents that support it.

vi. provide reasons for the two parties' meeting (for example, one of the two parties should have proof that he is an architect. The other should have documents as proof that he is a land owner. The architect has produced a construction plan for the land.)

3. *Specifying the Meeting Date and Time:*

i. Specifying the hour of the meeting as well as the date.

ii. Specifying the time of both parties' arrival and

the time of the first party's departure.
  iii. Specifying how long the meeting will last.
  iv. Specifying an alternative date and time.
   v. Not allowing a long period of time between making the meeting arrangements and the meeting itself.
4. Designating special signals between those who meet: If the two individuals meeting know one another's shape and appearance, it is sufficient to use a single safety sign. [In that case,] the sitting and arriving individuals inform each other that there is no enemy surveillance. The sign may be keys, beads, a newspaper, or a scarf. The two parties would agree on moving it in a special way so as not to attract the attention of those present.

If the two individuals do not know one another, they should do the following:
a. The initial sign for becoming acquainted may be that both of them wear a certain type of clothing or carry a certain item. These signs should be appropriate for the place, easily identified, and meet the purpose. The initial sign for becoming acquainted does not [fully] identify one person by another. It does that at a rate of 30%.
b. Safety Signal: It is given by the individual sitting in the meeting location to inform the second individual that the place is safe. The second person would reply through signals to inform the first that he is not being monitored. The signals are agreed upon previously and should not cause suspicion.
c. A second signal for getting acquainted is one in which the arriving person uses while sitting down. That signal may be a certain clause, a word, a sentence, or a gesture agreed upon previously, and should not cause suspicion for those who hear it or see it.

B. *The Stage of the Meeting [itself]:* The following measures should be taken:
  1. Caution during the meeting.
  2. Not acting unnaturally during the meeting in order not to raise suspicion.
  3. Not talking with either loud or very low voices ([should be] moderate).
  4. Not writing anything that has to do with the meeting.
  5. Agreeing on a security plan in case the enemy raids the location.
C. *After the Meeting:* The following measures should be taken:
  1. Not departing together, but each one separately.
  2. Not heading directly to the main road but through secondary ones.
  3. Not leaving anything in the meeting place that might indicate the identity or nature of those who met.

Meeting in-person has disadvantages, such as:
  1. Allowing the enemy to capture those who are meeting.
  2. Allowing them [the enemy] to take pictures of those who are meeting, record their conversation, and gather evidence against them.
  3. Revealing the appearance of the commander to the other person. However, that may be avoided by taking the previously mentioned measures such as disguising himself well and changing his appearance (glasses, wig, etc.)

Third Means: The Messenger: This is an intermediary between the sender and the receiver. The messenger should possess all characteristics mentioned in the first chapter regarding the Military Organization's member.

These are the security measures that a messenger should take:
  1. Knowledge of the person to whom he will deliver the message.
  2. Agreement on special signals, exact date, and specific time.

3. Selecting a public street or place that does not raise suspicion.
4. Going through a secondary road that does not have check points.
5. Using public transportation (train, bus, . . .) and disembarking before the main station. Likewise, embarking should not be done at the main station either, where there are a lot of security personnel and informants.
6. Complete knowledge of the location to which he is going.

Fourth Means: Letters: This means (letters) may be used as a method of communication between members and the Organization provided that the following security measures are taken:

1. It is forbidden to write any secret information in the letter. If one must do so, the writing should be done in general terms.
2. The letter should not be mailed from a post office close to the sender's residence, but from a distant one.
3. The letter should not be sent directly to the receiver's address but to an inconspicuous location where there are many workers from your country. Afterwards, the letter will be forwarded to the intended receiver. (This is regarding the overseas-bound letter).
4. The sender's name and address on the envelope should be fictitious. In case the letters and their contents are discovered, the security apparatus would not be able to determine his [the sender's] name and address.
5. The envelope should not be transparent so as to reveal the letter inside.
6. The enclosed pages should not be many, so as not to raise suspicion.
7. The receiver's address should be written clearly so that the letter would not be returned.
8. Paying the post office box fees should not be forgotten.

Fifth Means: Facsimile and Wireless: Considering its modest capabilities and the pursuit by the security apparatus of its members and forces, the Islamic Military Organization cannot obtain these devices. In case the Organization is able to obtain them, firm security measures should be taken to secure communication between the members in the country and the command outside. These measures are:

1. The duration of transmission should not exceed five minutes in order to prevent the enemy from pinpointing the device location.
2. The device should be placed in a location with high wireless frequency, such as close to a TV station, embassies, and consulates in order to prevent the enemy from identifying its location.
3. The brother, using the wireless device to contact his command outside the country, should disguise his voice.
4. The time of communication should be carefully specified.
5. The frequency should be changed from time to time.
6. The device should be frequently moved from one location to another.
7. Do not reveal your location to the entity for which you report.
8. The conversation should be in general terms so as not to raise suspicion.

Transportation Means:

The members of the Organization may move from one location to another using one of the following means: a. Public transportation; b. Private transportation.

Security Measures that Should Be Observed in Public Transportation:

1. One should select public transportation that is not subject to frequent checking along the way, such as crowded trains or public buses.
2. Boarding should be done at a secondary station, as main stations undergo more careful surveillance.

Likewise, embarkment should not be done at main stations.

3. The cover should match the general appearance (tourist bus, first-class train, second-class train, etc).

4. The existence of documents supporting the cover.

5. Placing important luggage among the passengers' luggage without identifying the one who placed it. If it is discovered, its owner would not be arrested. In trains, it [the luggage] should be placed in a different car than that of its owner.

6. The brother traveling on a "special mission" should not get involved in religious issues (advocating good and denouncing evil) or day-to-day matters (seat reservation, . . .).

7. The brother traveling on a mission should not arrive in the [destination] country at night because then travelers are few, and there are [search] parties and check points along the way.

8. When cabs are used, conversation of any kind should not be started with the driver because many cab drivers work for the security apparatus.

9. The brother should exercise extreme caution and apply all security measures to the members.

SIXTH LESSON
TRAINING
*The following security precautions should be taken during the training:

The Place:

The place should have the following specifications:

1. Distance from the populated areas with the availability of living necessities.

2. Availability of medical services during the training.

3. The place should be suitable for the type of training (physical fitness, shooting, tactics).

4. No one except the trainers and trainees should know about the place.
5. The place should have many roads and entrances.
6. The place should be visited at suitable times.
7. Hiding any training traces immediately after the training.
8. Guarding the place during the training.
9. Appropriateness of the existing facilities for the number of training members.
10. Exclusion of anyone who is not connected with the training.
11. Taking all security measures regarding the establishment.
12. Distance of the place from police stations, public establishments, and the eyes of informants.
13. The place should not be situated in such a way that the training and trainees can be seen from another location.

The Trainees:
1. Before proceeding to the training place, all security measures connected with an undercover individual should be taken. Meanwhile, during training at the place, personnel safety should be ensured.
2. Selecting the trainees carefully.
3. The trainees should not know one another.
4. The small size of groups that should be together during the training (7–10 individuals).
5. The trainees should not know the training place.
6. Establishing a training plan for each trainee.

The Trainers:
All measures taken with regard to the commanders apply also to the trainers. Also, the following should be applied:
1. Fewness of the trainers in the training place. Only those conducting the training should be there, in order not to subject the training team to the risk of security exposure.

2. Not revealing the identity of the trainer to trainees.
3. Keeping a small ratio of trainees to trainer.
4. The training team members should not know one another.

SEVENTH LESSON
WEAPONS:
MEASURES RELATED TO BUYING AND
TRANSPORTING THEM

Prior to dealing with weapons, whether buying, transporting, or storing them, it is essential to establish a careful, systematic and firm security plan that plan deals with all stages. It is necessary to divide that task into stages: First Stage: Prior to Purchase; Second Stage: Purchasing; Third Stage: Transport; Fourth Stage: Storage.

1. *Prior to Purchase Stage:* It is necessary to take the following measures:
   a. In-depth knowledge of the place where weapons will be purchased, together with its entrances and exits.
   b. Verifying there are no informants or security personnel at the place where purchasing will take place.
   c. The place should be far from police stations and government establishments.
   d. Not proceeding to the purchasing place directly by the main road, but on secondary streets.
   e. Performing the exercises to detect the surveillance.
   f. One's appearance and clothing should be appropriate for the place where purchasing will take place.
   g. The purchasing place should not be situated in such a way that the seller and buyer can be seen from another location. To the contrary, the purchasing place should be such that the seller and buyer can see the surrounding area.
   h. Determining a suitable cover for being in that place.
   i. The place should not be crowded because that would facilitate the police hiding among people, monitoring the arms receiving, and consequently arresting the brother purchasing.

 j. In case one of the parties is unable to arrive, it is essential to prearrange an alternative place and time with the seller.

 k. Selecting a time suitable for the purchase so that it does not raise suspicion.

 l. Prior to purchasing, the seller should be tested to ensure that he is not an agent of the security apparatus.

 m. Preparing a place for storage prior to purchasing.

2. *The Purchase Stage:*

 a. Verifying that the weapons are in working condition.

 b. Not paying the seller the price for the weapons before viewing, inspecting, and testing them.

 c. Not telling the seller about the mission for which the weapons are being purchased.

 d. Extreme caution should be used during the purchasing operation in the event of any unnatural behavior by the seller or those around you.

 e. Not lengthening the time spent with the seller. It is important to depart immediately after purchasing the weapons.

3. *The Transport Stage:*

 a. Avoid main roads where check points are common.

 b. Choose a suitable time for transporting the weapons.

 c. Observers should proceed on the road ahead of the transportation vehicle for early warning in case of an emergency.

 d. Not proceeding directly to the storage place until after verifying there is no surveillance.

 e. During the transport stage, weapons should be hidden in a way that they are inconspicuous and difficult to find.

 f. The route for transporting the weapons should be determined very carefully.

 g. Verifying the legality of the vehicle, performing its maintenance, checking its gasoline and water levels, etc.

 h. Driving the car normally in order to prevent accidents.

EIGHTH LESSON
MEMBER SAFETY

Defining Members' Safety:

This is a set of measures taken by members who perform undercover missions in order to prevent the enemies from getting to them.

It is necessary for any party that adopts Jihad work and has many members to subdivide its members into three groups, each of which has its own security measures. The three groups are: 1. The overt member; 2. The covert member; 3. The commander.

Measures that Should Be Taken by the Overt Member:

1. He should not be curious and inquisitive about matters that do not concern him.
2. He should not be chatty and talkative about everything he knows or hears.
3. He should not carry on him the names and addresses of those members he knows. If he has to, he should keep them safe.
4. During times of security concerns and arrest campaigns and especially if his appearance is Islamic, he should reduce his visits to the areas of trouble and remain at home instead.
5. When conversing on the telephone, he should not talk about any information that might be of use to the enemy.
6. When sending letters, he should not mention any information that might be of use to the enemy. When receiving letters, he should burn them immediately after reading them and pour water on them to prevent the enemy from reading them. Further, he should destroy any traces of fire so the enemy would not find out that something was burned.

Measures that Should Be Taken by the Undercover Member:

In addition to the above measures, the member should . . .

1. Not reveal his true name to the Organization's members who are working with him, nor to the [Islamic] Da'wa [Call].

2. Have a general appearance that does not indicate Islamic orientation (beard, toothpick, book, [long] shirt, small Koran).

3. Be careful not to mention the brothers' common expressions or show their behaviors (special praying appearance, "may Allah reward you," "peace be on you" while arriving and departing, etc.)

4. Avoid visiting famous Islamic places (mosques, libraries, Islamic fairs, etc.)

5. Carry falsified personal documents and know all the information they contain.

6. Have protection preceding his visit to any place while moving about (apartment, province, means of transportation, etc.).

7. Have complete and accurate knowledge of the security status related to those around him in his place of work and residence, so that no danger or harm would catch him unaware.

8. Maintain his family and neighborhood relationships and should not show any changes towards them so that they would not attempt to bring him back [from the Organization] for security reasons.

9. Not resort to utilizing letters and messengers except in an emergency.

10. Not speak loudly.

11. Not get involved in advocating good and denouncing evil in order not to attract attention to himself.

12. Break the daily routine, especially when performing an undercover mission. For example, changing the departure and return routes, arrival and

departure times, and the store where he buys his goods.

13. Not causing any trouble in the neighborhood where he lives or at the place of work.

14. Converse on the telephone using special code so that he does not attract attention.

15. Not contracting the overt members except when necessary. Such contacts should be brief.

16. Not fall into the enemy's excitement trap, either through praising or criticizing his Organization.

17. Performing the exercises to detect surveillance whenever a task is to be performed.

18. Not park in no-parking zones and not take photographs where it is forbidden.

19. Closing all that should be closed before departing the place, whether at home or his place of undercover work.

20. Not undergo a sudden change in his daily routine or any relationships that precede his Jihad involvement. For example, there should not be an obvious change in his habits of conversing, movement, presence, or disappearance. Likewise, he should not be hasty to sever his previous relationships.

21. Not meet in places where there are informers, such as coffee shops, and not live in areas close to the residences of important personalities, government establishments, and police stations.

22. Not write down on any media, specially on paper, that could show the traces and words of the pen by rubbing the paper with lead powder.

Measures that Should Be Taken by the Commander:

*The commander, whether in overt or covert work, has special importance for the following reasons:

1. The large amount of information that he possesses.

2. The difficulty of the command in replacing the commander.
3. Therefore, all previously mentioned security precautions regarding members should be heightened for the commander. Many resources should be reserved for protecting the commanders.

*Important Note: Married brothers should observe the following:
1. Not talking with their wives about Jihad work.
2. The members with security risks should not travel with their wives. A wife with an Islamic appearance (veil) attracts attention.

NINTH LESSON
SECURITY PLAN
Defining Security Plan:

This is a set of coordinated, cohesive, and integrated measures that are related to a certain activity and designed to confuse and surprise the enemy, and if uncovered, to minimize the work loss as much as possible.

Importance of the Security Plan:

The work will be successful if Allah grants that. The more solid is the security plan, the more successful [the work] and the fewer the losses. The less solid the security plan, the less successful [the work] and the greater the losses.

Specifications of the Security Policy: A number of conditions should be satisfied to help the security plan to succeed. These are: [It should be]

A. realistic and based on fact so it would be credible to the enemy before and after the work.

B. coordinated, integrated, cohesive, and accurate, without any gaps, to provide the enemy [the impression of] a continuous and linked chain of events.

C. simple so that the members can assimilate it.

D. creative.

E. flexible.

F. secretive.

The Method of Implementing the Security Plan: There should be a security plan for each activity that is subject to being uncovered by the enemy. For example, the brother who is charged with a certain mission might be arrested. It is, therefore, essential that a security plan be designed for him through which he will be able to deny any accusation. Likewise, for the group assigned a collective mission, there should be a security plan to which all members are committed. Each member would then find out, learn, and be trained in his role to ensure his assimilation of it.

In this lesson, we shall cover many examples of security plans related to certain matters: 1. Security plan for an individual mission. 2. Security plan for a group (important meeting). 3. Security plan for a group mission (assassination operation).

1. *Example of a security plan for an individual mission* (training in Afghanistan):

Prior to Departure: Traveling through an airport, the brother might be subjected to interrogation. It is essential that he be taught the answers to the following anticipated questions:

A. What are the reasons for your travel?

B. How did you get the money for travel?

C. How long is the travel period?

D. Who will meet you in the arrival country?

E. What will you be doing in the arrival country?

(There are different degrees of interrogation)

During Travel (transit country): The brother should be taught the answers to the following questions:

A. Why are you going to Pakistan?

B. Do you belong to any religious organizations?

C. How did you get the travel money?

D. Who got you the visa to Pakistan?

E. What will you be doing in Pakistan?

F. With whom will you be staying in Pakistan?

Arrival Country (Pakistan): The brother should be taught the answers to the following questions:

A. Why did you come to Pakistan?
B. How long will you be spending in Pakistan?
C. With whom will you be staying?

ELEVENTH LESSON
ESPIONAGE
(I) INFORMATION-GATHERING USING OPEN METHODS
Definition of Espionage[5]:

It is the covert search for and examination of the enemy's news and information for the purpose of using them when a plan is devised. In [the book titled] "Nile Al-Aoutar wa Fath Al-Bari," [it is said that] the spy is called an eye because his work is through his eyes, or because of his excessive preoccupation with observation, as if all his being is an eye.

Espionage in the era of the prophet—Allah bless and keep him— and his honored companions: The prophet—Allah bless and keep him—used informants in most of his attacks. As Abou Soufian's caravan, that was coming from Damascus, was approaching, the prophet—Allah bless and keep him—wanted to know the caravan's destination. While the prophet was in Madina, he sent Talha Ibn Obaidallah and Said Ibn Zeid to the Damascus route to gather information about the caravan. On their way back to Madina, and at the conclusion of the Badr battle, they met the prophet—Allah bless and keep him—in Terban, as he was descending from Badr to take Madina. [Though] they did not participate in the battle, they nevertheless got their share of the [spoils].

In his attacks, the prophet—Allah bless and keep him—would find out the enemy's intention. In the Hodaibiya [battle] days, though he did not want war, he exercised caution by sending a special 40-man reconnaissance group, headed by A'kkasha Ibn Mohsen Al-Azda. One of that group's fore-

[5]For details, refer to *The Spying Journal: Religious Duty and Human Necessity.*

runners found a man who led them to the enemy's livestock. They captured 200 camels from that livestock and brought them to Madina.

The prophet—Allah bless and keep him—had local informants in Mecca who told him everything, big and small, that might harm the Muslims' welfare. Among those [enemies] were his uncle Al-Abbas Ibn Abd Al-Mutlib, and Bashir Ibn Soufian Al-Atki. Al-Khulafa Arrashidun [Mohammed's successors] advised their commanders about the importance of using scouts and informants to learn the enemy's secrets. Abou Bakr Al-Siddik—may Allah be pleased with him—said to his commander Amro Ibn Al-A'ss—may Allah be pleased with him—, "Send your informants to bring you Abou Obeida's news. If he is victorious over his enemy, then you fight those that are in Palestine. If he needs soldiers, then dispatch one battalion after another for him."

Omar Ibn Al-Khattab—may Allah be pleased with him—advised his commander Saad Ibn Abou Wakkas—may Allah be pleased with him—saying, "If you step foot on your enemies' land, get spies for them. Choose those whom you count on for their truthfulness and advice, whether Arabs or inhabitants of that land. Liars' accounts would not benefit you, even if some of them were true; the deceiver is a spy against you and not for you." Khaled Ibn Al-Walid—may Allah be pleased with him—used to take informants and spies with him in each of his wars against the Christian Orthodox. He chose them carefully and treated them well.

Principle of Moslems Spying on Their Enemies: Spying on the enemy is permitted and it may even be a duty in the case of war between Moslems and others. Winning the battle is dependent on knowing the enemy's secrets, movements, and plans. The prophet—Allah bless and keep him—used that method. He would send spies and informants. Perhaps, he—Allah bless and keep him—even went himself as in the major Badr attack. Al-Khulafa Arrashidun [Mohammed's successors] also ordered it [spying]. Since Islam is superior to all human conditions and earthly religions, it permits spying for itself but not for others. Majestic Allah says, "Not equal are the companions of the fire and the companions of the garden," and the prophet says, "Islam is supreme and there is nothing above it." Islam, therefore, fights so the word of Allah can become supreme. Others fight for worldly gains and lowly and inferior goals.

An Important Question: How can a Muslim spy live among enemies if he maintains his Islamic characteristics? How can he perform his duties to Allah and not want to appear Muslim?

Concerning the issue of clothing and appearance (appearance of true religion), Ibn Taimia—may Allah have mercy on him—said, "If a Muslim is in a combat or godless area, he is not obligated to have a different appearance from [those around him]. The [Muslim] man may prefer or even be obligated to look like them, provided his action brings a religious benefit of preaching to them, learning their secrets and informing Muslims, preventing their harm, or some other beneficial goal."

Resembling the polytheist in religious appearance is a kind of "necessity permits the forbidden" even though they [forbidden acts] are basically prohibited. As for the visible duties, like fasting and praying, he can fast by using any justification not to eat with them [polytheist]. As for prayer, the book (Al-Manhaj Al-Haraki Lissira Al-Nabawiya) quotes Al-Bakhari that "he [the Moslem] may combine the noon and afternoon [prayers], sunset and evening [prayers]. That is based on the fact that the prophet—Allah bless and keep him—combined [prayers] in Madina without fear or hesitation."

Though scholars have disagreed about the interpretation of that tradition, it is possible—though Allah knows best—that the Moslem spy combines [prayers]. It is noted, however, that it is forbidden to do the unlawful, such as drinking wine or fornicating. There is nothing that permits those[6].

Guidelines for Beating and Killing Hostages: Religious scholars have permitted beating. They use a tradition ex-

[6]*Al-Morabitoun* magazine, Issue No. 6

plained in Imam Mosallem's manuscript, who quotes Thabit Ibn Ans that Allah's prophet—Allah bless and keep him—sought counsel when he was informed about Abou Soufian's arrival. Abou Bakr and Omar spoke, yet he [the prophet] did not listen. Saad Ibn Ibada said, "Do you want us, O Allah's prophet, who controls my life? If you order us to subdue the camel we would do it, or beat and follow them to Al-Ghimad lakes (5-day trip beyond Mecca), we would do it, too." The prophet—Allah bless and keep him—called on the people, who then descended on Badr. They were met by Kureish camels carrying water. Among their takers was a young black [slave] man belonging to the Al-Hajjaj clan. They took him [as hostage]. The companions of the prophet—Allah bless and keep him—started asking him about Abou Sofian and his companions. He first said, "I know nothing about Abou Soufian but I know about Abou Jahl, Atba, Sheiba, and Omaya Ibn Khalaf." But when they beat him he said, "O yes, I will tell you. This is the news of Abou Soufian . . ." Meanwhile, the prophet—Allah bless and keep him—, who was praying, started to depart saying, "Strike him if he tells you the truth and release him if he lies." Then he said, "That is the death of someone [the hostage]." He said that in the presence of his companions and while moving his hand on the ground.

In this tradition, we find permission to interrogate the hostage for the purpose of obtaining information. It is permitted to strike the nonbeliever who has no covenant until he reveals the news, information, and secrets of his people.

The religious scholars have also permitted the killing of a hostage if he insists on withholding information from Moslems. They permitted his killing so that he would not inform his people of what he learned about the Muslim condition, number, and secrets. In the Honein attack, after one of the spies learned about the Muslims' kindness and weakness, then fled, the prophet—Allah bless and keep him—permitted [shedding] his blood and said, "Find and kill him." Salma Ibn Al-Akwaa followed, caught, and killed him.

The scholars have also permitted the exchange of hostages for money, services, and expertise, as well as secrets of the enemy's army, plans, and numbers. After the Badr attack, the prophet—Allah bless and keep him—showed favor to some hostages, like the poet Abou Izza, by exchanging most of them for money. The rest were released for providing services and expertise to the Muslims[7].

Information Sources: Any organization that desires to raise the flag of Islam high and proud, must gather as much information as possible about the enemy. Information has two sources:

1. *Public Source:* Using this public source openly and without resorting to illegal means, it is possible to gather at least 80% of information about the enemy. The percentage varies depending on the government's policy on freedom of the press and publication. It is possible to gather information through newspapers, magazines, books, periodicals, official publications, and enemy broadcasts. Attention should also be given to the opinion, comments, and jokes of common people.

Truman, a past American President, said, "We attribute our great advance to our press, because it gives America's enemies the capability of learning what we have not officially publicized about our plans and even our establishments."

In 1954, Allan Dulles [PH], Director of American Intelligence [CIA], said, "I am ready to pay any amount of money to obtain information about the Soviet Union, even as little as what the Soviet Union obtains by simply reading American newspapers."

The one gathering public information should be a regular person (trained college graduate) who examines primary sources of information published by the enemy (newspapers, magazines, radio, TV, etc.). He should search for information directly related to the topic in question.

The one gathering information with this public method

---

[7]Abdullah Ali Al-Salama: *Military Espionage in Islam,* pp. 253–258.

is not exposed to any danger whatsoever. Any brother can gather information from those aforementioned sources. We cannot label that brother a "Moslem Spy" because he does not make any effort to obtain unpublished and covert information.

TWELFTH LESSON
ESPIONAGE
(2) INFORMATION-GATHERING USING COVERT METHODS

Information needed through covert means: Information needed to be gathered through covert means is of only two types:

First: Information about government personnel, officers, important personalities, and all matters related to those (residence, work place, times of leaving and returning, wives and children, places visited)

Second: Information about strategic buildings, important establishments, and military bases. Examples are important ministries such as those of Defense and Internal Security, airports, seaports, land border points, embassies, and radio and TV stations.

General security measures that should be taken by the person gathering information: During the process of gathering information, whether about governing personalities or establishments, the person doing the gathering must take the following security measures:

1. Performing the exercises to detect surveillance while executing the mission. These exercises are not well defined, but are dependent on the time, place, and the ability to be creative. These exercises include the following:
   a. Walking down a dead-end street and observing who is walking behind you. Beware of traps.
   b. Casually dropping something out of your pocket and observing who will pick it up.
   c. Walking fast then stopping suddenly at a corner and observing who will be affected.

    d. Stopping in front of store windows and observing who is watching you.

    e. Getting on a bus and then getting off after it departs and observing who will be affected.

    f. Agreeing with one of your brothers to look for whoever is watching you.

C. *Gathering Information Through Recruitment:* Recruiting agents is the most dangerous task that an enlisted brother can perform. Because of this dangerous task, the brother may be killed or imprisoned. Thus, the recruitment task must be performed by special types of members.

There are a number of motives that might entice an uncommitted person to take part in intelligence work. These motives are:

1. Coercion and entanglement
2. Greed and love for money
3. Displaying courage and love of adventure
4. Love of amusement and deviance
5. Mental and political orientation
6. Fear of being harmed

The Organization may use motives No. 2, 3, 5, and 6 in recruitment.

Candidates for Recruitment Are:

1. Smugglers
2. Those seeking political asylum
3. Adventurers
4. Workers at coffee shops, restaurants, and hotels
5. People in need
6. Employees at borders, airports, and seaports

Types of Agents Preferred by The American Intelligence Agency [CIA]:

1. Foreign officials who are disenchanted with their country's policies and are looking towards the U.S. for guidance and direction.
2. The ideologist (who is in his county but against his government) is considered a valuable catch and a good candidate for American Intelligence Agency [CIA].

3. Officials who have a lavish lifestyle and cannot keep up using their regular wages, or those who have weaknesses for women, other men, or alcoholic beverages. The agent who can be bought using the aforementioned means is an easy target, but the agent who considers what he does a noble cause is difficult to recruit by enemy intelligence.
4. For that purpose, students and soldiers in Third World countries are considered valuable targets. Soldiers are the dominating and controlling elements of those countries.

PRISONS AND DETENTION CENTERS
IF AN INDICTMENT IS ISSUED AND THE TRIAL BEGINS, THE BROTHER HAS TO PAY ATTENTION TO THE FOLLOWING:
1. At the beginning of the trial, once more the brothers must insist on proving that torture was inflicted on them by State Security [investigators] before the judge.
2. Complain [to the court] of mistreatment while in prison.
3. Make arrangements for the brother's defense with the attorney, whether he was retained by the brother's family or court-appointed.
4. The brother has to do his best to know the names of the state security officers, who participated in his torture and mention their names to the judge. [These names may be obtained from brothers who had to deal with those officers in previous cases.]
5. Some brothers may tell and may be lured by the state security investigators to testify against the brothers [i.e. affirmation witness], either by not keeping them together in the same prison during the trials, or by letting them talk to the media. In this case, they have to be treated gently, and should be offered good advice, good treatment, and pray that God may guide them.

6. During the trial, the court has to be notified of any mistreatment of the brothers inside the prison.

7. It is possible to resort to a hunger strike, but it is a tactic that can either succeed or fail.

8. Take advantage of visits to communicate with brothers outside prison and exchange information that may be helpful to them in their work outside prison [according to what occurred during the investigations]. The importance of mastering the art of hiding messages is self evident here.

   - When the brothers are transported from and to the prison [on their way to the court] they should shout Islamic slogans out loud from inside the prison cars to impress upon the people and their family the need to support Islam.

   - Inside the prison, the brother should not accept any work that may belittle or demean him or his brothers, such as the cleaning of the prison bathrooms or hallways.

   - The brothers should create an Islamic program for themselves inside the prison, as well as recreational and educational ones, etc.

   - The brother in prison should be a role model in selflessness. Brothers should also pay attention to each other's needs and should help each other and unite vis a vis the prison officers.

   - The brothers must take advantage of their presence in prison for obeying and worshiping [God] and memorizing the Qora'an, etc. This is in addition to all guidelines and procedures that were contained in the lesson on interrogation and investigation. Lastly, each of us has to understand that we don't achieve victory against our enemies through these actions and security procedures. Rather, victory is achieved by obeying Almighty and Glorious God and because of their many sins. Every brother has to be careful so as not to commit sins and everyone of us has to do his best in obeying Almighty God, Who said in his Holy Book: "We will, without doubt, help Our messengers and those who believe (both) in this world's life and the one Day when the Witnesses will stand forth."

May God guide us.

[Dedication]

To this pure Muslim youth, the believer, the mujahid (fighter) for God's sake, I present this modest effort as a contribution from me to pave the way that will lead to Almighty God and to establish a caliphate along the lines of the prophet.

The prophet, peace be upon him, said according to what was related by Imam Ahmed: "Let the prophecy that God wants be in you, yet God may remove it if He so wills, and then there will be a Caliphate according to the prophet's path [instruction], if God so wills it. He will also remove that [the Caliphate] if He so wills, and you will have a disobedient king if God so wills it. Once again, if God so wills, He will remove him [the disobedient king], and you will have an oppressive king. [Finally], if God so wills, He will remove him [the oppressive king], and you will have a Caliphate according to the prophet's path [instruction]. He then became silent."

THE IMPORTANCE OF TEAMWORK:

1. Team work is the only translation of God's command, as well as that of the prophet, to unite and not to disunite. Almighty God says, "And hold fast, all together, by the Rope which Allah (stretches out for you), and be not divided among yourselves." In "Sahih Muslim," it was reported by Abu Horairah, may Allah look kindly upon him, that the prophet, may Allah's peace and greetings be upon him, said: "Allah approves three [things] for you and disapproves three [things]: He approves that you worship him, that you do not disbelieve in Him,

and that you hold fast, all together, by the Rope which Allah, and be not divided among yourselves. He disapproves of three: gossip, asking too much [for help], and squandering money."

2. Abandoning "team work" for individual and haphazard work means disobeying that orders of God and the prophet and falling victim to disunity.

3. Team work is conducive to cooperation in righteousness and piety.

4. Upholding religion, which God has ordered us by His saying, "Uphold religion," will necessarily require an all out confrontation against all our enemies, who want to recreate darkness. In addition, it is imperative to stand against darkness in all arenas: the media, education, [religious] guidance, and counseling, as well as others. This will make it necessary for us to move on numerous fields so as to enable the Islamic movement to confront ignorance and achieve victory against it in the battle to uphold religion. All these vital goals can not be adequately achieved without organized team work. Therefore, team work becomes a necessity, in accordance with the fundamental rule, "Duty cannot be accomplished without it, and it is a requirement." This way, team work is achieved through mustering and organizing the ranks, while putting the Amir (the Prince) before them, and the right man in the right place, making plans for action, organizing work, and obtaining facets of power . . .

Atta's Last Will

On the day of the attacks on the World Trade Center, a travel bag that had missed its connecting flight was found at Logan Airport in Boston. It belonged to suicide pilot Atta, who steered the Boeing 767, American Flight 11, into the north tower. Atta's last will, from 1996, was among the papers found in the bag, together with a document that reads like a primer for terrorists on suicide missions.

I, Mohamed, son of Mohamed al-Amir Awad al-Sajjid, ask that the following take place after my death.

I believe in Mohamed the Divine Envoy of God and I have not the slightest doubt that the time will come when God shall resurrect all men from their graves. It is my desire that my family as well as those who read this fear the Almighty God and be not distracted by worldly matters; that they fear God and strive to follow His Prophet if they are true believers. To honor my memory, they should follow the example of (the prophet) Abraham, who brought his son to die, as a good Muslim. When I die, those who inherit my belongings should consider the following:

1. Those who lay out my body shall be good Muslims. This will recommend me to God and His forgiveness.

2. Those who lay out my body shall close my eyes and pray that I rise to Heaven. They shall dress me in new clothes and not leave me in those in which I died.

3. No one should cry on my behalf, or scream or tear apart their clothes or beat their faces—these are all foolish gestures.

4. No one who quarreled with me in the past shall be permitted to visit me, kiss me, or to take leave of me after my death.

5. Neither pregnant women nor unclean persons shall be allowed to take leave of me—I reject it.

6. No woman shall beg pardon for me after my death. I am not responsible for animal sacrifices in front of my open corpse—this violates the tenets of Islam.

7. Those who sit at my wake shall honor God and pray that I be in the company of His angels.

8. Those who wash my body shall be good Muslims.

Let there be not too many unless absolutely necessary.

9. Whoever washes my body near my genitals shall wear gloves so that I am not touched there.

10. The clothes I shall wear at my death shall consist of three pieces of white cloth, but not silk or other expensive material.

11. Women shall not be admitted to my burial nor later find themselves at my grave.

12. The burial shall take place quietly, for God said that He desired calm and quiet on three occasions: while reading the Koran, during burials, and while falling to the ground for prayer. The burial shall take place quickly and in the presence of many who are praying for me.

13. I shall be buried together with other good Muslims, my face turned towards Mecca.

14. I wish to lie on my right side. Earth shall be tossed onto me three times, with these words: "You come from dust, you are dust, you return to dust. And from dust shall arise a new person." Thereafter, every one shall call out God's name and bear witness that I died a Muslim, believing in God's religion. All who take part in my burial shall pray for my forgiveness.

15. For an hour shall people stay by my grave, that I might enjoy their company; an animal shall be sacrificed and the meat distributed to the needy.

16. The custom exists of remembering the dead every forty days or once a year. I ask you not to do this since it does not befit Islamic practice.

17. During the burial, no one shall write verses on paper and carry them in their pocket as talismans. This is superstition. It is better to use that time to pray to God.

18. The assets I leave behind shall be distributed according to Islamic practice—as the Almighty God instructed us: one third to the poor and the needy. My books shall become the possessions of a mosque. The executors of my will shall be leaders among the Sunni.

Whoever it be should come from the region in which I grew up, or be a person whom I followed in prayer. Should the ceremony not correspond to the Islamic faith, they who so decided shall be made accountable. Those whom I leave behind shall fear God and not be fooled by worldly things, but instead pray to God and be true believers. Whoever does not abide by this my last will or who violates the commandments of religion will in the end be held responsible.

Written thus on April 11, 1996, by Islamic calendar Dhu al-Kada in the year 1416.

Written by:
Mohamed al-Amir Awad al-Sajjid

Witness: Abd al-Ghani Muswadi
[signature]

Witness: al-Mutasadik Munir
[signature]

Primer for Terrorists on Suicide Missions
"The Sky Smiles, My Young Son"

Spiritual Handbook for the Suicide Attack on the World Trade Center

Among the papers found in Atta's travel bag was a reader or primer for terrorists on suicide missions—a bizarre document of religious delusion that spells out how to behave when you sacrifice yourself during a mass murder.

Work and group work (that is, work for the sake of the Prophet) shall have priority since this is *Sunna* [wisdom]. We are obligated to pursue this work. Do it nor for your own sake, but for the sake of God the

Almighty. One example is Ali Ibn Abi Talib—God bless his soul. He quarreled with an infidel, someone who spit upon Ali—God bless his soul. At first, Ali did not want to draw his sword against the infidel; later he did. After the quarrel, some of his followers asked—why did you not draw the sword against the infidel right away? Ali—God bless his soul—answered: when he first spat at me, I was reluctant to react right away for fear I would be taking revenge on account of myself, and I wished rather to do it for God's sake.

God says man should be without wishes on earth, yet he will reward you in the end, when you die.

When your work is done and everything has gone well, everyone will take each other's hands and say that this was a deed done in the name of God. You shall not instill fear or cause confusion among other brothers but shall talk to them, calm them and encourage them. No one can do better than read the verses of the Koran, for God said that you fight in His name and that you shall surrender what you have in your current life for a better life in Heaven. In a different verse, God says: do not regard as dead men who have died acting in God's name . . . (for they continue to live in Heaven).

The brothers who treat each other with high regard shall be contented and console one another and their hearts shall be filled with joy. The end is near and the heavenly promise within reach. Open your hearts, welcome death in the name of God. And the last thing to do is to remember God, and your last words should be that there is no God but Allah and that Mohamed is His prophet. Afterwards I shall meet God in Heaven. Should you look upon the masses of the Unfaithful, know that God—despite the high number of Unfaithful—will help see that the Faithful triumph against the majority. God said: As soon as the Faithful take on the fight against the Unfaithful, the Faithful shall remember that God is with them and that they shall prevail.

Then the second phase:

When the time comes for the taxi driver to drive you to (M), tell him something about the city and the other places. When you arrive and you see (M) and when you get out of the cab, pray to God and pray to God wherever you go, and smile and have faith that God is always with the Faithful and that the angels will protect you even though you do not notice it. Pray that God has created all and pray that you carry out what God has asked of you. Pray that you do so because the Unfaithful does not recognize the true God and that you have nothing to do with him.

Once you have prayed these prayers all will go well for you, for the power of God is with you, and God promised his followers after they spoke these prayers:

1. that this took place because of God's blessings and because of his forgiveness;

2. that nothing shall happen to the men who execute his plan;

3. that you followed the teachings of God. God says that you have His blessings and His forgiveness and that nothing evil will happen to you as long as you follow the Almighty, he who created all, since the deeds and words of the Unfaithful shall not help them and shall not harm you, God is willing for you are faithful. The Faithful fear no one, and those who fear are sons and daughters of the devil, who fear the devil himself, and are slaves of the devil. Those who fear God and follow Him and take action according to His will shall be the righteous in the end. God said that the devil shall overwhelm those who follow him.

All western civilizations that enjoy power are very weak in their core. Hence, do not be afraid and do not fear if you are faithful, since the Faithful live only in fear of God the Almighty, who holds power over all.

The Faithful hold their belief trusting that the Unfaithful will be conquered in the end. Remember that God will defeat and vanquish the Unfaithful. Remember the promise of the Almighty, and you must say it one thousand times—and no one will notice whether you say it or not—for the honor of God remember His promise that the Faithful who believe with their hearts shall enter Heaven. Remember too how the Prophet—God bless him—said that if you took Heaven and Earth in one hand and God in the other, the hand that holds God shall be on top. You can smile as you recite God's words and the glory of His Word is that you need not say it loud or recite it but you can say it in thoughts. It suffices that you try to elevate Islam and to fight under its banner, as did the Prophet—God bless his soul—and his followers.

Don't give the impression of being confused, instead be strong and happy with confidence and an open heart because you are engaged in work that pleases God and that He will bless. The day in Heaven shall come, God's will, and you shall encounter this verse in Heaven:

The sky smiles, my young son, for you march towards Heaven. Wherever you go, whatever you do, always remember and pray to God, since God always remains with His followers who believe in Him and God will make it easy for you and will bless you and He will crown your work with success and in the end, you will be the victor.

The third phase:

In the plane, as soon as you get on, you should pray to God, because you do this for God, and everyone who prays to God shall prevail since you do this for God. As the almighty Prophet has said, a deed for God is worth more than the entire world and more than every thing on this earth.

As soon as you board the airplane and have taken

your seat, remember that which you were told earlier and devote yourself to remember God. God says that when you are surrounded by several nonbelievers, you must sit quietly and remember that God will make victory possible for you in the end.

When the airplane moves, as soon as it starts to move slowly, start praying the prayers of traveling Muslims, because you travel in order to meet God and to enjoy the journey. You will notice that the plane will stop and then start flying again. This is the hour in which you will meet God, and pray to God the way God stated in His Book: God help me to do this and let us win over the unfaithful nations, and in another saying of God: God, forgive us our trespasses and help us to succeed in what we attempt to do, allow us vanquish the unfaithful peoples and, as the Prophet Mohamed—God bless his soul—said, God, vanquish them and let us conquer and bring down the unfaithful, that they lower their heads.

Pray for yourself and for your Muslim brothers and for the final victory and fear not, for soon you will encounter God. Everyone should be ready to do his part, and your deed shall be endorsed by the will of God. When you begin your task, hit hard like a hero, for God does not welcome men who do not finish a task once begun. You will not return to earth and you will plant fear into the hearts of the infidels, as God said, hit very hard in the neck, in the knowledge that Heaven awaits you, waits for you and that there you will lead a better life, and angels are calling your name and are wearing their finest clothes for you.

As Mustafa, one of the Prophet's followers said, kill and do not think of the possessions of those you will kill. That will only distract you from the true purpose of your task and this is dangerous for you.

The evening before you perform your deed:

1. You shall recite that you are dying for God. Shave

all excess hair from your body, perfume your body and wash your body.

2. Look at your plan carefully and know it well. Expect a reaction and expect resistance from the enemy.

3. Recite the verses about forgiveness and what God holds in store for martyrs, for they shall enter paradise.

4. Remember that this night—the night before the deed—you must listen and obey because you will confront a grave situation, and the only one path that exists is to listen and to grant 100% obedience. Tell yourself that it is your duty to do so, understand it in its true spirit and convince yourself that you must commit this deed. God said that you shall follow his orders and those of his Prophet and that you shall not resist, for resisting will lead to failure. Be patient, for God is with those who are patient.

5. Get up during the night and pray for victory; then God will make everything easy and protect you.

6. Always beware and remember. It is best to recite the Koran and to know that you will at last leave the earth and soon enter Heaven.

7. Cleanse your heart of all bad feelings that you might hold and forget all about your life in this world since all you have done in this world will soon be ending. The time is ripe for the true deed. We have wasted our lives and now the opportunity and hour have come to devote ourselves to God and to obey Him.

8. Open your heart, for you are but a short moment away from the goodness of eternal life filled with positive values in the company of martyrs. This is the best company in which to find yourself. We ask for God's blessing and are hopeful, for God the Almighty loves hopeful men who do God's work.

9. Remember what you do and say in case you are caught. In case you are caught, it is not because of your mistakes and it is not your fault. It happened because God had His reasons and God will uplift you

and forgive all your sins. This is God's will only for the time being. Rejoice, for you will receive your reward from God the Almighty. God promises that all of His fighters shall enter Heaven.

10. Always think of what God said, you have hoped to become a martyr before you encountered Him and now you shall . . . (the dots mean that we both know it, and thus I will not write it). After that, remember the verses of the Koran that signify that the smaller group shall conquer the larger, that such is the will of God. As God said when He was with you, you shall not be vanquished and if you are vanquished, God is the only one who will uplift you.

11. Remind yourself through prayer, alone and with your Muslim brothers, and always remember your brothers in your prayers, in the morning and at night.

12. Remember your luggage, your clothes, the knife and the things you need, your identification papers, your passport, and all your documents.

13. Check your weapon before your trip because you will need it for the execution of your act.

14. Wear your best clothes and thereby follow the example of your forebears, who wore their best clothes before battle. Tie your laces very tight and wear socks, so that the shoes fit snugly on your feet. All of this is self-evident, and God will protect you.

15. In the morning, pray together in the group since that is a good reward and after the deed, each of you will recall that you prayed with them. Do not leave your house unless you are washed and clean, for the angels will forgive you if you are clean and have prayed to God. God said it was a good practice to be well shaven and that is how it is written in the book.

The Bin Laden Videotape

[In this translation provided by the U.S. government, the transcript and annotations were independently prepared by

George Michael, translator, Diplomatic Language Services, and Dr. Kassem M. Wahba, Arabic language program co-ordinator, School of Advanced International Studies, Johns Hopkins University. They collaborated on their translation and compared it with translations done by the U.S. government for consistency. There were no inconsistencies in the translations.]

In mid-November, Osama bin Laden spoke to a room of supporters, possibly in Kandahar, Afghanistan. These comments were videotaped with the knowledge of bin Laden and all present. Note: The tape is approximately one hour long and contains three different segments: an original taping of a visit by some people to the site of the downed U.S. helicopter in Ghazni province (approximately 12 minutes long); and two segments documenting a courtesy visit by bin Laden and his lieutenants to an unidentified Sheik—since identified as Ali Saeed al-Ghamdi—who appears crippled from the waist down. The visit apparently takes place at a guesthouse in Kandahar. The sequence of the events is reversed on the tape: The end of his visit is in the beginning of the tape with the helicopter site visit in the middle and the start of the Osama bin Laden visit beginning approximately 39 minutes into the tape. The tape is transcribed below according to the proper sequence of events.

Due to the quality of the original tape, it is NOT a verbatim transcript of every word spoken during the meeting, but does convey the messages and information flow.

Editor's note: 39 minutes into the tape—the first segment of the bin Laden meeting—begins after footage of the helicopter site visit.

AL-GHAMDI: *[. . . inaudible . . .]* You have given us weapons, you have given us hope and we thank Allah for you. We don't want to take much of your time, but this is the arrangement of the brothers. People now are supporting us more, even those ones who did not support us in the past, support us more now. I did not want to take that much of your time. We praise Allah, we praise Allah. We came from

Kabul. We were very pleased to visit. May Allah bless you both at home and the camp. We asked the driver to take us, it was a night with a full moon, thanks be to Allah. Believe me it is not in the countryside. The elderly . . . everybody praises what you did, the great action you did, which was first and foremost by the grace of Allah. This is the guidance of Allah and the blessed fruit of jihad.

BIN LADEN: Thanks to Allah. What is the stand of the Mosques there *[in Saudi Arabia]*?

AL-GHAMDI: Honestly, they are very positive. Sheik Al-Bahrani *[phonetic]* gave a good sermon in his class after the sunset prayers. It was videotaped and I was supposed to carry it with me, but unfortunately, I had to leave immediately.

BIN LADEN: The day of the events?

AL-GHAMDI: At the exact time of the attack on America, precisely at the time. He (Bahrani) gave a very impressive sermon. Thanks be to Allah for his blessings. He (Bahrani) was the first one to write at war time. I visited him twice in Al-Qasim.

BIN LADEN: Thanks be to Allah.

AL-GHAMDI: This is what I asked from Allah. He *[Bahrani]* told the youth: "You are asking for martyrdom and wonder where you should go *[for martyrdom]*?" Allah was inciting them to go. I asked Allah to grant me to witness the truth in front of the unjust ruler. We ask Allah to protect him and give him the martyrdom, after he issued the first fatwa. He was detained for interrogation, as you know. When he was called in and asked to sign, he told them, "don't waste my time, I have another fatwa. If you want me, I can sign both at the same time."

BIN LADEN: Thanks be to Allah.

AL-GHAMDI: His position is really very encouraging. When I paid him the first visit about a year and a half ago, he asked me, "How is Sheik bin Laden?" He sends you his special regards. As far as Sheik Sulayman 'Ulwan is concerned, he gave a beautiful fatwa, may Allah bless him. Miraculously, I heard it on the Quran radio station. It was strange because he [*'Ulwan*] sacrificed his position, which is equivalent to a director. It was transcribed word-by-word. The brothers listened to it in detail. I briefly heard it before the noon prayers. He [*'Ulwan*] said this was jihad and those people were not innocent people [*World Trade Center and Pentagon victims*]. He swore to Allah. This was transmitted to Sheik Sulayman Al [*'Umar*] Allah bless him.

BIN LADEN: What about Sheik Al-[*Rayan*]?

AL-GHAMDI: Honestly, I did not meet with him. My movements were truly limited.

BIN LADEN: Allah bless you. You are welcome.

AL-GHAMDI: [*Describing the trip to the meeting*] They smuggled us and then I thought that we would be in different caves inside the mountains so I was surprised at the guest house and that it is very clean and comfortable. Thanks be to Allah, we also learned that this location is safe, by Allah's blessings. The place is clean and we are very comfortable.

BIN LADEN: [*. . . inaudible . . .*] when people see a strong horse and a weak horse, by nature, they will like the strong horse. This is only one goal; those who want people to worship the lord of the people, without following that doctrine, will be following the doctrine of Muhammad, peace be upon him. Those youth who conducted the operations did not accept any *fiqh* [Islamic jurisprudence] in the popular terms, but they accepted the fiqh that the prophet Muhammad brought. Those young men [*. . . inaudible . . .*] said in deeds, in New York and Washington, speeches that overshadowed all other speeches made everywhere else in the world. The speeches are understood by both Arabs and non-Arabs—even by Chinese. It is above all the media said. Some of them said that in Holland, at one of the centers, the number of people who accepted Islam during the days that followed the operations were more than the people who accepted Islam in the last eleven years. I heard someone on Islamic radio who owns a school in America say: "We don't have time to keep up with the demands of those who are asking about Islamic books to learn about Islam." This event made people think *[about true Islam]* which benefited Islam greatly.

AL-GHAMDI: Hundreds of people used to doubt you and few only would follow you until this huge event happened. Now hundreds of people are coming out to join you. I remember a vision by Sheik Salih Al-*[Shuaybi]*. He said: "There will be a great hit and people will go out by hundreds to Afghanistan." I asked him *[Salih]*: "To Afghanistan?" He replied, "Yes." According to him, the only ones who stay behind will be the mentally impotent and the liars (hypocrites). I remembered his saying that hundreds of people will go out to Afghanistan. He had this vision a year ago. This event discriminated between the different types of followers.

BIN LADEN: *[. . . inaudible . . .]* we calculated in advance the number of casualties from the enemy, who would be killed based on the position of the tower. We calculated that the floors that would be hit would be three or four floors. I was the most optimistic of them all. *[. . . inaudible . . .]* due to my experience in this field, I was thinking that the fire from the gas in the plane would melt the iron structure of the building and collapse the area where the plane hit and all the floors above it only. This is all that we had hoped for.

AL-GHAMDI: Allah be praised.

BIN LADEN: We were at *[. . . inaudible . . .]* when the event took place. We had notification since the previous Thursday that the event would take place that day. We had finished our work that day and had the radio on. It was 5:30 P.M. our time. I was sitting with Dr. Ahmad Abu-al-*[Khair]*. Immediately, we heard the news that a plane had hit the World Trade Center. We turned the radio station to the news from Washington. The news continued and no mention of the attack until the end. At the end of the newscast, they reported that a plane just hit the World Trade Center.

AL-GHAMDI: Allah be praised.

BIN LADEN: After a little while, they announced that another plane had hit the World Trade Center. The brothers who heard the news were overjoyed by it.

AL-GHAMDI: I listened to the news and I was sitting. We didn't . . . we were not thinking about anything, and all of a sudden, Allah willing, we were talking about how come we didn't have anything, and all of a sudden the news came and everyone was overjoyed and everyone until the next day, in the morning, was talking about what was happening and we stayed until four o'clock, listening to the news every time a little bit different, everyone was very joyous and saying "Allah is great," "Allah is great," "We are thankful to Allah," "Praise Allah." And I was happy for the happiness of my brothers. That day the congratulations were coming on the phone non-stop. The mother was receiving phone calls continuously. Thank Allah. Allah is great, praise be to Allah.

[Quoting the verse from the Koran]

AL-GHAMDI: "Fight them, Allah will torture them, with your hands, he will torture them. He will deceive them and he will give you victory. Allah will forgive the believers, he is knowledgeable about everything." No doubt it is a clear victory. Allah has bestowed on us . . . honor on us . . . and he will give us blessing and more victory during this holy month of Ramadan. And this is what everyone is hoping for. Thank Allah America came out of its caves. We hit her the first hit and the next one will hit her with the hands of the believers, the good believers, the strong believers. By Allah it is a great work. Allah prepares for you a great reward for this work. I'm sorry to speak in your presence, but it is just thoughts, just thoughts. By Allah, who there is no god but him. I live in happiness, happiness . . . I have not experienced, or felt, in a long time. I remember, the words of Al-Rabbani, he said they made a coalition against us in the winter with the infidels like the Turks, and others, and some other Arabs. And they surrounded us like the days . . . in the days of the prophet Muhammad. Exactly like what's happening right now. But he comforted his followers and said, "This is going to turn and hit them back." And it is a mercy for us. And a blessing to us. And it will bring people back. Look how wise he was. And Allah will give him blessing. And the day will come when the symbols of Islam will rise up and it will be similar to the early days of Al-Mujahedeen and Al-Ansar (similar to the early years of Islam). And victory to those who follow Allah. Finally said, if it is the same, like the old days, such as Abu Bakr and Othman and Ali and others. In these days, in our times, that it will be the greatest jihad in the history of Islam and the resistance of the wicked people. By Allah my Sheik. We congratulate you for the great work. Thank Allah.

BIN LADEN: Abdallah Azzam, Allah bless his soul, told me not to record anything *[. . . inaudible . . .]* so I thought that was a good omen, and Allah will bless us *[. . . inaudible . . .]*. Abu-Al-Hasan Al-*[Masri]*, who appeared on Al-Jazeera TV a couple of days ago and addressed the Americans saying: "If you are true men, come down here and face us." *[. . . inaudible . . .]* He told me a year ago: "I saw in a dream, we were playing a soccer game against the Americans. When our team showed up in the field, they were all pilots!" He said: "So I wondered if that was a soccer game or a pilot game? Our players were pilots." He (Abu-Al-Hasan) didn't know anything about the operation until he heard it on the radio. He said the game went on and we defeated them. That was a good omen for us.

AL-GHAMDI: May Allah be blessed.

SULAYMAN [ABU GUAITH]: I was sitting with the Sheik in a room, then I left to go to another room where there was a TV set. The TV broadcast the big event. The scene was showing an Egyptian family sitting in their living room, they exploded with joy. Do you know when there is a soccer game and your team wins, it was the same expression of joy. There was a subtitle that read: "In revenge for the children of Al Aqsa', Osama bin Laden executes an operation against America." So I went back to the Sheik *[meaning OBL]* who was sitting in a room with 50 to 60 people. I tried to tell him about what I saw, but he made gesture with his hands, meaning: "I know, I know . . ."

BIN LADEN: He did not know about the operation. Not everybody knew *[. . . inaudible . . .]*. Muhammad *[Atta]* from the Egyptian family *[meaning the Al Qaeda Egyptian group]*, was in charge of the group.

AL-GHAMDI: A plane crashing into a tall building was out of anyone's imagination. This was a great job. He was one of the pious men in the organization. He became a martyr. Allah bless his soul. The plane that he saw crashing into the building was seen before by more than one person. One of the good religious people has left everything and come here. He told me, "I saw a vision, I was in a huge plane, long and wide. I was carrying it on my shoulders and I walked from the road to the desert for half a kilometer. I was dragging the plane." I listened to him and I prayed to Allah to help him. Another person told me that last year he saw, but I didn't understand and I told him I don't understand. He said, "I saw people who left for jihad . . . and they found themselves in New York . . . in Washington and New York." I said, "What is this?" He told me the plane hit the building. That was last year. We haven't thought much about it. But, when the incidents happened he came to me and said, "Did you see . . . this is strange."

BIN LADEN: The brothers, who conducted the operation, all they knew was that they have a martyrdom operation and we asked each of them to go to America but they didn't know anything about the operation, not even one letter. But they were trained and we did not reveal the operation to them until they are there and just before they boarded the planes. Those who were trained to fly didn't know the others. One group of people did not know the other group. *[. . . inaudible . . .]*

[Someone in the crowd asks OBL to tell the Sheik about the dream of (Abu-Da'ud).]

BIN LADEN: We were at a camp of one of the brother's guards in Kandahar. This brother belonged to the majority of the group. He came close and told me that he saw, in a dream, a tall building in America, and in the same dream he saw Mukhtar teaching them how to play karate. At that point, I was worried that maybe the secret would be revealed if everyone starts seeing it in their dream. So I closed the subject. I told him if he sees another dream, not to tell any-body, because people will be upset with him.

[Another person's voice can be heard recounting his dream about two planes hitting a big building.]

BIN LADEN: They were overjoyed when the first plane hit the building, so I said to them: be patient. The difference between the first and the second plane hitting the towers was twenty minutes. And the difference between the first plane and the plane that hit the Pentagon was one hour.

AL-GHAMDI: They *[the Americans]* were terrified thinking there was a coup.

[Note: Ayman al-Zawahiri says first he commended OBL's awareness of what the media is saying. Then he says it was the first time for them (Americans) to feel danger coming at them.]

BIN LADEN: *[reciting a poem]*: I witness that against the sharp blade. / They always faced difficulties and stood to-gether . . . / When the darkness comes upon us and we are bit by a Sharp tooth, I say . . . / "Our homes are flooded with blood and the tyrant Is freely wandering in our homes" . . . / And from the battlefield vanished The brightness of swords and the horses . . . / And over weeping sounds now We hear the beats of drums and rhythm . . . / They are storming his forts And shouting: "We will not stop our raids / Until you free our lands. . . ."